VOICES

INTERMEDIATE PLUS

DANIEL BARBER AND MAREK KICZKOWIAK

NATIONAL GEOGRAPHIC LEARNING

Australia · Brazil · Canada · Mexico · Singapore · United Kingdom · United States

NATIONAL GEOGRAPHIC LEARNING

National Geographic Learning,
a Cengage Company

**Voices Intermediate Plus Student's Book,
1st Edition**
Daniel Barber and Marek Kiczkowiak

Publisher: Rachael Gibbon

Commissioning Editor: Kayleigh Buller

Content Editor: Yvonne Molfetas

Director of Global Marketing: Ian Martin

Product Marketing Manager: Caitlin Thomas

Heads of Regional Marketing:
  Charlotte Ellis (Europe, Middle East and Africa)
  Irina Pereyra (Latin America)
  Justin Kaley (Asia)
  Joy MacFarland (US and Canada)

Production Manager: Daisy Sosa

Media Researcher: Leila Hishmeh

Art Director: Brenda Carmichael

Operations Support: Hayley Chwazik-Gee

Manufacturing Manager: Eyvett Davis

Composition: Composure

Audio Producer: New York Audio

Contributing writer: Billie Jago (Endmatter)

Advisors: Anna Blackmore, Bruna Caltabiano, Dale Coulter

© 2022 Cengage Learning, Inc.

ALL RIGHTS RESERVED. No part of this work covered by the copyright herein may be reproduced or distributed in any form or by any means, except as permitted by U.S. copyright law, without the prior written permission of the copyright owner.

"National Geographic", "National Geographic Society" and the Yellow Border Design are registered trademarks of the National Geographic Society ® Marcas Registradas

For permission to use material from this text or product, submit all requests online at **cengage.com/permissions**
Further permissions questions can be emailed to **permissionrequest@cengage.com**

Student's Book with Online Practice and Student's eBook:
ISBN: 978-0-357-45869-3

Student's Book:
ISBN: 978-0-357-44327-9

National Geographic Learning
Cheriton House, North Way,
Andover, Hampshire, SP10 5BE
United Kingdom

Locate your local office at **international.cengage.com/region**

Visit National Geographic Learning online at **ELTNGL.com**
Visit our corporate website at **www.cengage.com**

Printed in Greece by Bakis SA
Print Number: 01 Print Year: 2021

Contents

1 Your life — 10

2 Breaking the rules — 22

3 Imagining the future — 34

4 Good taste — 46

5 Let's play — 58

6 Accidents and incidents — 70

7 Going shopping — 82

8 Working life — 94

9 History revisited — 106

10 Believe your eyes! — 118

Scope and sequence

		GRAMMAR AND 'FOCUS ON'	VOCABULARY	PRONUNCIATION
1	**Your life** Pages 10-21	auxiliary verbs in questions and short answers; short questions	education	stressing auxiliaries; saying groups of consonants
2	**Breaking the rules** Pages 22-33	past tenses; *be/get used to* + something / doing something	crime	pronouncing *-ed* words; saying long and short 'o'
3	**Imagining the future** Pages 34-45	talking about predictions; talking about data: prepositions	making predictions	saying contracted forms of *will* and *going to*; pronouncing long vowels
4	**Good taste** Pages 46-57	modifying comparative and superlative adjectives; negative prefixes for adjectives	table manners	changing your pronunciation; saying /k/, /p/ and /t/ in stressed syllables
5	**Let's play** Pages 58-69	*could have, should have* and *would have*; talking about past ability: *could, was able to* or *managed to*?	being competitive	pronouncing *have* in past modal verbs; saying 'o' in stressed syllables

READING	LISTENING	WRITING	COMMUNICATION SKILL	CRITICAL THINKING	USEFUL LANGUAGE
an article about childhood memories; skimming online articles	explorers talk about their education; understanding different accents	a description of an influential person; proofreading	establishing rapport	asking questions to evaluate evidence	linking to what the other person says; saying why someone is important to you
a blog post about unusual laws; understanding the meaning of new words from context	a podcast about crimes gone wrong; understanding fast speech	a crime story; describing actions	understanding power distance	identifying the writer's tone of voice	adverbs with past tenses; using adverbs to make a story more interesting
profiles about people who are innovating; scanning for specific information	conversations about the future of languages and films; understanding fillers in conversations	a personal development plan; using a mind map to brainstorm ideas	giving helpful feedback	comparing solutions	talking about uncertain plans and predictions; expressing feedback; talking about achieving your goals
an extract from a travel journal; identifying supporting stories	explorers talk about table manners; understanding fast speech: assimilation	a review of a restaurant; organizing a restaurant review	saying no	analysing descriptive writing	ways of saying 'no'; a restaurant review
a blog post about collaborative games; identifying supporting examples	a radio show about esports; using context to understand new words	an opinion essay; organizing a paragraph in a formal text	communicating clearly in a group	relating information to your own experience	explaining games; clarifying misunderstandings; linking opposing points of view in a formal essay

Scope and sequence

			GRAMMAR AND 'FOCUS ON'	VOCABULARY	PRONUNCIATION
6	**Accidents and incidents** Pages 70-81		reporting what people say; discussing present habits	accidents	saying auxiliary verbs at the end of sentences; saying /ʃ/, /dʒ/ and /tʃ/
7	**Going shopping** Pages 82-93		have/get something done; cost, price, worth	buying things	stressing the object with have/get something done; saying longer vowels before voiced consonants
8	**Working life** Pages 94-105		noun phrases; compound words	work	saying /ɜː/ and /ɑː/; saying /r/ at the end of syllables
9	**History revisited** Pages 106-117		pronouns; the passive voice with by	history	stressing pronouns; saying /ɜː/ with and without 'r'
10	**Believe your eyes!** Pages 118-129		quantifiers; verbs of the senses: looks, sounds, smells, feels, seems	being honest	understanding vowels across accents; changing meaning by stressing different words

READING	LISTENING	WRITING	COMMUNICATION SKILL	CRITICAL THINKING	USEFUL LANGUAGE
an article about accidental inventions; activating prior knowledge before reading	explorers talk about accidents they've had; understanding a sequence of events	a formal email of complaint; organizing information in a formal complaint email	balancing fluency and accuracy	analysing conclusions	talking about surprising information; saying what action you would like to be taken
an article and infographic about vending machines; identifying facts and speculation	an explorer talks about shopping; understanding approximate numbers	an online advert for an item you want to sell; omitting words to shorten a text	finding solutions when negotiating	identifying and evaluating the writer's purpose	recommending where to get things done; negotiating; selling items online
an article about the glass ceiling; taking notes using symbols and abbreviations	explorers talk about their work; synthesizing ideas across listening passages	the 'About me' section of an online professional profile; using the -ing form to turn verbs into nouns	dealing with different working styles in teams	evaluating a writer's statements	adapting to different working styles within a team; your professional profile
an extract from a novel and an interview with an author; understanding reference words	an explorer talks about the Maya; taking notes when listening	a biography of an historical figure; paraphrasing sources	adapting your argument to suit your listener	synthesizing from multiple sources	persuading people; describing historical figures and their achievements
a timeline about optical illusions; scanning to interpret visual information	an explorer talks about being honest; understanding reference	formal and informal invitations; writing formal and informal invitations	saving face	applying knowledge to new situations	being tactful in sensitive situations; accepting and declining invitations

Reflect and review *Page 130*
Vocabulary reference *Page 135*
Grammar reference *Page 140*
Irregular verbs *Page 154*
Extra speaking tasks *Page 156*
Audioscripts *Page 158*

Meet the explorers

ALYEA PIERCE

Lives: US
Job: I'm a poet and educator who focuses on the untold stories within the African diaspora (global communities descended from people from Africa). As an Afro-Caribbean female writer, I enjoy helping young people find their voices through creative writing and theatre.
Where is 'home'? Home for me is anywhere close to nature and art.
Find Alyea: Unit 2

FRANCISCO ESTRADA-BELLI

Lives: US
Job: I'm an archaeologist – this means I explore the history of an area by digging up what people left behind. I run an archaeological project in the Maya Biosphere Reserve in Guatemala. I have written about the Maya civilization and I'm also a research professor at Tulane University in New Orleans.
Describe yourself in three words: Archaeologist, explorer, father
Find Francisco: Unit 9

ANUSHA SHANKAR

Lives: US
Job: I'm a wildlife biologist – and interested in how animals live in extreme conditions. I'm a researcher at the University of Alaska Fairbanks and my research is on hummingbirds and how they save energy.
Describe yourself in three words: Salsa dancing biologist!
Find Anusha: Unit 5

IMOGEN NAPPER

Lives: UK
Job: I am a marine scientist – this means I study what happens in the sea. I specialize in plastic pollution. I am working to identify technology that can catch the tiny plastic fibres that enter the water when clothes are washed.
What do you do to relax? Play my guitar (badly)!
Find Imogen: Unit 4

BRIAN BUMA

Lives: US
Job: I'm an ecology professor and author. I study changes to the planet – from wildfires to landslides to the movements of wildlife – in response to changing climates. I am currently doing research into the effects of snow loss on forests around the world.
What do you do in your free time? Snowboard, mountain bike, build guitars
Find Brian: Unit 8

JEFF MARLOW

Lives: US
Job: I'm a geobiologist, and my curiosity has led me everywhere from the edge of a volcanic lake in the South Pacific to the bottom of the sea. I have also written and directed a short film about NASA's Mars rover, Curiosity.
What did you want to do when you were younger? I wanted to find life beyond Earth, ideally as a NASA astronaut.
Find Jeff: Unit 10

JOE CUTLER

Lives: US
Job: I am a conservationist and I work with the Nature Conservancy in Gabon. I have undertaken seven fish sampling expeditions and collected hundreds of fish species, including many new to science. Using this information, I provide advice to governments and organizations on balancing development and freshwater conservation.
Describe yourself in three words: Freshwater fish guy
Find Joe: Unit 6

PABLO (POPI) BORBOROGLU

Lives: Argentina
Job: I'm a marine biologist and I specialize in penguins and marine conservation. I am founder and president of the Global Penguin Society, an international conservation organization that protects the world's penguins through science, habitat protection on both land and sea, and education.
What's your fondest memory? Listening to my grandmother's stories about penguins when she visited them one hundred years ago in Patagonia.
Find Popi: Unit 7

MARY GAGEN

Lives: UK
Job: I am a professor of geography and I work on climate change and forests. I study ancient woodlands around the world. I am also passionate about science education and regularly run workshops to bring young people into a science lab.
What do you do in your free time? I live by the sea and most of my free time is spent in the water or hiking along the cliff paths.
Find Mary: Unit 3

NIRUPA RAO

Lives: India
Job: I am a botanical illustrator, which means I draw and paint plants and trees. My recent work includes a project on the trees of south Indian rainforests, and a children's book that helps young readers explore the wonderful world of plants.
Do you have any fears? I actually have a fear of snakes, which is quite inconvenient since I come across them a lot in my work!
Find Nirupa: Unit 8

MIKE GIL

Lives: US
Job: I am a marine biologist. I am interested in understanding how animal social networks can shape ecosystems that provide valuable services to people. I'm also very involved in teaching people about science.
What do you always take with you when you travel? No matter what: a toothbrush and a positive attitude – both simply make life better anywhere.
Find Mike: Unit 1

PAOLA RODRÍGUEZ

Lives: Mexico
Job: I am a coral reef researcher – this means I study how this tiny tropical sea creature will be affected by global climate change and look for ways to protect it from changes in the sea.
What did you want to do when you were younger? I wanted to be an ice skater.
Find Paola: Unit 4; Unit 6

TSIORY ANDRIANAVALONA

Lives: Madagascar
Job: I am a palaeontologist with a special interest in shark fossils. I co-founded an organization to inspire young people to take an interest in science and technology and encourage the next generation to make positive change for my home country, Madagascar.
What did you want to do when you were younger? I wanted to be an archaeologist or a detective.
Find Tsiory: Unit 1

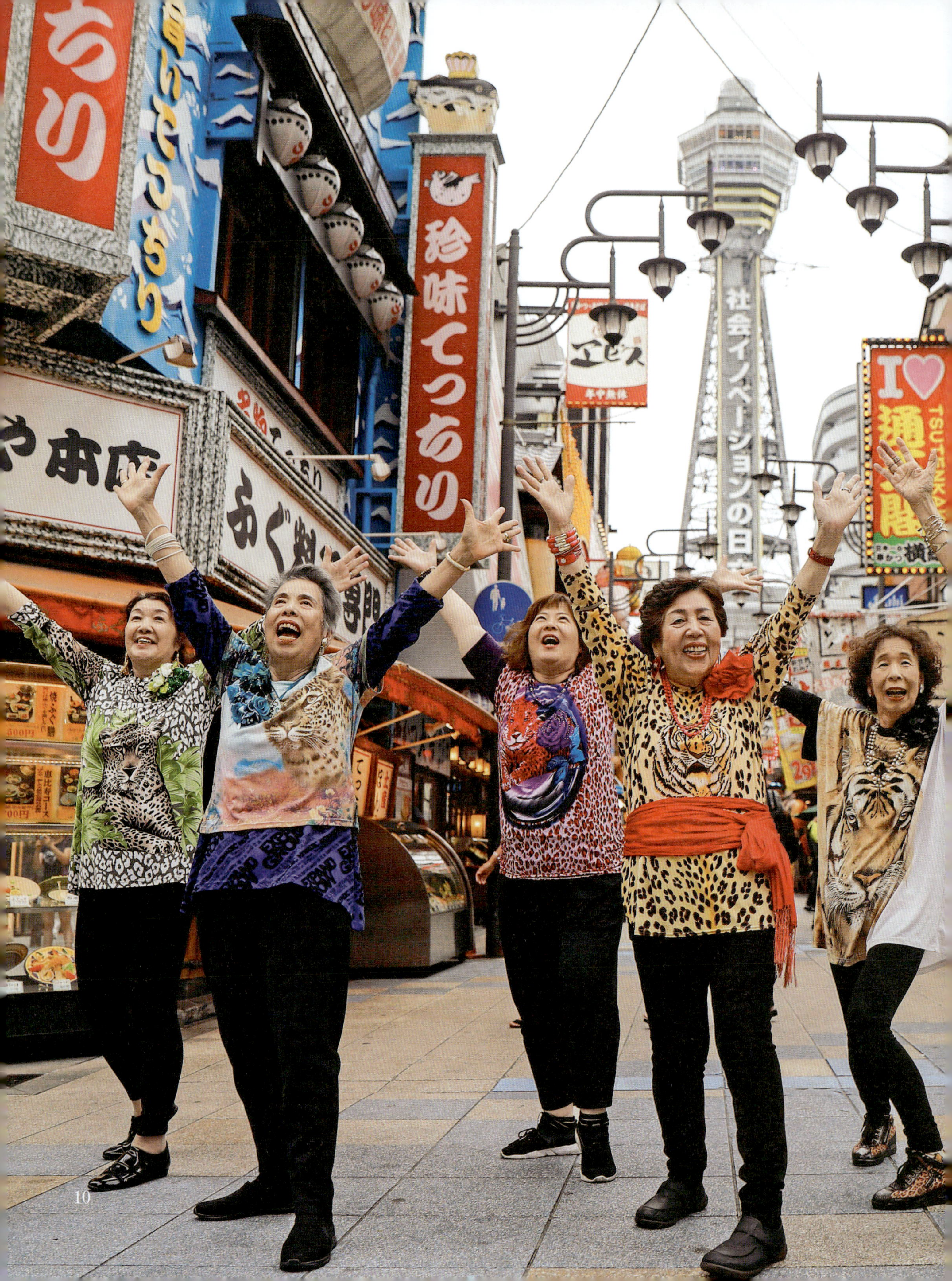

珍味てっちり
社会イノベーションの日
エビス
や本店

1
Your life

Grandmothers perform hip-hop to welcome G20 leaders to a summit in Osaka, Japan.

GOALS

- Skim an article to identify the main ideas
- Practise asking questions and giving short answers
- Talk about education at different ages
- Understand different accents
- Establish good rapport with people of all ages
- Write a description of an influential person

1 Work in pairs. Look at the photo and discuss the questions.
   1 What are the people in the photo doing?
   2 Would you enjoy doing this? What about older people you know, e.g. your grandparents?

WATCH ▶

2 ▶ 1.1 Watch the video. Are the sentences true (T) or false (F)?

NATIONAL GEOGRAPHIC EXPLORERS

MIKE GIL   TSIORY ANDRIANAVALONA

1 Tsiory wants to go back to when she was a child.
2 Mike likes two aspects about his life now.
3 Both Mike and Tsiory are looking forward to relaxing when they are older.

3 ▶ 1.1 Watch the video again. Write the four questions Mike and Tsiory answered.

4 Make connections. Ask and answer the questions you wrote in Exercise 3.

11

1A Remembering childhood

LESSON GOALS
- Skim an article to identify the main ideas
- Ask questions to evaluate evidence
- Talk about childhood memories

READING

1 Work in pairs. Discuss the questions.
1 What is your earliest memory?
2 What is your happiest childhood memory? Why is it important for you?

2 Look at the Reading skill box. In what situations would you skim a text? Why?

READING SKILL
Skimming online articles

Sometimes, you might not be interested in every detail of a text, but more in the general message. In that situation, you don't need to read every word. Often, the main idea of the text will be in the first or last few sentences. In online articles, it is common for the main idea to be in the first sentence or two immediately below the title. The first sentence of each paragraph will also often have the main idea of the paragraph. Understanding these can help you understand the main idea of the whole text too.

3 Use the tips from the Reading skill box to skim the online article on page 13. Choose which sentence best expresses the main idea of the text.
1 Childhood memories that are invented can be dangerous.
2 Many childhood memories are not real but invented.
3 We should try to forget false childhood memories.

4 Use the tips from the Reading skill box to match the sentences (a–g) with the paragraphs in the article (1–7).
a Use these tips to find out if what you remember actually happened.
b Some people believe what scientists know is very unlikely.
c Almost half of us seem to remember events from very early childhood.
d Some early memories might not be true.
e We can make people remember things that never happened.
f These are my happiest childhood memories.
g What should I do with my false memories?

5 Work in pairs. Think about the memories you described in Exercise 1. After reading the article, how sure are you that these are real memories? How do you know?

6 Look at the Critical thinking skill box. Choose two paragraphs from the article and in pairs think of questions you could ask to evaluate the presented evidence.

CRITICAL THINKING SKILL
Asking questions to evaluate evidence

It is important to think critically about the evidence an author provides in a text to help you, for example, decide how objective it is or whether it applies to your context. To evaluate evidence in a text, it can be helpful to ask yourself questions about it, such as:
- Where does the evidence come from: a scientific paper or a newspaper article?
- Where was the study conducted and how many people took part?
- To what extent do the results apply to the general population?
- Does the writer report the evidence correctly? Do they leave out any important details or change some facts?

SPEAKING

7 Prepare to describe two childhood memories to a classmate. One of them must be a memory of yours and one must be made up. Work in pairs. Give each other as much detail as possible about each memory. Then ask questions to decide which of your classmate's memories is true.

I remember being on a beach and looking down at my feet, which were covered in sand. I was collecting shells in a bucket. I was with my big sister and my parents.

EXPLORE MORE!

Choose one of the memories you discussed in class today. Talk to your family to find out if they remember it the same way as you.

How true are your early childhood memories?

1 *Our childhood memories might be some of the happiest and most important. But what if it turns out they're not real but completely made up?*

[1] I remember running around as a child without shoes in the summer rain. I also remember learning to draw castles with my grandpa. Oh, and collecting leaves with my grandma and planting flowers with my mum (and getting dirty in the process!). These childhood memories seem completely real. I can still feel the warm rain pouring down on me, and hear my grandpa's gentle voice as he teaches me.

[2] However, it seems that our earliest memories may not be true. Researchers have shown that while young children do form memories, they don't last long. In fact, at around the age of seven, something called childhood amnesia happens and we forget a lot of our earliest memories. It's true that those memories from my first few years of life are just blurry images and impressions.

[3] The interesting thing is, though, that many people do claim to have very vivid memories of events that took place before the age of seven. In fact, in one study about 40% of people said they remembered events from when they were three or younger. Even more strangely, 10% of the people studied were certain they remembered an event that happened in their first year of life.

[4] So on the one hand, scientists are pretty sure we can't remember much before the age of three, and we forget a lot of what happened before the age of seven. On the other hand, some people claim they remember being in a pram! One possible explanation is that as humans, we need to construct a life story. We fill any gaps in our story with made-up events, and these then turn into memories. Maybe my early memories of drawing with my grandpa were created when my relatives told me about this. But how do invented stories become real memories?

[5] Researchers have shown that it's possible to create false memories and these can feel so real that they affect how you behave in real life. For example, scientists have been able to stop people from eating certain foods by making them believe it had made them sick as a child.

[6] So how do you know whether a memory is true or false? Most memories from before the age of two are most likely false. If you can, look at family photos or videos or ask your family if they remember this. You could also look more closely at the details of the memory to see if they make sense.

[7] And if the memory turns out to be false? You can still keep it. I like remembering my grandpa's hands, voice and face as he gently helps me draw a better castle, even though my mum is sure we never drew together.

1B
Friends for life

LESSON GOALS
- Talk about friends you've had
- Ask questions and give short answers using auxiliary verbs
- Stress auxiliary verbs when appropriate

LISTENING AND GRAMMAR

1 Match the photos with the types of friend (1–4). Then name one of your friends for each type.
   1 workmates
   2 childhood friends
   3 school friends
   4 friends for life

2 Work in pairs. Take turns to ask and answer the questions about the friends you chose in Exercise 1.
   1 How did you meet?
   2 Why did you become friends?
   3 Are you still in touch? Why? / Why not?

3 🎧 1.1 Listen to two conversations. Which type of friend is each conversation about?

4 🎧 1.1 Complete the extracts from the conversations. Then listen again to check.
   1 A: ¹_____ you remember that friend Jacek I told you about?
      B: Yeah, I think I ²_____.
   2 A: But you two lost touch a while back, ³_____ you?
      B: We ⁴_____, yes.
   3 A: But ⁵_____ he living abroad now?
      B: He ⁶_____, but I think he moved back.
   4 A: We haven't spoken since she left.
      B: ⁷_____ you? I think that's a shame.
      A: Yeah, so ⁸_____ I.
   5 B: She ⁹_____ ask about you, you know.

14

5 Match your answers from Exercise 4 (1–9) with the uses of auxiliary verbs (a–g). Then read the Grammar box to check.

a emphasizing or correcting a point
b asking a positive question
c asking a short question to show interest/surprise
d agreeing using *so* or *neither*
e giving a short answer
f asking a negative question
g checking if we are right with a tag question

> **GRAMMAR** Auxiliary verbs in questions and short answers
>
> Auxiliary verbs (**be, do, have**) are typically used to:
> - ask positive questions
>
> *Do you remember …?*
>
> - ask negative questions
>
> *But **isn't** he living abroad now?*
>
> - give short answers
>
> *I **have**, but she just refuses to talk to me now.*
>
> - ask short questions to show surprise or interest
>
> ***Does** he? Oh, **did** she?*
>
> - check if what we're saying is true with tag questions
>
> *You two lost touch a while back, **didn't you**?*
>
> - agree with someone using *so* or *neither*
>
> *So did I, to be honest.*
>
> - give emphasis
>
> *She **does** ask about you, you know.*

Go to page 140 for the Grammar reference.

6 🎧 1.2 Choose the correct options to complete the conversation. Then listen to check.

Camila: Luis and I have known each other for over 30 years now.
Paula: ¹ *Have / Did / Has* you? Wow! Is it true that you weren't always best friends?
Camila: It ² *does / is / has*!
Luis: I actually didn't like you when we first met.
Camila: Neither ³ *had / was / did* I!
Paula: So how ⁴ *did / do / had* you become friends?
Luis: Well, it was a long process, ⁵ *was / wasn't / didn't* it?
Camila: It definitely ⁶ *was / did / were*. ⁷ *Did / Have / Do* you want to tell the story, Luis?
Luis: Well, as you said, it ⁸ *didn't / had / did* have a bit of a shaky start to it. One day …

PRONUNCIATION

7 🎧 1.2 Listen to the conversation in Exercise 6 again. Underline the auxiliary verbs that are stressed. Then read the Clear voice box to check.

> **CLEAR VOICE**
> **Stressing auxiliaries**
>
> In questions, auxiliary verbs are not normally stressed. Also, when you are agreeing with someone using *so* or *neither*, the main stress will be on the pronoun, not on the auxiliary (*So did **I***). However, auxiliaries are stressed:
> - in short questions to show surprise or interest: ***Have** you?*
> - in tag questions: *It was a long process, **wasn't** it?*
> - in short answers: *It **is**!*
> - when you want to give emphasis: *It **did** have a bit of a shaky start to it.*

8 Work in groups of three. Act out the conversation from Exercise 6. Stress the auxiliary verbs when appropriate. Change roles twice.

SPEAKING

9 Work in pairs. Discuss the difference between:
1 a friend and an acquaintance
2 a best friend and a close friend
3 a flatmate and a roommate
4 a partner and a couple
5 a workmate and a colleague

10 Complete the questions about friends with your own ideas. Write two more questions using words from Exercise 9.
1 Have you ever made friends _____ ?
2 Have you lost touch with any of _____ ?
3 Don't you think that _____ ?
4 You enjoy _____ , don't you?
5 When you were a child, did you _____ ?

11 Work in pairs. Take turns to ask and answer your questions from Exercise 10. Respond using the correct auxiliary verb and correct stress, and give some extra information.

A: Have you ever made friends with someone you haven't met in real life?

B: Yes, I have. There are people online that I call 'friends', but I've never met them in real life.

1C Back to school

LESSON GOALS
- Understand different accents
- Talk about education
- Say groups of consonants clearly
- Use short questions to ask for more information

SPEAKING

1 Work in pairs. Look at the infographic and write three questions to ask your partner. Then discuss your questions together.

Do you think maths is popular in this country too?

LISTENING

NATIONAL GEOGRAPHIC EXPLORERS

2 ∩ 1.3 Listen to Tsiory Andrianavalona and Mike Gil discuss their education. Write down at least one similarity and one difference with your own education. Then compare in pairs.

3 Work in pairs. Tell your partner about a time when you found it difficult to understand someone's pronunciation. Then read the Listening skill box for advice.

LISTENING SKILL
Understanding different accents

Most people who speak English do not speak it as their first language, so you will hear many different accents. To better understand them, be positive and don't give up. If other people's accents seem strange to you, it is only because you are not familiar with them. Notice how they say certain sounds (e.g. the /r/ in *remember*), words (e.g. *three* might sound like *tree* or *free*) or phrases (*get you* might sound like *getcha*). Listen to accents you find difficult by watching films, for example.

4 ∩ 1.4 Listen to Tsiory and Mike. How do they pronounce the underlined words? How would you pronounce them?

1 Tsiory: … during <u>mathematics</u> and <u>physics</u> classes, when I was <u>terrified</u> …
2 Tsiory: I <u>lived</u> about 1 kilometre <u>from</u> school, and walked <u>that</u> distance back and forth four times a day …
3 Mike: I <u>hated</u> 'busy work' that <u>required</u> no imagination or <u>thought</u> to complete.
4 Mike: I just <u>got</u> it <u>done</u> quickly and moved on to do fun things, like <u>hanging</u> out with friends …

Education around the world

Maths is the most popular school subject among students in many countries, including India and Saudi Arabia.

How many hours a year do 12-year-old students spend in school?

Philippines: 1,467
Mexico: 1,167
Netherlands: 1,067
Australia: 1,014
Paraguay: 1,011
Tunisia: 900
Zimbabwe: 753
Finland: 713

Finnish children do on average only 3.5 hours of homework a week, yet score in the top 6 in the world in international tests.

Bilingual children tend to do better than monolingual children in many types of tests.

Bonjour!
Xin chào!

A school in Lucknow, India is the largest in the world with 52,000 pupils!

750 million people in the world have difficulty reading and writing.

There are about 1.5 billion people learning English around the world.

How are you?
Hello!
My name's Niko.
Bye!
What's your name?

VOCABULARY AND PRONUNCIATION

5 Read about Isabel and Alex. How are their education journeys similar or different from Tsiory's and Mike's / your own education?

> 'I didn't complete high school because I got married very young. But thanks to a UNESCO programme, I was able to restart my education last year. I go to **evening classes** and will hopefully soon **graduate** from high school. I am then planning to go to university and study medicine. **Getting a degree** will help me provide a better future for me and my children.'
>
> *(Isabel, 32)*

> 'I'm from a small village and the **education system** in my area was a bit old-fashioned. We were expected to **memorize** a lot of facts without really understanding them. I found it difficult to **pay attention** in class. But I **revised hard for my exams** and somehow managed to **get good grades**. Now I'm at university, my learning experience is the complete opposite to that of my school days. I am learning about a subject I love in depth and it's easy to **stay focused**.'
>
> *(Alex, 21)*

6 Use the words in bold from Exercise 5 to complete the sentences. Then change the sentences so that they are true for you and discuss in pairs.

1 I was one of those students who rarely _____ attention in class.
2 My parents often got quite angry when I got bad _____.
3 Although my sister never _____ from university, she now runs a successful business.
4 It's quite common where I come from for people to do _____ classes or courses online.
5 I think the _____ system in my country is quite good compared to most countries.
6 I find it hard to stay _____ when I'm studying because there are so many distractions.
7 In school we have to _____ a lot of facts, especially in history and geography class.
8 I spend a lot of time _____ for exams.

Go to page 135 for the Vocabulary reference.

7 🎧 1.5 Look at the Clear voice box. Then listen to these words and underline the consonant groups. Practise saying them.

attention   degree   exchange   facts
grades   succeed   system

CLEAR VOICE
Saying groups of consonants

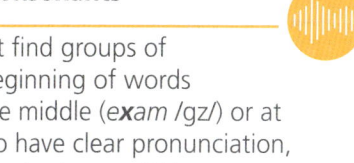

In English, you might find groups of consonants at the beginning of words (g*r*aduate /gr/), in the middle (e*x*am /gz/) or at the end (ha*rd* /rd/) To have clear pronunciation, it's important that you try to say all the consonant sounds in the group.

8 Find more words about education that have groups of consonants. Practise saying them.

SPEAKING AND GRAMMAR

9 Read the Focus on box. Then write a short question in response to the sentences (1–3).
1 My brother finally got his degree last week.
2 I'd love to go on an exchange.
3 I need to study for my exam.

FOCUS ON   Short questions

There are many short questions you can ask in a conversation to show you are listening and ask for more information. Many have a question word (e.g. *where*) + a preposition (e.g. *to*).

Who with?	What for?	What in?
How long for?	Who by?	Where to?

Go to page 141 for the Focus on reference.

10 Work in pairs. Tell each other about your experience in school. Talk about some or all of these ideas. Use short questions to ask for more information.
- your (least) favourite subjects and why you felt that way about them
- subjects you had to do and subjects you wanted to do
- a funny story that happened to you or a friend at school

1D Establishing good rapport

LESSON GOALS
- Understand how to establish good rapport with people of all ages
- Find things in common when talking to a person you don't know
- Practise speaking to someone you've just met

SPEAKING

1 Work in pairs. Follow the instructions.
1 Look at the photo of people who are meeting for the first time. Make a list of things they could be talking about.
2 Decide which of the questions (a–f) you might ask someone when meeting them for the first time. Which questions do you think are appropriate? Give reasons.
   a You're looking good for your age. How is your health?
   b University? What are you studying?
   c Interesting job. How much do you earn?
   d That dress looks fantastic on you! How much did you pay for it?
   e Dar es Salaam? Beautiful city. Have you always lived there?
   f Nice phone! I was going to get one. Where did you get it?

LISTENING

2 🎧 1.6 Listen to two people meeting for the first time. Which of these subjects do they discuss?

clothes   the man's job   the woman's job
a phone app for watching the stars   the 'star tour'
useful equipment   the weather   what they are going to see

3 🎧 1.6 Listen again. Discuss the questions in pairs.
1 Do you think they get on well? What do they have in common?
2 What helps them start a friendly relationship?
3 What makes it more difficult to establish a good relationship?
4 Do you usually find it easy to speak to new people? Why? / Why not?
5 Do you usually find it easy or difficult to get on with people much older or younger than you? Why? How important is it to establish good relationships with these people?

MY VOICE ▶

4 ▶ 1.2 Watch the video about establishing rapport (a friendly relationship). Tick the reasons for establishing rapport (1–10).
1 to ask questions
2 to discuss safe topics
3 to work together more effectively
4 to find things in common
5 to build trust
6 to listen actively
7 to understand each other better
8 to make teamwork more enjoyable
9 to show interest
10 to build stronger communities

5 Work in pairs. Look at the Communication skill box and discuss the questions (1–2).

COMMUNICATION SKILL
Establishing rapport

To establish rapport with new people, you need to show an interest in them and what they say. You need to find suitable topics of conversation and to keep the conversation going. Use these tips to help you start and continue your conversations.

- **Active listening:** Listen carefully to the other person and think about what they are saying. Think of ways to respond with questions and comments that show you are interested.
- **Key words:** Identify key words the other person says that you can ask about in follow-up questions (questions that ask for more information).
- **Things in common:** Talk about things you have in common. If you can't think of something, look around you for common subjects, such as the place you are in, friends you share, the food, etc.
- **Safe topics:** Stick to topics that in your opinion are safe, such as why you are here together or the things you can see around you. Look for signs that the other person is uncomfortable discussing a topic, such as staying silent or disagreeing. If this is the case, be prepared to change the subject.

1 Which of the tips do you already do?
2 Which tip do you think would be the most difficult for you to follow? Why?

6 Work in pairs. Read the exchanges. Underline the key words that A could use to keep the conversation going. Then write a follow-up question for A to ask B.
1 A: Where in Australia do you live?
   B: I live in Melbourne now, but I was in Perth before. I moved last year.
2 A: How well do you know the museum? Have you been here before?
   B: Oh, yes, several times. I think it's my favourite museum in Colombia.
3 A: How did you and Bouchra meet?
   B: I was working in a port in Tangiers, and Bouchra owned a company there.

7 🎧 1.7 Listen to the conversations to find out how the exchanges in Exercise 6 continued. Were the follow-up questions similar or different to yours?

8 🎧 1.7 Look at the Useful language box. Then listen to the conversations in Exercise 6 again and underline the expressions you hear.

> **Useful language** Linking to what the other person says
>
> I'm so glad you said you like …
> Going back to what you were saying about …
> It's funny you mentioned …, because …
> Speaking of …

SPEAKING

9 **OWN IT!** Work in pairs. Roleplay two people meeting each other for the first time at a party. Student A: Go to page 156. Student B: Go to page 157. Before you talk to your partner, think about how you can use the tips from the Communication skill box and the Useful language to keep the conversation going.

A: So how do you know the host?
B: He's a friend of a friend. How do you know him?

10 Discuss how well you established rapport with your partner. Use questions 1–3 from Exercise 3 to help you.

1E A big influence on me

LESSON GOAL
- Proofread your writing
- Say why someone is important to you
- Write a description of an influential person

SPEAKING

1 Think about two people who have influenced you. Use these ideas or your own ideas. Write two sentences about each person. Then read them to your partner. Can they work out who the sentences are about?

---
aunt/uncle   brother/sister   childhood friend   colleague
famous person   parent/grandparent/guardian   teacher

She's been a real inspiration to me. I've always looked up to her ever since I was a child.

READING FOR WRITING

NATIONAL GEOGRAPHIC EXPLORER

2 Read Mike Gil's description of a person that has influenced him. In which paragraphs (1–3) does he talk about the things below (a–g)? Two things are not mentioned.

a the history of their relationship
b the last time Mike saw the person
c the person's background
d what impresses Mike about the person
e what Mike has learned from the person
f what the person does for a living
g what the person is like

[1] My mother is my hero. She's had such a positive impact on my life. She helped my brother and me to believe that we could achieve whatever we wanted in life if we worked at it. She raised my brother and me as a single parent because my parents divorced when I was eight years old, and even though we didn't have much support or resources, she provided us with a life full of love and encouragement. Seeing my mom's* generosity and ability to make a working-class family feel fortunate has been a real inspiration to me, to say the least.

[2] My mom is from northern New Jersey, which means she comes across as a tough woman, who speaks her mind. But she is also extremely caring and has a deep love for people and nature. She is also fun-loving and regularly reminds me not to take life too seriously.

[3] My mom taught me to love myself and to stand up for what I believe in, no matter how difficult the path ahead may seem. She has shown me just how far the love and support of one champion can get you in life. This has played a central role in my teaching and science communication, through which I aim to teach, inspire and help others.

* *mom* US, *mum* British

3 Look at the Writing skill box. Then read the description of an influential person and use the tips to find eight mistakes.

WRITING SKILL
Proofreading

When you finish writing, it is important to proofread, or check for mistakes. Here are some tips that might help you.

- If you try to check everything at once, you may miss things. Make a list of things to check, e.g. prepositions. Check one thing at a time.
- Read it aloud – you might be able to hear mistakes you don't see.
- If you start proofreading immediately after finishing writing, you may not see the mistakes. Take a break first!
- Record the typical mistakes you make in writing and look for these in your work.
- Ask someone else to check it for you – they may spot what you can't see any more.

> My biggest influence is my partner, Lucia. I met her at university when I was eighteen years, but we didn't become a couple for two years later.
>
> Lucia is very friendly and outgoing person. Unlike me, she is never to shy to talk to new people, make friends and show how kind she is. I must admit, I trust people less than she does, which is something I very admire about her. She always makes people feel welcome.
>
> Lucia is an inspiration of me. For example, I don't think I would be as generous if she wasn't around, because she always thinks of other people before herself. She's also the reason I'm interested in animals, plants and the natural world (Lucia is biologist). I now often stop to listen to a bird singing and try to identify it! But perhaps the most important way that Lucia influences me is that I want to be a better person because she is in my live.

4 Work in pairs. Compare the mistakes you found. Discuss which tips you used and which were the most helpful.

5 Make notes about one of the influential people you chose in Exercise 1. Use the Useful language to help you. Write about:
- who they are.
- how you know them.
- what their personality is like.
- what you admire about them.
- how they have influenced you.

Useful language Saying why someone is important to you

She is the only person who understands me.
He's the reason why I studied law.
She means so much to me because she believed in me when no one else did.
She's an amazing writer because the characters are always so real.
I admire her for her determination.
If I could swim like her, I'd be a very happy woman!
My passion for dance comes from his classes too.

WRITING TASK

6 WRITE Write a description of an influential person. Organize the information into three or four paragraphs.

7 CHECK Use the checklist. I have …
- ☐ organized the information into 3–4 paragraphs.
- ☐ described who the person is and what they are like.
- ☐ explained why the person is influential in my life.
- ☐ used some of the Useful language.
- ☐ checked my work and corrected any mistakes.

8 REVIEW Work in pairs. Read your partner's description and proofread his/her writing. Then ask your partner questions to find out more about his/her influential person.

Go to page 130 for the Reflect and review.

EXPLORE MORE!

Think of a famous person you admire. Write three questions you'd like to ask them. Search online to see if you can find their answers to any of your questions.

A kingfisher perches proudly on a 'No fishing' sign with a fish in its beak.

2

Breaking the rules

GOALS

- Understand the meaning of new words from context
- Tell stories and talk about the past
- Understand fast speech
- Talk about crime and punishment
- Understand power distance
- Write a story

1 Work in pairs. Discuss the questions.
   1 Can you think of any rules for public spaces in your country?
   2 Have you ever broken any of them?

WATCH ▶

2 ▶ 2.1 Watch the video. Underline the types of rules that Alyea talks about.

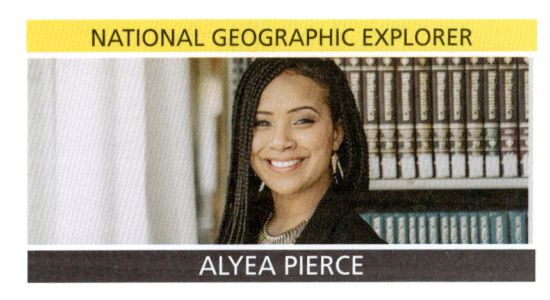

NATIONAL GEOGRAPHIC EXPLORER

ALYEA PIERCE

games rules   household chores   rules one gives to oneself
school rules   social rules   work regulations

3 ▶ 2.1 Watch the video again. Is Alyea someone who likes to follow or break the rules?

4 Make connections. How similar are your attitudes about rules to those of Alyea's?

2A Unusual laws from around the world

LESSON GOALS
- Understand the meaning of new words from context
- Identify the writer's tone of voice
- Discuss different rules for a city

READING

1 Work in pairs. Read the four laws from around the world. There is one that is invented. Can you work out which one it is?
   1 You must not annoy someone by flying a kite in Melbourne, Australia.
   2 It is illegal to bring your pet lion to the cinema in Baltimore, US.
   3 You have to give your mother flowers at least once a year in Phnom Penh, Cambodia.
   4 You can have a drink on a terrace in a café in Seville, Spain but you can't play dominoes.

2 Read the blog post on page 25 quickly to check which of the rules in Exercise 1 is invented.

3 Read the blog post again. Answer the questions.
   1 Why can't you name your child 'Apple' in Denmark?
   2 How might a tourist end up breaking the law in Venice, Italy?
   3 Is it legal to fly a kite in a public space in Melbourne if nobody else is there?
   4 What are you allowed to do on Spanish *terrazas* instead of playing dominoes?

4 Look at the Reading skill box. Use context to work out the meaning of the words/phrases in bold in the blog post.
   1 You must do this: _____
   2 You must not do this: _____

READING SKILL
Understanding the meaning of new words from context

It's often possible to work out the meaning of new words from context. To help you, consider the topic of the text and each paragraph, and the words before or after the new word. It's not always necessary to understand the exact meaning of the word to understand the text as a whole. It might be enough to decide, for example, if the new word is positive or negative, or what part of speech it is.

5 Look at the Critical thinking skill box. Underline the words in the box that best describe the writer of the blog post's tone of voice. Then circle any words or phrases in the blog post that helped you decide.

CRITICAL THINKING SKILL
Identifying the writer's tone of voice

By identifying the writer's tone of voice – their attitude to the topic – you often get important clues about their intention: are they trying to inform, entertain or criticize, for example? Here are some common tones that may be expressed in writing:
- conversational
- enthusiastic
- formal
- funny
- professional
- informative
- critical
- informal
- serious
- entertaining

To help you identify tone, look for words, sentences and opinions that express these attitudes.

6 Why do you think the writer chose this tone of voice? How does the tone affect your feelings about the laws he/she describes?

LISTENING AND SPEAKING

NATIONAL GEOGRAPHIC EXPLORER

7 🎧 2.1 Listen to Alyea Pierce. Which laws does she suggest for her city?

8 Work in pairs. Discuss what effect you think the laws Alyea suggested would have on her city.

9 Imagine you are law-makers for *your* city. Write five new laws and explain why you think they are important.

Citizens are obliged to go running every morning between 6 and 6.30 a.m. This is good for your health.

EXPLORE MORE!

Find unusual laws or rules that your country or region has. What might be their origin?

Children flying kites in a botanic garden in Australia.

The strange world of law

1 If you think law is always predictable, you might be in for a surprise. We took a tour of the world to find the most unusual laws. Here are our favourites.

No unusual baby names please!
Want to give your child an unusual name? Think twice! In Denmark it is **illegal** to use a name for
5 your child that's not on the list of names officially approved by the government. So if you wanted to imitate Gwyneth Paltrow and name your newborn Apple, that's **not allowed**. It's a fruit. Well, at least Danish children are less likely to be embarrassed by their name.

Don't feed those birds!
Wherever you find tourists, you can usually find pigeons looking for food. If you're a Venetian
10 pigeon, though, you're out of luck. Since 2008, feeding the pigeons has been **banned** in Venice. Maybe they should try Rome instead?

Keep your lion in its cage, sir
Where can you see lions? On an African savannah. In the zoo. On TV. And in the cinema. No, not in a film, but sitting next to you. Well, at least that's what law-makers in Baltimore, US must have
15 worried about when they **prohibited** bringing your pet lion to the cinema with you. The poor thing is **obliged to** stay home. Perhaps it could watch TV instead.

Let's go fly a kite ... or not!
It's a windy day in Melbourne, Australia – the perfect day to fly your kite. You go to a park, to see how high the kite will fly. Someone complains that you're annoying them and, before you know
20 it, you've broken the law. That's right – there is **a ban on** flying a kite in a public place in the Australian state of Victoria, if it annoys someone else. You'd better apologize quickly!

Singing yes, dominoes no
If you've ever been to Seville, Spain, I'm sure you've noticed that the *terrazas* are always full of people eating, chatting and otherwise enjoying themselves. Unfortunately, if you're a fan of
25 the game dominoes, you're **required to** play it at home. Seville has **outlawed** the game on the *terrazas* because of the noise the dominoes pieces can cause. Talking, whistling or singing, however, are not **forbidden**.

♥ 12   👍 10   😟 6   😃 3   💬 1

Comment ...

2B They hacked my laptop!

LESSON GOALS
- Understand articles about cybercrimes
- Talk about events in the past
- Say final consonant groups in -ed words

READING AND GRAMMAR

1 Work in pairs. Answer the questions.
  1 Do you know what a 'cybercrime' is? Can you think of any examples?
  2 What's a 'cryptocurrency'?

2 Read the newspaper articles. Then match the articles with the crimes (a–c). One article can be matched with two options.
  a fraud: the crime of getting money by lying to people
  b blackmail: forcing people to pay by saying you will hurt them in some way
  c hacking: breaking into someone else's computer system without permission to find out information or do something illegal

3 Work in groups. Discuss the questions.
  1 Do you think the articles give good advice? What other advice would you recommend?
  2 Has anything similar happened to you, or to someone you know?

4 Look at the Grammar box. Match the sentences (1–5) with the rules in the Grammar box (a–e).
  1 Carrie was reading her emails when a message appeared on her screen.
  2 Then one day Ruja just disappeared. Her investors tried to contact her repeatedly.
  3 Ruja Ignatova told thousands of people she had invented a cryptocurrency.
  4 A virus called CryptoWall 2.0 had installed itself on her computer.
  5 If she hadn't paid, she would have lost several months of files.

1 Follow the money

In 2016, Ruja Ignatova, also known as 'the Cryptoqueen', told thousands of people she had invented a cryptocurrency, a form of digital money, which would be more successful than Bitcoin, and persuaded them to buy into the idea. People around the world invested between 4 and 15 billion euros in 'OneCoin', believing that they would make lots of money.

Then one day Ruja just disappeared. Her investors tried to contact her repeatedly. But she had run away, along with the money. Unlike Bitcoin, the OneCoin company hadn't created the database that is needed for a digital currency to work – called a 'blockchain'. OneCoin was worthless, and many innocent people lost their money.

The advice? Don't trust get-rich-quick schemes! If it looks too good to be true, it probably is!

2 The clock is ticking

Carrie* was reading her emails when a message appeared on her screen: 'Your files are encrypted. To get the key to decrypt files you have to pay $500.' It was true: she couldn't open any of her 5,726 personal documents and photos. Several computer professionals failed too. And she only had a week to pay the hackers!

Somehow, a nasty software virus called CryptoWall 2.0 had installed itself on her computer and was stopping her from opening any files. Carrie decided to pay. If she hadn't paid, she would have lost several months of files because she hadn't backed up her computer recently.

* not her real name

The advice? Make regular backups of your data, and stay away from email attachments you don't trust.

WANT YOUR DATA BACK? PAY US THE MONEY!

GRAMMAR Past tenses

a Use the **past simple** to describe events in the past that happen one after the other.
*I **backed up** my computer then I **shut** it **down**.*

b Use the **past continuous** for a longer action that is interrupted by another action in the past simple.
*I realized someone **was using** my bank account when I saw €200 disappear mysteriously.*

c Use the **past perfect** to describe an event that happened before a point in the past.
*I didn't buy those things. Someone **had copied** my card.*

d Use the **past perfect** to report what someone says in the past simple or present perfect.
*He asked me whether I **had** ever **been** the victim of online crime before.*

e Use the **past perfect** to talk about unreal situations in the past.
*If the bank **hadn't blocked** my card so quickly, I could have lost it all!*

Go to page 141 for the Grammar reference.

5 Find and correct the mistakes in the sentences.
1 Someone tried to steal my card while I had taken money out of the cash machine.
2 She thought the email was from her bank, so she was clicking the link.
3 If he backed up his computer, he wouldn't have lost the files.

PRONUNCIATION

6 🎧 2.2 Look at the Clear voice box. Then listen and repeat the words.

CLEAR VOICE
Pronouncing -ed words

If an -ed word has a /t/ or /d/ sound before -ed, then -ed is pronounced /ɪd/, adding an extra syllable, e.g. *decided, invested*. When there isn't a /t/ or /d/ sound before -ed, the 'e' in -ed is not pronounced, so the final consonants are in groups:

/-md/ seemed	/-kt/ backed up
/-nd/ turned on	/-skt/ asked
/-vd/ received	/-pt/ stopped
/-ld/ installed	/-lpt/ helped
/-ndʒd/ changed	/tʃt/ attached

Identify consonant groups that are difficult for you to say. Practise the individual sounds, then in groups.

7 Work in pairs. Take turns to choose a verb and ask your partner to say the past form correctly.

activate block call change create fail
invent kill need prove seem switch

SPEAKING

8 Look at the Useful language box. Then find words/phrases in the box that have similar meanings to the words/phrases (1–6).
1 at first   4 finally
2 at the same time   5 when
3 without warning   6 little by little

Useful language Adverbs with past tenses

Past simple
He was writing an essay when **all of a sudden**, the screen went black.
Initially / In the end, he thought it must be the screen.
He **gradually** realized that something was wrong.

Past perfect
By the time he realized the laptop had a virus, the hackers had already stolen a lot of his data.

Past continuous
He took it to a repair shop. **Meanwhile**, the hackers were shopping online with his credit card.

9 Work in pairs. Student A: Go to page 156. Student B: Go to page 157. Read the notes about a cybercrime story. Then tell your partner the story. Use the Grammar box and the Useful language to help you.

Attila Nemeth decided he would hack the hotel's computers to persuade them to give him the job he had applied for.

2C
Crimes gone wrong

LESSON GOALS
- Understand fast speech
- Talk about crimes, criminals and punishments
- Say long and short 'o'

SPEAKING

1 Work in pairs. Look at the headlines and discuss what you think the stories might be about. Try to give as much detail as possible.

1 **Career change criminal applies for cop job**

2 **The uninvited house guest**

3 **Caught after a text message**

4 **Don't announce your plan on social media!**

LISTENING

2 🎧 2.3 Listen to the podcast. Which stories from Exercise 1 are mentioned? In what order?

3 🎧 2.3 Listen to the podcast again. Answer the questions.
1 How did the first criminal get caught so quickly?
2 Why didn't the second offender manage to steal anything from the supermarket?
3 Why did the second criminal go to prison if he hadn't stolen anything?
4 What two things surprised the couple when they arrived home from their holiday?
5 What punishment did the last offender get?

4 🎧 2.4 Look at the Listening skill box. Then listen to extracts 1–3 from the podcast and complete the sentences with the words you hear.

LISTENING SKILL
Understanding fast speech

In fast speech, people might not say the first consonant in words beginning with 'h' (e.g. *him*) and 'th' (e.g. *them*), so 'his' will sound like 'is' /ɪz/ and 'them' like 'em' /əm/. This happens when the previous word ends in a consonant. So, for example, 'caught him' will sound like 'caughtim' /ˈkɔːtɪm/ and 'caught them' like /ˈkɔːtəm/. Paying attention to this can help you understand fast speech better.

1 This guy was caught _____ home with a stolen phone.
2 And that's only an hour after he'd _____.
3 But before _____ it, he posted a photo of himself on social media.

VOCABULARY

5 Write these words from the podcast in the correct place in the mind map.

be/get caught   be sentenced to   break   break into
fine   guilty   innocent   rob   robber   victim   warning

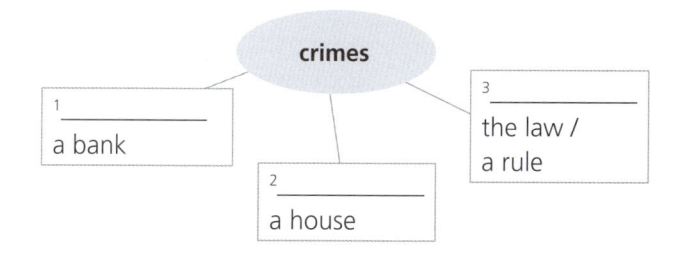

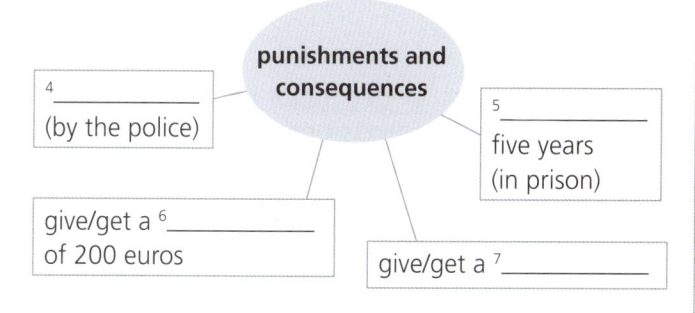

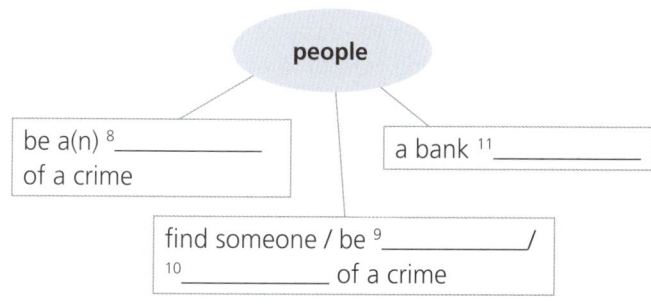

crimes
- 1 _____ a bank
- 2 _____ a house
- 3 _____ the law / a rule

punishments and consequences
- 4 _____ (by the police)
- 5 _____ five years (in prison)
- give/get a 6 _____ of 200 euros
- give/get a 7 _____

people
- be a(n) 8 _____ of a crime
- a bank 11 _____
- find someone / be 9 _____ / 10 _____ of a crime

Go to page 135 for the Vocabulary reference.

6 Complete the stories with words and phrases from Exercise 5.

When Mike Watson decided to 1_____ a man on the street, he was going for the expensive watch he'd seen on his wrist. Unfortunately for him, it turned out the watch was a fake, so Watson returned it to the 2_____. He then went to play football with his friends, and that's where the police 3_____ him. Of course, he claimed to be 4_____ – after all, he'd given the watch back.

In Germany, a man tried to 5_____ his neighbour's apartment. While opening the front door with his own credit card, he woke up the neighbours and the card broke. He ran away, leaving half of the card behind. All the details were on the card, so the police knew he was 6_____. To make matters worse, when the police got to the 7_____ house, they found the other half of the card on the table. The man was 8_____ two years in prison.

7 Work in pairs. Close your books. Retell one of the crime stories from this lesson to each other.

PRONUNCIATION

8 🎧 2.5 Look at the Clear voice box. Underline the words with a long 'o' /ɔː/ sound. Then listen to check. Practise saying the words, paying attention to the difference between the short and long 'o'.

all   caught   law   lost   order   robbed
short   stop   warning   your

CLEAR VOICE
Saying long and short 'o'

English has long and short vowels. One of them is the long /ɔː/, for example in *warning* /ˈwɔːnɪŋ/, and a short /ɒ/, for example in *rob* /rɒb/. To be easy to understand, it is important you make this difference between long and short sounds clear.

SPEAKING

9 Work in pairs. Prepare a short news report sharing two stories about stupid crimes. The stories can be real or invented. Use these ideas or your own ideas. Decide:
- what the criminal tried to do.
- how the criminal got caught.
- the punishment.

break into a museum	her own mobile phone
the owner of the boat	a secret camera
the security alarm	a 'smart' fridge
tried to steal the data	the victim's dog

2D Understanding power distance

LESSON GOALS
- Understand power distance
- Talk about getting used to new experiences
- Discuss your own attitude to power distance

> Good morning, Sir. I would like to apply for my papers.
>
> Please, call me Pablo.

> Erm, OK Sir ... I mean, Pablo!

SPEAKING

1 Work in pairs. Look at the cartoon and read about the two situations. Then answer the questions (1–4).

'When I moved to Spain, I had to go to the town hall to arrange my official papers. Where I come from, doing anything like this is a formal thing, and there is a distance between you and people in positions of power. We show respect by calling people Mr or Mrs. But the man I spoke to called me "Roman" and smiled and joked as if I was his friend.'

(Roman, from Poland)

'I recently made friends on social media with a biologist from Nepal who is studying the same plants as me. I am a professor and he wanted my help with his PhD application, and I was happy to help. When he first got in touch, he called me "Sir". Even though I asked him to call me David, he insisted on "Sir" in our messages. I still can't understand why.'

(David, from Austria)

1. How do you think Roman and David felt in these situations? Why? Would you feel the same?
2. What about the man Roman spoke to and David's online friend? What do you think they thought about Roman and David?
3. What do these stories tell you about the attitudes to authority of the four countries involved?
4. Would you say people in your country respect distances between people in positions of power and those who are not?

MY VOICE ▶

2 ▶ 2.2 Watch the video about power distance. Then choose the correct options to complete the sentences.

1. Examples of authority figures include parents, teachers and *managers / shop assistants*.
2. 'Power distance' describes our thoughts and beliefs about *authority / age differences*.
3. People in low-power-distance cultures have a more *equal / changing* view of relationships between people in a group.
4. When meeting someone from another culture, you should first of all identify *your own / the other person's* attitude to authority.
5. Be prepared to *keep / change* your attitude to power distance.

3 ▶ 2.2 Look at the Communication skill box, then watch the video again. Which of the tips from the box is not mentioned in the video?

COMMUNICATION SKILL
Understanding power distance

Be aware of your own attitude to authority and learn about other people's attitudes:
- observe their behaviour
- find out about what is typical of their culture
- ask questions with interest and polite curiosity

Be prepared to change your own communication style or behaviour. If you are not sure, assume a high-power-distance approach.

Try to be patient with people who behave differently from what you're used to.

4 🎧 **2.6** Listen to a conversation between Dirk and Zainab. What advice from the Communication skill box is Dirk asking about?

GRAMMAR

5 Look at the phrases in bold in the sentences (1–3) and answer the questions (a–d). Then read the Focus on box to check your answers.
1. Back home I **used to** call them by their first name.
2. I'll need to **get used to** being more formal then.
3. It's just that I**'m** not **used to** such special treatment.

a. Which structure means 'to already be familiar with a situation'?
b. Which structure means 'to change or adapt to a new, unusual situation'?
c. Which structure means you did something as a habit in the past?
d. What different structures come after *used to*?

> **FOCUS ON** *be/get used to* + something / doing something
>
> Use *get used to* (sth / doing sth) to talk about adapting to things that are difficult for you because they are unusual.
> *Some of the rules at my new company seem strange to me, but I'm **getting used to** them.*
> Use *be used to* (sth / doing sth) to say that someone is already familiar with a situation.
> *I'm used to eating rice or noodles for breakfast, so having cereal is very strange!*
> *Be/Get used to* is followed by a noun or the *-ing* form. Compare with the verb *used to*, which is always followed by a verb in the infinitive.
> *People **used to recognize** a power distance between young and old, but this is changing.*

Go to page 142 for the Focus on reference.

6 Complete the sentences with the correct form of *be* or *get*.
1. He _____ used to his students calling him by his first name now. He's worked in this country for years.
2. It feels strange to work so closely with the boss, but I _____ used to it eventually.
3. I've always made my own decisions, so this new job is quite hard for me to _____ used to.

SPEAKING

7 OWN IT! Complete the questionnaire. Decide whether each response shows high-, medium- or low-power distance. Go to page 157 to check your answers. Then compare your responses in pairs.

Authority and power distance

1 You are a teacher. You expect your students to call you …
  a by your first name. b by your family name.
  c 'Sir'/'Madam'.

2 You are a chemistry student. Your teacher gave you clear instructions of how to carry out an experiment. You want to try a different way. You …
  a ask your teacher if it is a good idea.
  b follow the instructions.
  c do the experiment your way, without asking.

3 You are a young person. You meet a friend of your father's. You decide to call him …
  a Mr Bellinger.   b Steve.   c Sir.

4 You are a team manager in a company. In a meeting, you explain an idea you have. A young employee in your team disagrees with it and suggests an alternative. You …
  a explain that you are only discussing your idea.
  b thank them and invite other comments and suggestions.
  c ask them politely to speak to you later.

8 Work in pairs. Think of different situations when there is power distance: at work, school or in your private life. Continue this list with as many ideas as you can think of. Then tell your partner about your own experiences in one or more of these situations.

Situations where there is power distance
-answering the phone
-going out with colleagues

EXPLORE MORE!

Do you think your country has a low or high power distance culture? Search online to see if you can find out.

2E Crime story

LESSON GOALS
- Describe people's actions
- Use adverbs to make a story more interesting
- Write a crime story

SPEAKING

1 Work in pairs. Discuss the questions.
  1 Look at the picture. What do you think might be happening?
  2 Do you enjoy reading or watching crime stories? Why? / Why not?
  3 What elements should a good crime story have?

READING FOR WRITING

NATIONAL GEOGRAPHIC EXPLORER

2 2.7 Read and listen to Alyea Pierce read out the story. Then answer the questions in pairs.
  1 Who do you think is the man 'yelling angrily' at the thief?
  2 What do you think might happen next?

She quietly pushed the front door open and stopped for a moment to listen to the sounds of the house. Everything was silent.

Now she had only 30 seconds to disable the alarm. She rushed over to the alarm. She had practised this for hours at home, but now she felt her hands shaking nervously.

Then suddenly it was done. The alarm switched off with a quiet click.

She grabbed her bag of tools and crept upstairs. The bedroom was large and there were paintings on all the walls. She swiftly crossed the room. She knew exactly where she was going. She had studied the plans carefully.

She was standing in front of a huge painting of a man on a horse. She gently pressed an invisible button under the bottom left-hand corner of the frame. The painting moved aside silently. Behind it was a tiny self-portrait. 'Small, but worth millions,' she whispered aloud excitedly.

She glanced at her watch. She'd only been in the house for five minutes.

As she was about to reach for her tools and get the painting off the wall, she sensed someone's eyes on her back. And then she heard a male voice yell angrily: 'Put your hands up and turn around slowly.'

She tried to act calmly, but as soon as she heard the voice, she knew who it was.

3 Look at the Writing skill box. Then complete the definitions (1–6) with these words. Use the story to help you.

WRITING SKILL
Describing actions

When writing a story, you can use many different verbs to describe the things that happened or that people did. These verbs can help you describe the actions better and make the story more real and interesting. For example, rather than 'look at' something, you could also *glance*, which means 'to look quickly'.

creep   glance   grab   rush   whisper   yell

1 _____ to look at something quickly
2 _____ to say something quietly
3 _____ to pick something up quickly
4 _____ to say something very loudly
5 _____ to move in a hurry
6 _____ to walk slowly and carefully so you are not noticed

4 Complete the sentences with the correct form of the verbs from Exercise 3.
1 The policeman _____ at the man to put his hands up, but he ran down an alleyway.
2 Rebecca tried to _____ up the old stairs, but the wood creaked with every step.
3 She _____ as many banknotes as she could, jumped on the bike and rode away.
4 The thief _____ towards the door, but Keeler got there first and blocked him.
5 She only had to _____ at the woman's expression to know she was hiding something.
6 Sergio could hear police officers behind the door. 'Any ideas how we get out of this one?' he _____.

5 Writers often use adverbs, e.g. *suddenly*, to make a story more interesting. Underline all the adverbs in the story in Exercise 2. Where are they typically placed in relation to verbs? Check the meaning of any new words in a dictionary.

6 Use an adverb from the Useful language box to modify the underlined verbs.
1 The plan <u>had been prepared</u>: what could possibly go wrong?
2 His boss <u>yelled</u> at him. How stupid of him to use the same password again!
3 Without warning, the lights <u>turned on</u>. Someone was coming!
4 She knew exactly what to do next, <u>took out</u> a tool and started working on the safe.

Useful language   Using adverbs to make a story more interesting

Although he was yelling **angrily** at him, Tom tried to act **calmly**.
She had **carefully** studied the plans, but now **suddenly** felt her hands shaking **nervously**.
He **confidently** walked across the room and **quietly** pushed the door open.
She smiled **happily** as she crept **slowly** out of the room.

WRITING TASK

7 🎧 2.8 Listen to Alyea talking about how to write a good crime story. Which piece of advice that she gives do you think is the most important?

8 You are going to write a crime story. Choose one of the titles or think of your own. Make notes on who the person is, where they are, what they are doing and why. Share your ideas with a partner.
1 'The robbery of the century'
2 'The guest in room 113'
3 'The good hacker'

9 WRITE Write your story.

10 CHECK Use the checklist. I have …
☐ followed some of Alyea's advice from Exercise 7.
☐ used descriptive verbs.
☐ made the story more interesting by using adverbs.
☐ divided the story into paragraphs.

11 REVIEW Work in pairs. Read your partner's story. What do you like the most about it? Did your partner follow some or all of Alyea's advice?

Go to page 130 for the Reflect and review.

EXPLORE MORE!
Read a crime story of your choice. What did you like the most/least about it?

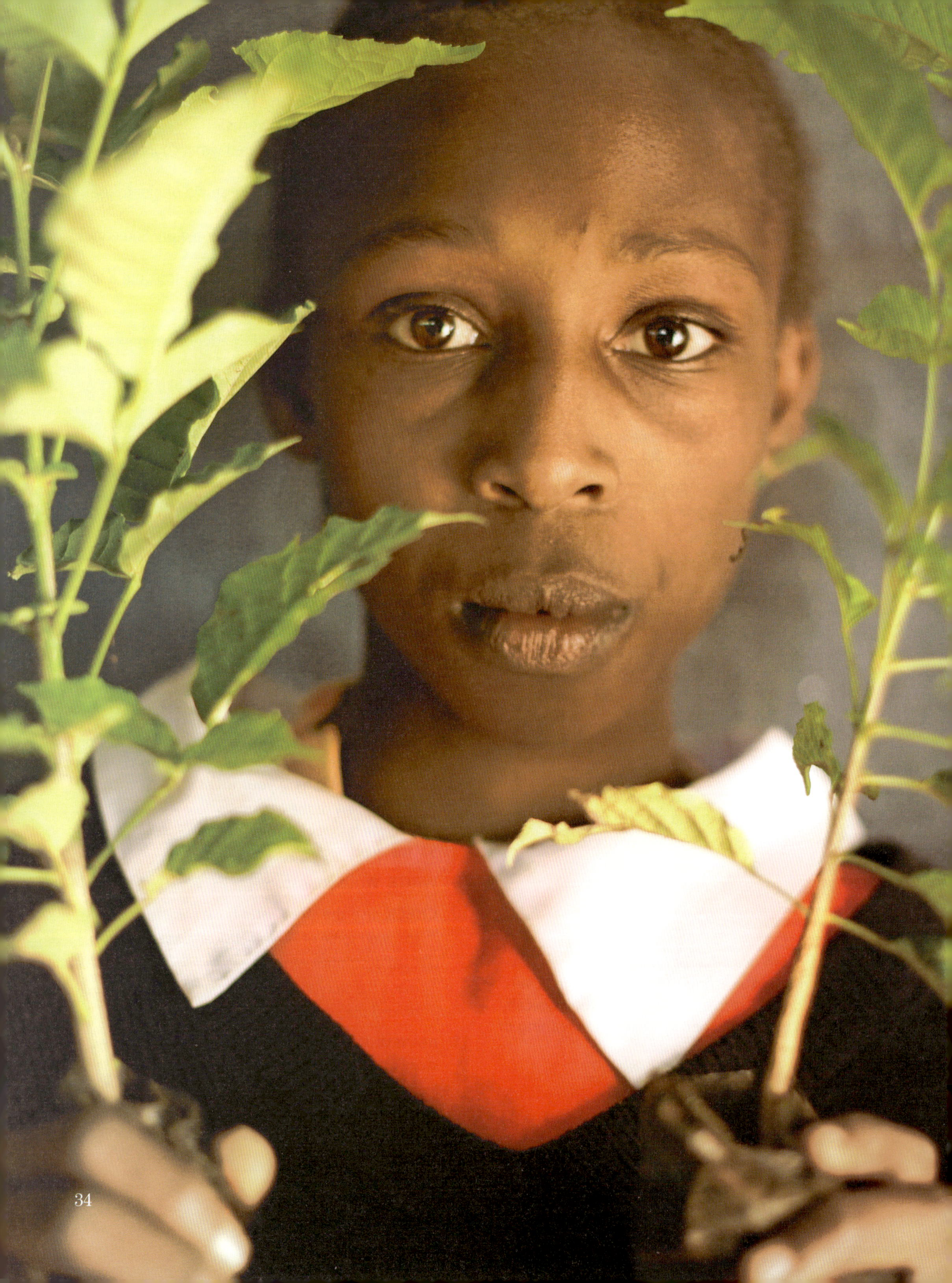

3

Imagining the future

GOALS

- Scan a text for specific information
- Talk about predictions
- Discuss future trends
- Understand fillers in conversations
- Give helpful feedback
- Write a personal development plan

1 Work in pairs. Discuss the questions.
  1 Look at the photo and the caption. How is the girl preparing for the future?
  2 What do you imagine the world will look like in ten or twenty years' time?

WATCH ▶

2 ▶ 3.1 Watch the video. Choose the correct options to complete the sentences.

NATIONAL GEOGRAPHIC EXPLORER

MARY GAGEN

  1 Mary is *positive / negative* about our ability to change how we live to protect the planet.
  2 Mary *prepares / does not prepare* for the future.
  3 Because she works from home a lot, she decided to buy *a camper van / a new computer*.

3 Make connections. Do you agree with Mary? Are you preparing for the future? What could/should you do?

A girl participating in the TIST programme in Kenya, which teaches people about the value of trees in cleaning the air, reducing soil erosion and building community values.

3A Innovating the future

LESSON GOALS
- Scan a text for specific information
- Compare solutions to solve a problem
- Discuss solutions to a possible future problem

READING

1 Work in pairs. Discuss the questions.
  1 What changes would you like to make to ensure a better future for yourself, your community and/or your country?
  2 If you had to choose one idea, which would you do? Why?

2 Read the profiles on page 37. For each one, write:
  - the problem(s) the person is solving.
  - how they are solving the problem(s).

3 Look at the Reading skill box. Then scan the profiles quickly to find what these numbers and names mean.

200	2010	6,000	725,000,000	8,000,000
Komunitas Motor Literasi		Ocean Sole		South Central

READING SKILL
Scanning for specific information

We often read for specific information such as numbers, names and details. In these situations, it may not be necessary, or quick enough, to read everything. Effective reading in this sense means quickly scanning the text to find the information. Once you have found where in the text it is, you can read that sentence carefully.

NATIONAL GEOGRAPHIC EXPLORER

4 🎧 **3.1** Look at the Critical thinking skill box. Then listen to Mary Gagen comparing the solutions in the profiles. Which of these points of view (1–5) does she use to evaluate the solutions? What does she think of the solutions?
  1 how it educates people about the problem
  2 how it involves the local community
  3 how long the solution might last
  4 how many other problems it helps solve
  5 how much it costs

CRITICAL THINKING SKILL
Comparing solutions

To decide how effective different solutions are, you can compare them by evaluating each from different points of view, e.g. price, effectiveness and speed. First you will need to decide on priorities: which points of view have the most importance in solving that specific problem? Then you can evaluate which solution is the most appropriate.

5 Work in pairs. Compare the solutions in the profiles from two points of view not discussed by Mary in Exercise 4. Which idea do you think would work best where you live?

SPEAKING

6 Work in pairs. Look at the possible future situation and the suggested solutions. Then evaluate the solutions using the points of view (1–5) from Exercise 4 and the advice in the Critical thinking skill box. Which solution do you think is best?

> **Problem:** The natural beauty of the area you live in is being spoiled by lots of rubbish that tourists throw on the ground. It's on the beaches, beside the road and in the natural parks. You'd like to solve the rubbish problem at the end of each holiday season and encourage visitors to respect your home.

> **Solution 1:** Put signs up and provide bins to encourage visitors not to drop rubbish.
> **Solution 2:** Organize rubbish collecting days for community volunteers and invite artists to do an art exhibition using the rubbish collected.
> **Solution 3:** Introduce fines for dropping rubbish and employ officers to enforce this.

7 Work with another pair. Compare your ideas. Do you agree on the best solution?

EXPLORE MORE!

Find out more about the work of Andri Gunawan, Julie Church or Ron Finley, or find out about another future innovator.

Nobody knows what the future has in store for us, but that doesn't mean we can't prepare for it. People are innovating in many different ways to create a better future for us all, by coming up with imaginative new ways of solving problems. Here are profiles about three of them.

Libraries on wheels

Andri Gunawan's school didn't have a library. His country, Indonesia, is made up of 6,000 inhabited islands spread over a huge distance, so in some places access to books can be challenging. That's why creative Indonesians such as Andri are doing it on their own. 'Many children drop out of school not because they aren't interested in reading, but because the access to books that they need is not there,' he says. He decided to do something about it and joined the *Komunitas Motor Literasi*, or Motor Literacy Community. About 200 motorcyclists volunteer their time and bikes to visit schools in remote areas. As well as distributing books, the group delivers literacy training, helping many young Indonesians learn to read so they can secure a more prosperous future.

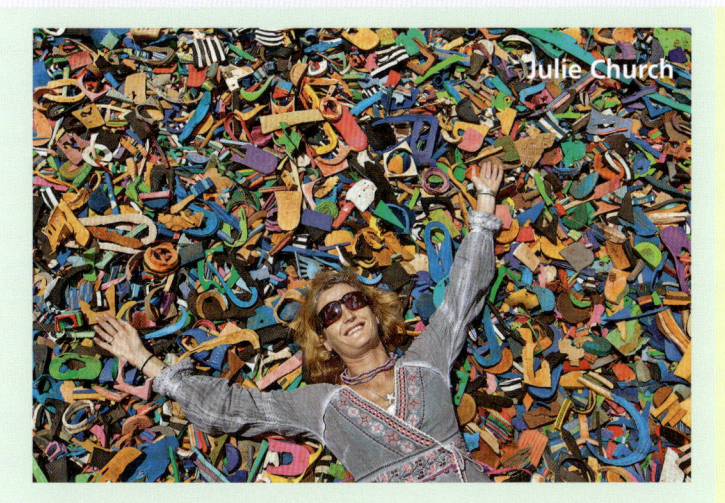

From flip-flops to art

Over 8 million tonnes of plastic enter the oceans every year. By 2050, there could be more plastic than fish in the oceans, according to the World Economic Forum. **Julie Church** set up a company in Kenya called Ocean Sole to address this problem by encouraging local people in Kenya to collect old flip-flops. These are then upcycled into various products, including art that has been exhibited in museums around the world. Julie explains the creative solutions to this problem: 'We've taken trash and we've made it into trade. We believe in trade not aid, and by doing so, we're making products that we're able to sell globally.' Apart from cleaning the environment, Ocean Sole has had a positive impact on the local community, creating jobs and supporting marine conservation. What's more, they organize school visits, educating children about the importance of protecting the environment.

Turning the L.A. streets into food

For **Ron Finley**, gardening isn't just about growing plants, it's about growing people. He lives in South Los Angeles, US, where quality fresh food can be hard to find. In 2010, he planted fruit and vegetables on some land between his house and the street. When the local authorities said what he was doing was illegal, he got the law changed. Ten years later, he has helped to create community gardens in unused spaces all over the city. He calculates that Los Angeles has more than 67 km² of such land – enough to grow 725 million tomato plants! Ron describes his gardens as 'a tool for the education, the transformation of my neighbourhood. You'd be surprised how kids are affected by this. Gardening is the most therapeutic and defiant act you can do, especially in the inner city. Plus you get strawberries.'

GLOSSARY:
defiant – refusing to do what you are told or expected to do
prosperous – successful; having more than enough money
upcycle – turn rubbish into things that are worth more because they are useful or beautiful
transformation – complete change of something so that it is better than before
therapeutic – if something is therapeutic, it makes you happier, more relaxed or healthier

3B Looking into the future

LESSON GOALS
- Understand predictions
- Talk about predictions
- Say contracted forms of *will* and *going to*

READING AND GRAMMAR

1 Work in pairs. Look at the illustration and discuss what predictions were made about the year 2020. Did the artist get anything right?

2 Read these old predictions about the future. Which have come true? Which do you find the most surprising?

> The telephone will be carried about by the individual, perhaps as we carry a watch today … I think the users will be able to see each other, if they want, as they talk. Who knows, but … it may actually translate from one language to another?
>
> Mark Sullivan, President of a telephone company (1953)

> In 2000, everyone is probably going to have a card instead of money. Each person might be given the same amount of money, which they will be able to spend by showing the card in shops.
>
> Writer Edward Bellamy (1888)

> I am convinced that within a century coffee [and] tea … will be no longer in vogue.
>
> Nikola Tesla (1937)

3 Work in pairs. Look at the predictions again and answer the questions. Then look at the first part of the Grammar box to check your answers.
   1 In addition to *will*, what other modal verbs do the people use to make predictions?
   2 What words do the speakers use to show they are not 100% certain of their predictions?
   3 What other verb structure is used to predict the future?

4 Look at these predictions. Which ones do you think will come true?
   1 As soon as the cost of computer-generated animation comes down, actors will be replaced by animations.
   2 Running out of milk will become a thing of the past if you get a 'smart fridge' that orders food for you.
   3 It won't be long before we will see living dinosaurs in zoos.
   4 We won't be able to grow enough food unless farmers can prepare for a hotter climate.
   5 People aren't going to trust human drivers when driverless cars have become the norm.
   6 I'll be old by the time people are living on Mars.

5 Look at the sentences in Exercise 4 again. Follow the instructions (1–4). Then look at the second part of the Grammar box to check your answers.
   1 Underline the time clauses.
   2 Circle the word or expression that introduces the time clause.
   3 Identify the two tenses used in the time clauses.
   4 Find a word or expression that means:
      a except if / if not
      b immediately after

38

GRAMMAR Talking about predictions

1

Use *will* or *going to* to make predictions.
*Users **will** be able to see each other as they talk.*
*All cars are **going to** be driverless in 50 years.*
Use *may*, *might* or words like *possibly* and *probably* to be less certain about the future.
*It **might** translate from one language to another.*
*Everyone is **probably** going to have a card instead.*

2

In sentences about the future with two clauses, use a present tense in the time clause.
***As soon as** the cost of CGI **comes down**, actors will be replaced by animations.*
Use the present perfect for a future event that will be finished before another future point.
*People aren't going to trust human drivers when driverless cars **have become** the norm.*

Go to page 142 for the Grammar reference.

6 Choose the correct options to complete the sentences.

1 I think that *when / after* our grandchildren are adults, the world *is / may be* a very different place!
2 Do you think you *can / might* own a house *as soon as / before* you are 30?
3 I don't think we *have / will have* discovered how to travel to the stars by the time we *are / will be* old.
4 Unless I *am / will be* ill, I don't think I *have wanted / will want* to retire.

7 Complete the sentences so that they are true for you. Then listen to your partner's sentences and ask about them.

1 I'll …
   by the time …
2 After I have …,
   I'm going to …
3 As soon as …,
   I'm going to …
4 I won't …
   unless …
5 When I …,
   I'm going to …
6 Before my …,
   I'll …

PRONUNCIATION

8 🎧 **3.2** Listen to the sentences and underline the words that are contracted by the speaker.

1 She is going to see him before the start of the show, so she will tell him then.
2 I will not be late. I promise. I am going to get the bus as soon as we have finished lunch.

EXPLORE MORE!

9 Look at the Clear voice box. Then practise conversations 1 and 2 in pairs. Say the first line fast, contracting where possible, then say it in full to be clearer. Then change roles.

CLEAR VOICE
Saying contracted forms of *will* and *going to*

In fast speech, *will/will not* and *am/is/are going to* can be contracted to '*ll/won't* and '*m/'s/'re gonna*. These contracted forms can be difficult to understand, so consider your listener. You may need to say them in their full forms to be clear.

1 A: It's going to rain at the weekend.
  B: I know. I was out shopping. I got very wet.
  A: No, I said it's going to rain next weekend.
  B: Oh!
2 A: The kitchen door is broken again.
  B: It's OK. I'll fix it.
  A: Oh, you have? That's great. Thanks.
  B: No, I will fix it. But I won't have time this afternoon, so it'll have to be tomorrow.

SPEAKING

10 Look at the Useful language box. Which expressions are used for more certain plans and predictions? Which are used for less certain future events?

Useful language Talking about uncertain plans and predictions
As far as I know, …
I'm convinced that …
I'm not sure whether …
It's likely that …
One thing is certain, …
There's a good/slight chance that …
There's no doubt that …

11 Work in groups. Discuss what life may be like in 50 years' time. Make predictions about three of these things. Use the Useful language to help you.

air travel   cities   education   health and medicine
language learning   leisure   money
shops and shopping   sports
work conditions (hours, types of work)

Choose something from the word box in Exercise 11 and find out more about the predictions people are making about it. Search online for 'the future of … (e.g. sport)'.

3C The future of languages

LESSON GOALS
- Discuss future trends
- Understand fillers in conversations
- Use prepositions to talk about data

THE FUTURE OF LANGUAGES

- Approximately **7,000** languages are currently spoken globally. In the 16th century, there were over **14,000**.
- Since 2014, the Wikitongues project has made video recordings of over **400** languages in order to save them.
- **62 million** people speak Spanish in the US (only Mexico has more Spanish speakers (121 million)). In 1980, there were **11 million**.
- **6.8 million** people took the HSK test of Chinese as a foreign language in 2018. In 1995, only about **12,600** students took it.
- Less than **1%** of internet content is in Arabic. But between 2001 and 2011 it grew by **2,500%**!
- Cornish, a language from Cornwall, UK, became extinct in the late 1700s. But there are now around **500** fluent speakers of Cornish.
- Less than **6%** of films shown in the US are in French (from **16%** in 2003). Films in Korean have more than doubled from **2%** to over **5%**.

Bonjour! Привет! Hi! Hej! 你好 ¡Hola! Dydh da!

SPEAKING

1 Work in pairs. Look at the infographic and discuss the questions.
1. Why do you think the number of world languages has decreased so much?
2. Why do you think interest in learning Chinese has grown so much?
3. How do you think these numbers might change in the next 100 years?

VOCABULARY

2 Read the predictions. Check the meaning of the bold phrases in a dictionary. Discuss in pairs which predictions you agree and disagree with. Give reasons.
1. Some people **estimate** there will be more Spanish speakers in the US than English speakers, but I think the number will **remain unchanged**.
2. The number of Cornish speakers **is set to** increase over the next 100 years.
3. We're going to **see a sharp growth** in the number of people taking the Chinese as a foreign language test.
4. If we **look at the data**, it's clear there will be a **steady drop** in the number of global languages.
5. **It's unlikely** that Arabic will become the most widely used language on the internet.
6. The percentage of films in Korean shown in the US is likely to **continue rising gradually**.
7. **It's only a rough estimate**, but I think Wikitongues might record all the world languages within the next 20 years.

3 Use the phrases from Exercise 2 to make three more predictions about the future of languages. Use your own ideas or these prompts. Then discuss your predictions in pairs.
- speakers of your mother tongue
- people learning English
- films made in your mother tongue and in English
- articles on Wikipedia in your mother tongue

Go to page 136 for the Vocabulary reference.

LISTENING

4 🎧 **3.3** Listen to extracts from two conversations. Complete the extracts with the words you hear.
1 _____, the US actually has 62 million Spanish speakers …
2 _____, the hope is that by recording these languages, they are preserving them.
3 A: So do you think Spanish-language films will _____ start growing a lot, _____?
B: Yes, it's possible. _____, it probably depends on …

5 Work in pairs. Look at the Listening skill box. Then discuss:
1 what fillers you often use in English.
2 what fillers you have got in your own language.

LISTENING SKILL
Understanding fillers in conversations

In conversations, it is common for speakers to pause to think or to change how they say something. Often you will then hear 'fillers', words that help speakers fill in the pauses. Some, e.g. *Basically* and *I mean*, are typically used at the beginning of a sentence. Others are used in the middle of a sentence, e.g. *like* and *sort of*.

6 🎧 **3.4** Listen to the complete conversations and choose the correct option (a, b or c) to complete the sentences.
1 One third of languages in the world have fewer than _____ speakers.
  a 1,000   b 2,000   c 5,000
2 The Wikitongues project is trying to _____ every language in the world.
  a speak   b teach   c record
3 In the US, the number of films in Korean _____ .
  a is on the rise   b remains unchanged
  c has decreased slightly
4 The film *Life in a Day* features over _____ languages.
  a 10   b 20   c 30

GRAMMAR

7 Complete the sentences with *of*, *by*, *to* or *in*. Then read the Focus on box to check.
1 The number of languages spoken around the world has decreased _____ 50% since the 16th century.
2 Recently, there has been an increase _____ the popularity of Māori, an indigenous language spoken in New Zealand.
3 The number of Māori speakers has risen from 20,000 _____ about 50,000.
4 There has been a rise _____ 2,500% in the percentage of internet content in Arabic.
5 I predict that the number of Cornish speakers in the UK will grow _____ 20% over the next five years.

FOCUS ON   Talking about data: Prepositions

Nouns describing changes such as a rise, fall, decrease, increase, decline or growth are typically followed by the prepositions *in* or *of*.
*There will be a sharp decline **in** the number of languages spoken around the world.*
*There was a rise **of** 10% in the percentage of internet content in Arabic last year.*

Verbs describing changes such as to rise, fall, decrease, increase, decline or grow are typically followed by the prepositions *by* or *to*.
*Spanish speakers in the US will grow **by** 60 million in the next 50 years.*
*The percentage of languages with fewer than 1,000 speakers has risen **to** 30%.*

Go to page 143 for the Focus on reference.

SPEAKING

8 Find out how one of these aspects of culture has changed over time. How do you think it will continue to change in the future? Tell your partner, using prepositions from the Focus on box.

art   books   dance   fashion   food
language   music   sports

EXPLORE MORE!

Search online for 'sounds of endangered languages'. Choose several to listen to. How do they sound?

3D
Giving helpful feedback

LESSON GOALS
- Discuss giving and receiving feedbac
- Pronounce long vowels clearly
- Practise giving and receiving feedback

SPEAKING

1 Work in pairs. Look at the photo and discuss the questions.
  1 What are the people in the photo talking about? What do you think the man is saying?
  2 Do you ever tell people what you think about things they've made, e.g. clothes, art or cooking? If so, do you ever comment on what's wrong, or do you only say how much you like it?
  3 Do you enjoy getting feedback (receiving people's opinions)? Why? / Why not?

2 Read about Ali. Then discuss the questions in pairs.

> Ali loves space and sci-fi and decides to make a podcast about it. When he puts his podcast online, his friend Sanjay calls him to give his opinion:
>
> 'Did you use the computer's microphone? That's why the sound quality was so poor. Why didn't you buy an external microphone? There were other problems that made it difficult to listen to. Like when you talked, you read from a script, and I would never do that. It made the podcast uninteresting. Plus you didn't have any music to introduce the podcast.'

  1 How do you think Ali was feeling *before* he spoke to Sanjay?
  2 Why do you think Sanjay gave Ali his opinion?
  3 If you were Ali, how would you feel after listening to Sanjay?
  4 Do you think Sanjay's feedback was useful?

MY VOICE ▶

3 ▶ 3.2 Watch the video about giving feedback. Then complete the summary.

Feedback is ¹_____ about something new, or someone's work or behaviour that tells you how good or useful it is. Feedback can help us ²_____ and develop. We give feedback to others to help and ³_____ them. Feedback often focuses on the ⁴_____, but the problem is that this means people might not feel in ⁵_____. If you give feedback that focuses on the future, people will feel that they are making ⁶_____. Feedback stops being a criticism and starts being ⁷_____.

4 ▶ 3.2 Watch the video again. Then complete the sentence with your own definition in pairs.
Feeding forward is …

A fashion design teacher assesses students' work in Cape Town, South Africa.

5 Look at the Communication skill box. Use the advice to rewrite Sanjay's feedback to Ali from Exercise 2 so that it is more helpful.

COMMUNICATION SKILL
Giving helpful feedback

When we offer our opinion about other people's performance, it should be because we want to help them. Here are some guidelines to make feedback more helpful.
- Before you offer help, first ask whether the person wants your feedback!
- Describe the facts, rather than giving opinions, and talk about problems and errors as opportunities for improvement.
- Limit your negative feedback to two or three points. Make sure the ideas you are suggesting are achievable.
- Don't forget to point out positive points too!
- After giving feedback, continue to offer help. Your practical support will mean a lot.

PRONUNCIATION

6 🎧 3.5 Look at the Clear voice box. Listen and repeat.

CLEAR VOICE
Pronouncing long vowels

English has five long vowels: /ɑː/, /iː/, /ɜː/, /ɔː/ and /uː/.

To be understood, it is important to make these long. This will help the listener hear the difference with short vowels (e.g. f**a**ll vs f**u**ll, r**ea**d vs r**i**d).

/ɑː/ **ar**gue, sm**ar**t, f**ar**
/iː/ d**e**cr**ea**se, m**ea**n, r**ea**d
/ɜː/ l**ear**n, c**er**tain, w**or**k
/ɔː/ t**a**lk, th**ough**t, f**or**ward
/uː/ t**u**ne, ch**oo**se, l**o**se

7 🎧 3.6 Listen to these words and circle the ones that have a long vowel. Then practise saying the words.

comment	continue	fall	feedback	improve
increase	languages	learn	negative
opinion	partner	remark	support

SPEAKING

8 Work in pairs. Read the situations (1–3) and discuss how Erika's, Nurzhan's and Julieta's feedback could be improved.

1. After a difficult meeting, Erika talks to her assistant, Stef: 'Were you planning to do the accounts later, or had you forgotten? And when I asked you to organize the client visit, I expected you to book the hotel.'

2. Nurzhan, an athletics coach, is talking to one of his runners after a race: 'You lost because you weren't thinking, Azi. The race was yours and you gave it all away in the last lap. What did I tell you about staying on the inside?'

3. Julieta is talking to her English student about an essay: 'Rosa, this is disappointing work from you. I expect more. Next time, all you need to do is organize your writing better.'

9 🎧 3.7 Listen to a conversation between Julieta and Rosa from Exercise 8 in which more helpful feedback is given. Underline the expressions in the Useful language box that you hear.

Useful language   Expressing feedback

Making helpful suggestions
Next time, you could try + -ing …
You might want to (do x next time) …
You'll be great as long as you remember to …

Offering support
Let me know (how I can help you).
I'll be happy to (talk to you about …) any time.
Don't hesitate to (ask for help).

10 OWN IT! Work in groups of three. Choose three situations from Exercises 2 and 8, or invent your own. Follow the instructions. Then change roles.

Student A: You are the person giving feedback. Use the techniques from the Communication skill box and the Useful language to help you.

Student B: You are the person receiving feedback. Listen carefully and ask questions when necessary.

Student C: Listen to the conversation. Use the form on page 156 to give feedback to Student A.

3E My future

LESSON GOALS
- Use a mind map to brainstorm ideas
- Talk about your goals and how to achieve them
- Write a personal development plan

SPEAKING

1 Work in pairs. Look at the personal goals (1–5). How similar or different are they to your own goals? Which important personal goals have you already achieved?
1 Travel to five foreign countries.
2 Be able to watch films in English without subtitles.
3 Get my driving licence by the end of the year.
4 Spend more time with my family and friends.
5 Start a new sport or get back to one I used to do.

NATIONAL GEOGRAPHIC EXPLORER

2 Look at the Writing skill box and Mary Gagen's mind map. Then discuss the questions in pairs.
1 Which goal from Exercise 1 does Mary want to focus on?
2 What problems and personal weaknesses might stop Mary from achieving her goal?
3 What personal strengths might help her?

WRITING SKILL
Using a mind map to brainstorm ideas

Before writing, a mind map can help you brainstorm ideas. Here are some tips for effective mind maps.
- Use images – they can help you get creative.
- Use colours – they help you divide ideas into categories.
- Let the ideas flow – don't worry if they don't make sense yet; you can edit them down and organize them later.
- Use key words – don't write full sentences yet; focus on words or short phrases.

READING FOR WRITING

3 Read Mary's personal development plan. How did Mary use the ideas from the mind map to organize her text?

Over the next year, I would really like to start surfing again. When I was younger, I surfed quite a lot, even though I wasn't very good at it! I am lucky that I already live close to the sea, so I can easily get to a surfing beach. One of my strengths is that I am a good swimmer and love the water, so I have no excuses!

However, what I am worried about is that it will be much harder to learn again, now I am older, than it was when I was younger. Deep down I worry that I might be too old to learn again! To help me tackle this issue, I am starting to go surfing again with two friends who want to learn as well. We are all starting together so we will motivate each other.

I also need to stop making an excuse to not go if it is a cold and rainy day or very windy. It can be really hard to motivate yourself to get in the freezing cold sea on a day like that, but you feel so much better afterwards.

To motivate myself, I need to remember that surfing is good for my wellbeing. It is good exercise, and I will feel better if I just go and do it!

Mary surfing in the Algarve, Portugal.

4 Read the plan again. Underline the phrases that Mary uses to talk about:
1 her strengths.
2 her weaknesses / dealing with her weaknesses.
3 achieving her goals.

5 Look at the Useful language box. Then complete the sentences (1–5) with one word.

> **Useful language** Talking about achieving your goals
>
> **Strengths**
> One of my main strengths is …
> I'm quite lucky that …
> I'm very good at …, so I can (easily) …
>
> **Weaknesses**
> Deep down I worry that I will …
> One thing I still need to work on is …
> I need to gain more skills, such as …
>
> **Achieving goals**
> (In order) to achieve …, I'm going to …
> To motivate myself, …

1 To _____ myself, I'm going to start a diary and write down my goals.
2 I need to _____ more skills before I can play my first public concert.
3 I hope that I can _____ this goal by the end of the year.
4 Deep _____ I worry that I'm never going to be good enough.
5 I'm quite _____ that my family always supports me.

6 Use a mind map to brainstorm ideas for your own personal development plan. Then discuss your ideas in pairs.

7 Use the Useful language to write five sentences for your personal development plan.
To gain the skills I need to pass the driving test, I can take regular lessons.

WRITING TASK

8 WRITE Write your personal development plan. Use the mind map from Exercise 6 and the sentences in Exercise 7.

9 CHECK Use the checklist. I have …
☐ discussed my personal goal(s).
☐ explained how my strengths can help me achieve my goals.
☐ talked about a possible problem and how I can deal with it.
☐ used some of the Useful language.

10 REVIEW Work in pairs. Read your partner's personal development plan. Can you think of any other ideas that could help your partner achieve their goals?

Go to page 131 for the Reflect and review.

EXPLORE MORE!
Put your personal development plan into practice. Keep notes about how it is going. Share your progress with a classmate.

Two women laughing together while working at an ice-cream parlour in Okinawa, Japan.

4
Good taste

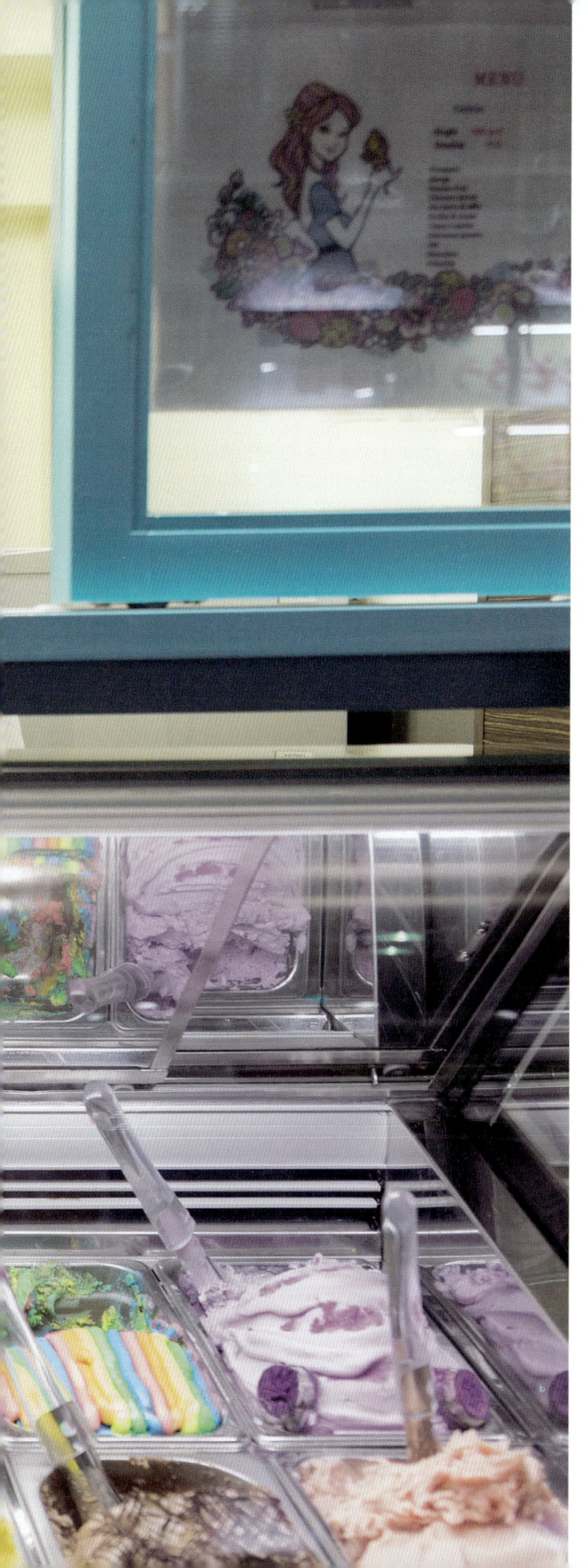

GOALS
- Identify supporting stories
- Compare different types of food
- Talk about good and bad table manners
- Understand assimilation in fast speech
- Recognize different ways of saying 'no'
- Write a review of a restaurant

1 Work in pairs. Discuss the questions.
 1 Do you enjoy eating ice cream? What's your favourite flavour?
 2 What other dishes do you love or hate? Why?

WATCH ▶

2 ▶ 4.1 Watch the video. Answer the questions.

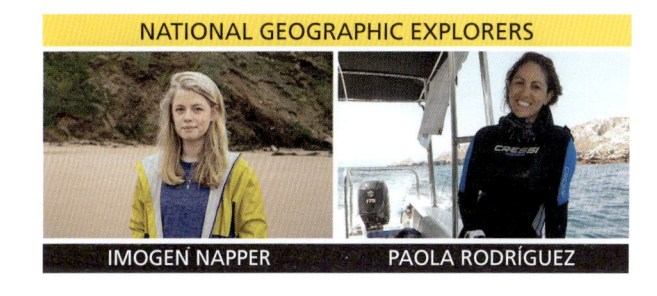

NATIONAL GEOGRAPHIC EXPLORERS

IMOGEN NAPPER   PAOLA RODRÍGUEZ

 1 What are Imogen's and Paola's favourite flavours?
 2 Which flavours would Imogen and Paola try?

cheese   chicken rice   coconut   Cornish clotted cream
insect   lobster   pizza   raw fish   spicy   walnut

3 Make connections. Discuss the questions.
 1 Which of the flavours would you try?
 2 How adventurous are you when it comes to trying new food? What food wouldn't you try?

47

4A Flavours of an ancient land

LESSON GOALS
- Identify supporting stories
- Analyse descriptive writing
- Organize a 'taste tour' for a visitor to your town

READING

1 Work in pairs. Discuss the questions.
  1 What's your favourite national cuisine?
  2 What's the most unusual food you've ever tried?

2 Read the extract from Christoph Niemann's travel journal on page 49. Find one thing:
  1 he found difficult to do.
  2 he did that was surprising.
  3 he did not enjoy.
  4 he learned about himself.

3 Read the extract again. Answer the questions.
  1 Who is likely to be the 'driver' going 'down the highway in the wrong direction' in paragraph 1?
  2 What part of the world is the writer from?
  3 What problem did the writer have greeting people?
  4 Why was the market seller impressed?
  5 Why was the writer surprised at the smell of the fermenting rice?

4 Find these words and phrases in the extract. Use them in the questions (1–3) instead of the phrases in bold. You may need to change other words. Then discuss the questions in pairs.

> encountered (line 49)   open-minded (line 21)
> shift in perspective (line 19)

  1 Travelling or meeting people from other places can often lead to a **change in the way you look at someone or something**. Have you experienced this?
  2 What challenges have you **come across** when travelling? How did you deal with them?
  3 Would you say you are **prepared to consider new ideas different to yours**?

5 Look at the Reading skill box. Find supporting stories in the extract for the arguments (a–c).
  a When you are away from home, some experiences can be strange and unpleasant for you.
  b Being away from home, it's possible to see how strange your normal life can be.
  c When you are away from home, you are the one who is strange.

READING SKILL
Identifying supporting stories

Writers often use stories to support their argument. These can include personal stories, historical accounts and even jokes. When reading a story within a longer article, ask yourself:
- What is the story saying about the person, place or theme?
- What argument does the story present? Does it help you follow or remember it better?
- Does the story help persuade you of the argument the article makes?

6 Look at the Critical thinking skill box. Then read the last three paragraphs of the extract to find examples of descriptive writing. Answer the questions in the box.

CRITICAL THINKING SKILL
Analysing descriptive writing

Writers use different techniques when describing places to help create the atmosphere. For example, they might make an unusual comparison (e.g. *fruits and vegetables were piled high like pyramids*). They can also encourage you to 'read' the story with your other senses by describing smells, feelings or emotions (e.g. *the air was filled with the aroma of food*). When reading a description, ask yourself:
- What feeling am I getting from the description and how does the writer achieve this?
- How effectively does the writer do this?
- Does the description affect (positively or negatively) my reaction to the text?

SPEAKING

7 Work in groups. Imagine a foreign visitor is coming to your town or area. Organize a 'taste tour' for them. Decide:
  1 what local dishes and drinks they must try to get the authentic taste of your area.
  2 which restaurants, markets and street sellers they need to go to.
  3 how to describe the local dishes so that the visitor understands what they are eating.

Along the Mekong

1. *Artist and traveller Christoph Niemann describes the sights and smells of a journey from Cambodia to Vietnam along the Mekong River.*

One of my favourite jokes goes like this: a man is listening to the radio in his car when the programme is interrupted: 'Attention! Attention! A driver is travelling down the highway in the wrong direction!' The man looks down the road, busy with oncoming traffic, and says to himself, 'What do you mean a driver? I see hundreds of them!'

I think about this joke whenever I travel to a new place that seems strange – when, in fact, I am the one who has just arrived from a foreign land and who is probably going down the road in the wrong direction.

As an artist, I'm conscious of the limitations that come from seeing the world through Western eyes. That's why I like to travel: because it requires – and inspires – a shift in perspective. So as I set off on a National Geographic Expeditions journey along the Mekong River, I had two main goals: 1 Be open-minded; 2 Don't embarrass yourself.

I failed at goal number two almost immediately. The first thing I learned about Cambodian good manners is that when saying hello (or thank you), you bring your hands together. It's a beautiful and simple sign of friendship. But I wasn't as graceful as others. Every time I attempted it, I found myself with my hands full. I was usually carrying a water bottle, a big camera or my backpack.

Food provided me with the perfect opportunity to achieve my other goal. These days, hardly anyone who lives in a big city needs to travel thousands of miles to enjoy Southeast Asian food. But being on the Mekong gave me the opportunity to see how the food related to the places and people.

Guided by a chef on a special taste tour of the local markets, I tried authentic dishes made by local people: a delicious dill omelette; a dessert of duck eggs; tapioca grilled banana; a paste of fermented fish, a popular Cambodian ingredient, cooked inside a banana leaf. The market seller was impressed that I tried it.

The markets were overflowing with produce. The fruits and vegetables were piled high like pyramids. Fish were arranged in neat rows like books on a shelf. The air was filled with the aroma of food: fried, barbecued or fermented.

In the towns and marketplaces of Cambodia and Vietnam, we encountered a range of memorable smells. On a visit to a fish farm in Vietnam, I stood next to a huge barrel in which homemade fish food was prepared – an experience my nose is not keen to repeat. The next afternoon, we watched the process of fermenting rice to make a local drink. Our guide opened the lid of a barrel, and I automatically turned away in expectation of the smell that came toward me. But then I was surprised: it could not be described as pleasant, and yet I loved it – the smell was one I'd known all my life from the dough my mum made for her traditional German strudel cake. I realized that sometimes a faraway place can teach you a lot about the strangeness of familiar tastes.

GLOSSARY:
aroma – a pleasant smell, e.g. from food
authentic – prepared in the traditional and original way
dough – the substance made of flour and water that you cook to make bread, etc.
fermented – if you ferment food, you leave it for the sugar to change in a chemical process

EXPLORE MORE!

Search online for more of Christoph Niemann's work, or him giving talks about his work. What interesting things has he encountered on his travels?

4B The tastiest meal ever?

LESSON GOALS
- Understand an interview about best and worst meals
- Modify comparative and superlative adjectives to talk about food
- Change your pronunciation to help the listener

LISTENING AND GRAMMAR

1 Work in pairs. Look at the text and discuss the questions.
  1 What's the most expensive, spiciest, biggest or smelliest food you've ever tried? How was it?
  2 What are the most important 'ingredients' of an enjoyable meal? Think about the atmosphere, place, food and people.

NATIONAL GEOGRAPHIC EXPLORERS

2 🎧 4.1 Listen to Imogen Napper and Paola Rodríguez discuss their best and worst meals. Answer the questions.
  1 What food/meals do Imogen and Paola mention?
  2 Did they like it? Why? / Why not?
  3 Which of Paola's or Imogen's meals would you like to try? Why?

3 🎧 4.1 Listen again. Are the sentences true (T) or false (F)?
  1 Plymouth has by far the best fish and chip shops Imogen has ever been to.
  2 The fish isn't as fresh in other places as it is at Imogen's favourite restaurant.
  3 Imogen's Thai curry was the spiciest meal she'd ever had.
  4 In San Andrés, *fruta del pan* is a lot less common than potato or rice with a meal.
  5 One of the most memorable meals Paola has ever had was a vegetarian meal her mum made.
  6 Paola was eating a bit more carefully than usual.
  7 Paola felt more and more full, but she kept eating anyway.

4 Read the sentences in Exercise 3 again and complete the tasks (1–3). Then read the Grammar box to check.
  1 Underline all the comparative and superlative forms.
  2 Circle all the words and expressions that make the comparative and superlative forms stronger or weaker.
  3 Tick (✓) the sentence where a comparative is used to mean *less than*.

« Fascinating food »

Saffron is the most expensive ingredient in the world. It takes 170,000 flowers to make one kilogram of it, which can cost up to $10,000 – much more than most caviar.

Hunan cuisine, from south China, is one of the spiciest in the world. It uses many ingredients which are often stewed, fried or smoked. Be prepared for a mouth explosion!

The largest serving of falafel on record was made in Ain Saadeh, Lebanon. It contained around 844,000 falafels and weighed 5,173 kilograms. It took 300 student chefs to make it, and no doubt many more people to eat it!

Surströmming, or fermented Baltic herring (a type of small fish), is a delicacy in Sweden, but some consider it the smelliest food in the world. A study found that even Japanese and Korean fermented fish dishes aren't as smelly as surströmming!

GRAMMAR Modifying comparative and superlative adjectives

You can use *a lot / much / a bit* to modify comparative adjectives.
*Potatoes or rice are **a lot** less common than 'fruta del pan'.*
You can use *by far / one of* to modify superlative adjectives.
*The fish is **by far** the most delicious I've ever had.*
Repeat the comparative with *and* to show that something keeps changing.
*Paola felt **more and more** full.*
Use *not as* + adjective + *as* to say that one thing is less than the other.
*The fish **isn't as fresh as** there.*
You can use comparatives and superlatives with adverbs.
*She was eating **more carefully than** usual.*

Go to page 144 for the Grammar reference.

5 Find and correct the mistakes in the sentences. Then rewrite the sentences so that they are true for you.
1 The Lighthouse is by far the better restaurant in my town.
2 My mother's cooking isn't as good than mine.
3 In my opinion, breakfast is lot more important than lunch or dinner.
4 One of worst food accidents I've ever had was when I left a big pot of ice cream in the sun.
5 If I had to choose, I'd say pizza is a bit more tasty than pasta.
6 I think the restaurants in my town are becoming more or more expensive.
7 Food tastes worse when it is cooked more slow than usual.

PRONUNCIATION

6 🎧 **4.2** Listen to the conversation. Then answer the questions in pairs.
1 How is *a lot* pronounced the first time it is spoken?
2 What does *a lot* sound like to the other person the first time it is spoken?
3 How does the first speaker change their pronunciation to help the other person understand?

7 Work in pairs. Look at the Clear voice box. Take turns to change your pronunciation when saying the sentences (1–3). Follow the instructions.
Student A: Say the sentence fast, not pronouncing the underlined final /t/.
Student B: Ask your partner to repeat.
Student A: Repeat the sentence, pronouncing the final /t/.
1 It's not the bes<u>t</u> burger on the menu.
2 It's by far the mos<u>t</u> delicious meal I've had.
3 It's the spicies<u>t</u> soup ever.

CLEAR VOICE
Changing your pronunciation

In order to be easily understood, it's important to adapt the way you speak if you notice the listener has not understood you (or if you think you may be misunderstood). For example, when people speak fast, the final /t/ is often not pronounced when the next word starts with a consonant (e.g. *a lot more* → /əlɒˈmɔː/). However, this can sometimes make your voice less clear, so you may need to change your pronunciation and say the final /t/ (e.g. *a lot more* → /əlɒt ˈmɔː/).

SPEAKING

8 Look at these dishes. Then follow the instructions.

> deep fried Nutella pies   fermented cabbage soup
> fried tarantula   mint chocolate chip pancakes
> oreo cookie pancakes   roasted iguana
> stuffed sheep stomach   tuna eyeball

1 Choose two dishes and ask as many people in the class as possible which one they'd rather have.
2 Ask people to give a reason, e.g. *I think it would be much saltier than the other one.*
3 Take notes on their answers.

9 Work in pairs. Report to each other what your classmates said. Which dishes were the most and least popular? Why?

EXPLORE MORE!

Search online for 'food of the future' and watch one of the videos. Then report to the class how different food in the future will be from the present.

4C Good table manners

LESSON GOALS
- Talk about good and bad table manners
- Use negative prefixes with adjectives
- Understand assimilation in fast speech

VOCABULARY

1 Work in pairs. Look at the different types of behaviour at the dinner table (1–6) and discuss the questions (a–c).
1. leaving food on your plate
2. leaving a tip in a restaurant
3. adding salt to a dish
4. taking the last piece of food without offering it to others first
5. using your phone at the table during a meal
6. waiting for everyone to sit at the table before you start eating

a Which types of behaviour show the best and worst table manners in your opinion? Why?
b What other bad table manners are there? What annoys you the most?
c Have you ever shown bad table manners without realizing? What happened?

2 Read the sentences. Which behaviour from Exercise 1 are they about? Which opinions do you agree and disagree with? Why?
1. I think it's **a sign of good manners** to eat everything. It shows the **host** you enjoyed it.
2. I think we **offended** the waiter by not giving him one last night.
3. It's **typical behaviour** these days, but I don't think it's **socially acceptable**. The other **guests** might feel you're ignoring them.
4. It might seem **impolite**, but sometimes I'm so hungry I can't wait!
5. This isn't **appropriate**. To **show some respect**, ask if anyone else wants it first.

3 🎧 4.3 Complete the conversations using the words in bold from Exercise 2. Then listen to check.
1. A: Oliver! You can't do that! That's very _____!
   B: Yes, show some good _____, please!
2. A: I'd like to thank the _____ for a lovely meal.
   B: Oh, please! Thank *you* all for being such wonderful _____!

3. A: Should I take a gift? I mean, what's socially _____ behaviour in this situation?
   B: Yes, that would be the _____ thing to do.
4. A: What's _____ behaviour at the table in your family?
   B: We normally wait for our parents to start eating before we do, to show them _____.
   A: Would they be _____ if you didn't wait for them?
   B: Yes, probably!

4 Think of two occasions when either you or someone you know showed bad manners. Write about what happened using words from Exercise 2. Then share your stories in groups.

Go to page 136 for the Vocabulary reference.

GRAMMAR

5 Read the Focus on box. Then write the opposite form of these adjectives. Use a dictionary to check your answers.

appropriate   certain   comfortable   direct   formal
organized   patient   polite   stressed

> **FOCUS ON** Negative prefixes for adjectives
>
> A prefix is something you add at the beginning of a word to change its meaning. Some common prefixes which create the opposite form of an adjective are *un-*, *in-*, *dis-* and *im-*.
> acceptable → **un**acceptable
> sensitive → **in**sensitive
> respectful → **dis**respectful
> possible → **im**possible

Go to page 145 for the Focus on reference.

6 Work in pairs. Discuss which types of behaviour in your country would be:
- disrespectful to older people.
- inappropriate in the classroom.
- impossible to understand for a foreigner.
- unacceptable as a guest.

A family enjoy lunch together at their home in Belo Horizonte, Brazil.

LISTENING

7 🎧 **4.4** Listen to how the phrases are said. Notice what happens to the underlined sounds. Then look at the Listening skill box to learn more about fast speech.

1 when I wa<u>s</u> younger
2 tha<u>t</u> you noticed
3 <u>D</u>o you remember …

LISTENING SKILL
Understanding fast speech: assimilation

In fast speech, the final /s/, /z/, /t/ and /d/ sounds can change to /ʃ/, /ʒ/, /tʃ/ and /dʒ/ when the next word begins with the letter 'y', or the sound /j/. So *was young* can sound like /wəʒˋjʌŋ/. Also, the following /j/ sound can sometimes disappear, so *get you* can sound like /ˈgetʃə/. Pay attention to this to understand fast speech more easily.

8 🎧 **4.5** Read the phrases and decide how the underlined sounds would be pronounced in fast speech. Then listen to check.

1 Bu<u>t</u> you know …
2 an<u>d</u> you eat it
3 abou<u>t</u> your experience

EXPLORE MORE!

Write an email to a friend who is planning to visit your country. Give them advice about 'good' and 'bad' manners.

NATIONAL GEOGRAPHIC EXPLORERS

9 🎧 **4.6** Listen to Paola Rodríguez and Imogen Napper discuss how 'good' table manners can differ from country to country. Which social mistakes from Exercise 1 do they mention?

10 🎧 **4.6** Listen again. Decide who did or does the things in sentences 1–5. Write *I* for Imogen or *P* for Paola.

1 I normally have lunch between 2 and 3 p.m.
2 I wasn't very good at eating with my hand.
3 I don't like it when people use their phone during a meal.
4 Friends don't need to let me know in advance if they want to come over.
5 I've got sick after eating red meat.

SPEAKING

11 Work in pairs. Create a class survey about (in)appropriate behaviour in different areas of life, e.g. in the street, at a friend's house, in class, playing sports or online. Follow the instructions.

1 In pairs, write at least five questions.
2 Individually, interview as many people in the class as possible.
3 Compare answers in your pairs.
4 Share your findings with the class.

4D Saying no

LESSON GOALS
- Recognize different ways of saying 'no'
- Pronounce /k/, /p/ and /t/ in stressed syllables
- Practise saying 'no' in international settings

SPEAKING

1 Work in pairs. Read the situations (1–3) and discuss the questions (a–c). Then put Sarah, Jun and Claire on the scale of how directly or indirectly they say 'no' to others.

DIRECT ◄──────────────► INDIRECT

1 Sarah goes for dinner at her friend Jochen's house. Jochen asks her if she wants a second serving of food and Sarah says 'No, that's OK.' Jochen says 'Oh, OK then.' Sarah is still hungry.
2 Paolo asks his friends to come to a party at the weekend. His friends all say yes, including Jun. But Jun doesn't turn up for the party.
3 Sandra invites Claire to her book club. Claire says she can't go and explains that she doesn't have time to read.

a What's the problem?
b Why has there been a miscommunication?
c How might each person be feeling?

2 Decide whether the sentences are true for you. Then put your name on the scale in Exercise 1.

1 I think you should always be honest, even if it might not be easy for the other person to hear.
2 I'm most polite when I am being indirect.
3 I usually talk to people in quite a direct way.
4 In my culture, people tend to communicate indirectly.

3 Roleplay the situations from Exercise 1 with your partner. Then change roles and repeat the conversations. What language did you use to say 'yes' and 'no'?

MY VOICE ▶

4 ▶ 4.2 Watch the video about the difficulties of saying and understanding 'no' in international settings. Then complete the summary with the words you hear.

If you don't feel comfortable saying 'no', you could ¹l_____, but there is a danger you can ²h_____ people. However, telling the truth might also ³o_____ others. So what do you do? You could say 'no' in a more ⁴i_____ way, but this may mean they ⁵m_____ you. To decide how directly you should say 'no', you could first think about how ⁶c_____ you and the other person are. Also, consider if there is any ⁷p_____ distance between you. You could also try to ⁸d_____ this issue with the other person. Finally, watch how they ⁹r_____ and be prepared to apologize or explain yourself. To sum up, remember that there is no ¹⁰r_____ way of saying 'no' and you may need to change how direct you are depending on the situation.

5 🎧 **4.7** Look at the Communication skill box. Then listen to the conversation between Patricia and Gabi and answer the questions.

COMMUNICATION SKILL
Different ways of saying 'no'

A person may say 'no' to you when they really mean 'yes', or they may say 'yes' when they really mean 'no'. In these situations, it is important to look for the hidden meaning.
- Look for signs that show the other person may not mean what they say, such as hesitation ('ums' and 'errs') and excuses.
- Think about how the other person is feeling. Might they be worried about losing face, for example?
- Try to be aware of how direct you tend to be. When saying 'no', you may need to be more or less direct than usual to make sure people understand you but are not offended by you.
- Enter international situations with an open-minded, polite and honest attitude.

1 What signs are there that Gabi does not mean exactly what she says?
2 Do you think Patricia is being sensitive enough to Gabi's feelings? Does she notice that Gabi does not want to help her? Why? / Why not?

PRONUNCIATION

6 🎧 **4.8** Listen to these words and circle the stressed syllable. Notice how the sound in bold is pronounced. Look at the Clear voice box to learn more.

im**p**olite   o**p**en-minded   **p**atient   res**p**ect
typical   un**c**omfortable

CLEAR VOICE
Saying /k/, /p/ and /t/ in stressed syllables

In syllables that are stressed, the sounds /k/, /p/ and /t/ are aspirated in English. This means that you feel a quick flow of air out of your mouth when saying them (put your hand in front of your mouth to check). Aspirating /k/, /p/ and /t/ is important, because otherwise the sounds might be heard as /g/, /b/ and /d/ and cause misunderstanding.

7 Practise saying the words in Exercise 6, aspirating when appropriate.

SPEAKING

8 Look at the Useful language box. Decide which ways of saying 'no' are more or less direct.

Useful language   **Ways of saying 'no'**
That's really kind, but I think I'd rather just …
Oh no! That's too much to ask.
No, thank you. I prefer to do it myself.
Oh please! I don't want to trouble you.
I'm grateful for the invitation, but really …
I'd love to …, but I have another arrangement, I'm afraid.
No.

9 **OWN IT!** Work in pairs. Act out the scenarios (1–4).
Student A: You ask B to do something. Insist more than once that B accepts your offer/request.
Student B: Say 'no' to A's offer/request. Use the Useful language to help you.
Change roles for each scenario.
1 A is B's manager. A invites B out for a meal with some other colleagues. B doesn't feel comfortable going for dinner with A.
2 A and B are friends and had an expensive meal. A knows that B doesn't have much money at the moment, so A offers to pay.
3 A and B are brothers. A has made some soup. They both know A is a terrible cook. A offers B some soup.
4 A is the boss of a café. B is one of the waiters. A wants B to work on New Year's Eve, but B has party plans!

10 Choose two scenarios to act out in front of another pair. Give feedback to the other pair on how well they managed to say 'no'.

EXPLORE MORE!

Notice all the times you say 'no' in your own language throughout a whole day. Each time, imagine the conversation in English.

4E I highly recommend it!

LESSON GOALS
- Organize a restaurant review
- Discuss positive and negative restaurant experiences
- Write a review of a restaurant

SPEAKING

1 Work in pairs. Discuss the questions.
   1 What would be your ideal restaurant experience? Think about who you are with, where you go, what kind of food you have, etc.
   2 Which of these would make a good or bad restaurant experience: slow service; big portions; loud music; spicy food; payment only by cash; a waiter who speaks your language?
   3 Have you ever written a review of a restaurant? Do you ever read reviews before choosing where to go? Why? / Why not?

READING FOR WRITING

2 Work in pairs. Follow the instructions. Then answer the questions.
   Student A: Read the review on this page.
   Student B: Read the review on page 157.
   1 Is the review positive or negative? What specifically did the writer like or dislike?
   2 If you were the restaurant owner, how would you feel after reading the review? What would you do to improve?

Alma P.
17 reviews • 2 photos

★★★★★ a month ago

Best meal ever!

I must say I didn't expect much, to be honest, but La Ermita turned out to be more than worth it.

The service was fabulous. The staff were very friendly, welcoming and attentive throughout. They also spoke very good English, which was a great plus, because my friend doesn't really speak much Spanish. Definitely the best service I've had in a restaurant.

The food was absolutely delicious. We had Spanish omelette, calamari, fried potatoes, fried fish, salad and olives. The only slightly negative point was that the portions were modest, to say the least, so we ended up getting an extra dish. So I'd recommend you order more dishes than you normally would.

I also loved the restaurant itself. It's very spacious and had a genuine Spanish feel to it. It's a shame we didn't have time for dessert, but next time I will make sure we order some.

So overall, we had a delightful time and one of the best meals we've ever eaten. It certainly exceeded our expectations. So a 5 out of 5. Highly recommended!

👍 Like

3 Look at the Writing skill box. Read both reviews again and tick the typical elements that are mentioned.

WRITING SKILL
Organizing a restaurant review

- Most restaurant reviews will share many common elements, such as a title, the writer's overall impression/recommendation, specific points about the food, etc. and suggestions for improvement.
- Often, a review will begin with a title and then the introduction, where the writer gives their overall opinion.
- Each paragraph that follows is about a specific topic, e.g. about the food, the staff and the restaurant itself, and might include suggestions for improvement.
- A restaurant review typically ends with some final thoughts, such as an overall recommendation.

4 Underline the positive adjectives and phrases in the reviews, and circle the negative ones. Use the Useful language box to check. Check the meaning of any new words in a dictionary.

Useful language   A restaurant review
Negative opinion
tasteless food
overpriced
small/modest portions
dreadful experience
didn't live up to our expectations
a (complete) let-down
it made a negative impression

Positive opinion
helpful/friendly/attentive staff
delicious food
an authentic/genuine feel to it
delightful experience
spacious interior
It's (more than/well) worth it
(It's) highly recommended
It exceeded our expectations

5 Work in pairs. Discuss the questions using the Useful language.
1. What's a restaurant that you would highly recommend?
2. Have you ever visited somewhere that didn't live up to your expectations? Why?
3. What's one of the most delightful or dreadful restaurant experiences you've had?
4. How can restaurant staff make sure they are helpful and friendly? Could they also be *too* friendly?
5. What helps create a genuine or authentic feel to a restaurant?

6 Write three true or false sentences about your restaurant experiences using the Useful language. Read the sentences to your partner. Can they work out which are true?

WRITING TASK

7 Think about a time you went to a restaurant and had a positive or negative experience. If you haven't been to a restaurant recently, imagine a good or a bad experience. Make notes on:
- the overall impression
- the service
- the food
- the restaurant itself
- any recommendations

8 **WRITE** Write a restaurant review. Use the Writing skill box and Useful language to help you.

9 **CHECK** Use the checklist. I have …
☐ a title and star rating.
☐ an introduction with my overall opinion.
☐ a review of the food, the staff and the restaurant itself.
☐ a conclusion with a final overall review.
☐ a separate paragraph for each element.
☐ a recommendation for improvement.
☐ used some of the Useful language.

10 **REVIEW** Exchange reviews with your partner. Give them at least one positive comment and one suggestion for improvement. Would you visit the reviewed restaurant? Why? / Why not?

Go to page 131 for the Reflect and review.

'Chessboxers' play a round of chess during training in Paris, France.

5

Let's play

GOALS

- Read to identify examples supporting an argument
- Talk about past regrets and possibilities
- Use context to understand new words when listening
- Talk about being competitive
- Communicate clearly in a group
- Write an opinion essay

1 Work in pairs. Discuss the questions.
1. What are the people doing in the photo? Would you call it a sport? Why? / Why not?
2. In your opinion, which of these activities are sports? Try to agree on a definition of 'sport'.

> chess   competitive dance   golf   horse racing
> motor racing   mountain climbing

WATCH ▶

2 ▶ 5.1 Watch the video. Answer the questions.

NATIONAL GEOGRAPHIC EXPLORER

ANUSHA SHANKAR

1. What did volleyball allow Anusha to do?
2. Why does Anusha enjoy watching 'artistic' sports?
3. Which type of game is her favourite?

3 Make connections. Are you a sporty person? What kinds of games and sports do you like playing? Why?

5A Play together nicely

LESSON GOALS
- Identify supporting examples
- Relate information to your own experience
- Explain how to play a game

READING

1 Work in pairs. Look at the photo. What kind of game do you think the people are playing? Do you enjoy playing games like this?

2 Read the blog post on page 61. Choose the best title.
  1 Competition or collaboration?
  2 The rise of collaborative games
  3 Collaboration – the future of games?

3 Look at the Reading skill box. Then find sentences in the blog post that provide supporting examples for the ideas (1–3).

READING SKILL
Identifying supporting examples

When a writer is building an argument, they may include examples to support their point of view. When you read, identify the examples that the writer is using and try to understand why they chose them. Ask yourself: What particular purpose does this example serve?

Examples that support ideas may begin 'for example' or 'such as', but often the example may not be clearly labelled. Look for specific information, like names, facts or personal anecdotes.

  1 Collaborative games are becoming more popular.
  2 Collaborative games follow most normal rules of game design.
  3 Video game players accepted the idea that collaboration is fun a long time ago.

4 Read the blog post again. Answer the questions.
  1 What rules must all good games follow, according to the writer? Can you think of any others?
  2 How have video games influenced board games?
  3 In which ways may collaborative games be better than competitive ones?

5 Look at the Critical thinking skill box. Then discuss the questions (1–3) in groups.

CRITICAL THINKING SKILL
Relating information to your own experience

Writers and speakers try to persuade you that their argument is right, so it is important to reflect on it and compare it with what you already know. This way, you can decide how much you agree with them.
- Identify statements of fact you read or hear. Are they true according to your own experience?
- Do the facts they claim match what you already know about the topic?
- Does any of the information contradict what you believe?

  1 What collaborative games and activities do you know or have you tried?
  2 Do you agree that collaboration 'makes a richer playing experience'?
  3 How convinced are you by the writer's conclusion about why we play games?

SPEAKING

NATIONAL GEOGRAPHIC EXPLORER

6 🎧 5.1 Listen to Anusha Shankar discuss two popular games in her country. Which sounds more fun? Do similar games exist in your country?

7 🎧 5.1 Look at the Useful language box. Then listen to Anusha again and write the next words she says after each phrase.

> **Useful language** Explaining games
> You have to / can't / must …
> It's a bit like … except that …
> The opposing team/player has to …
> The rules are quite …
> To play, you need …
> The objective/aim of the game is to …

8 Think of a childhood game or sport you have played. Use the Useful language to write five sentences about how to play your game. Then find someone in the class who doesn't know your game. Teach them how to play it.

EXPLORE MORE!

Find out about a collaborative board game, video game or other activity that you would like to play.

1 What's going on with all these collaborative games? Games have traditionally been competitive – mancala, *Monopoly*, Go … even Rock, paper, scissors! Isn't the aim of the game to beat your opponent? But *co-op* games are making their way into the top ten lists of board games. It turns out that there's a whole side to games I'd been missing all these years, and so had many game designers, it appears. All of a sudden, the world is playing games that break the first rule of game design: 'You must have a winner and a loser.'

In fact, collaborative games aren't breaking *all* the rules. Successful collaborative games still need to have clear objectives, as well as the opportunity for individual players within the team to show their skills. Like all good games, they need to develop, with a beginning, a middle and an end and, of course, they should be easy to play but difficult to play well and win!

10 A favourite example is *Forbidden Island*. You only need two people to play, and the rules are simple. The objective is to find the hidden treasures and escape before the island sinks. Players have roles with special skills. For example, only the diver is allowed to swim across flooded areas. Only by listening to suggestions and working as a team can you win.

So why the sudden growth in the collaborative board game market? Well, first, the designers may be
15 following designers in the digital gaming world, who realized long ago that the possibilities with online gaming could be both competitive and collaborative. Even classic games of the nineties like *Super Mario World* gave Mario and Luigi the option to work together. The board game revival is partly a reaction against video games by those of us who want more face-to-face personal interaction, but designers have also learned from the online gamers that working together can be as fun as defeating the scary monsters
20 by yourself.

Second, many of us will often catch up with friends and family online. People quickly realized that video get-togethers weren't always much fun without some structure, and games – both collaborative and competitive – took off. Competitive games aren't always healthy activities (the classic example is *Monopoly*, which in my family generally ends with no one speaking to each other for at least 24
25 hours), but there are some truly fantastic ideas for games you can play even when you're thousands of miles apart.

Reiner Knizia, designer of some of the most successful collaborative board games, believes that 'playing with each other and facing a common opponent … makes a much richer playing experience.' Collaboration brings out our greatest strengths as a species: the ability – and the desire – to solve
30 problems. Tess, a board-gaming friend of mine, says: 'It's sometimes frustrating when a teammate wants to do something you don't, but that's part of the fun – working together to find the best strategy.' The fact is that by using language, we can achieve things that we'd never be able to achieve alone. Games like this provide us with practice for the real-world battles that only together can we win.

Friends play a collaborative board game in Riga, Latvia.

5B
She should have scored!

LESSON GOALS
- Understand sports commentaries
- Talk about past regrets and possibilities
- Pronounce 'have' in past modal verbs

Amy Conroy in action at the women's final of the Wheelchair Basketball World Championships in Hamburg, Germany.

LISTENING AND GRAMMAR

1 Work in pairs. Look at these sports and discuss the questions.

> athletics   basketball   chess   football   ice-hockey
> karate   snowboarding   surfing   swimming   volleyball

1. Which of these sports have you played? Which would you like to try?
2. Which do you like/dislike watching on TV? Why?
3. Which are the most and least popular in your country?

2 🎧 5.2 Listen to three sports commentaries. Which sports are they about?

3 🎧 5.2 Listen again. Complete the sentences with the words that you hear.

1. That was a good effort, but he really _____ have passed the ball.
2. He knows he _____ have been in a much better position to shoot.
3. Kovacs really _____ have won this race with an earlier attack.
4. Being beaten by a 16-year-old Hungarian we hadn't even heard about before this World Cup _____ have been a huge surprise for the current world record holder.
5. He _____ have played the ball left. He _____ have played it right.

62

4 Answer the questions (1 and 2) about the sentences (1–5) in Exercise 3. Then read the Grammar box to check.
1 Are the sentences about past, present or future events?
2 Which modal verbs in the sentences refer to:
  a a regret?
  b an ability or possibility?
  c something that was certain?

> **GRAMMAR** *Could have, should have* and *would have*
>
> Use *could have* + past participle to talk about ability or possibility in the past.
> Kovacs really **could have won** this race with an earlier attack.
> Use *should/shouldn't have* + past participle to talk about regrets in the past.
> That was a good effort, but he really **should have passed** the ball.
> Use *would have* + past participle to imagine past results that we're certain of.
> He knows he **would have been** in a much better position to shoot.

Go to page 145 for the Grammar reference.

5 Complete the exchanges with *could have*, *should have* or *would have*.
1 A: I can't understand why she didn't score!
   B: Yes, she definitely _____ scored. There were no defenders around.
2 A: It's a real shame he didn't train enough.
   B: You're right. He _____ trained harder.
3 A: Do you think Josipov deserved to win?
   B: I don't think so. I'm sure Martinez _____ won the match if he hadn't got injured.
4 A: I really regret not listening to my coach.
   B: Well, what can I tell you? You really _____ listened to her. You had a good chance of winning.
5 A: The Pistons never stood a chance of winning.
   B: You think so? I really thought they _____ won it. They had some good opportunities.
6 A: It's a shame Lisa didn't win the chess tournament.
   B: Yes, I'm sure she _____ won if it wasn't for that tiny mistake.

PRONUNCIATION

6 🎧 **5.3** Listen to the sentence said by two different speakers. Answer the questions. Then read the Clear voice box to check.
I really thought she could have won that game.
1 How does each speaker say 'have'? Do they say it differently each time?
2 Who is easier to understand?

CLEAR VOICE
Pronouncing *have* in past modal verbs

In fast speech, *have* is often pronounced as /əv/ with *should, might, could* and *would*. So *should have* sounds like /ʃədəv/. This can make your pronunciation less clear, so sometimes you may need to say the full form of *have*, e.g. /ʃʊd hæv/, especially if you notice that the other person doesn't understand you.

7 Work in pairs. Act out the exchanges from Exercise 5. Follow the instructions.
Student B: Say the modal verb quickly as /əv/.
Student A: You didn't quite understand Student B, so ask them to repeat.
Student B: Adapt your pronunciation and say the full form of *have*.

SPEAKING

NATIONAL GEOGRAPHIC EXPLORER

8 🎧 **5.4** Listen to Anusha Shankar talk about an event she took part in. Answer the questions.
1 What event is Anusha talking about?
2 What happened during the event?
3 What regret does she have?

9 Think about a difficult event or competition you took part in or saw. It does not have to be related to sports. Think about:
1 what happened and why the event was important.
2 what didn't happen but *should, could* or *would* have happened.
3 how you felt.

10 Work in groups of three. Tell each other about the event/competition. What would you have done in that situation? How would you have felt? Is there anything your classmate could have done differently?

5C Games for gamers

LESSON GOALS
- Use context to understand new words when listening
- Talk about being competitive
- Say 'o' in stressed syllables
- Talk about past ability

SPEAKING

1 🎧 5.5 Work in pairs. Look at the photo and try to work out which sports might be played in the stadium. Then listen to a commentary from the event. Did you work out the sport correctly?

LISTENING

2 🎧 5.6 Listen to a radio show about esports. What reasons are given for and against including esports in the Olympic games?

LISTENING SKILL
Using context to understand new words

When listening, there may be words you don't understand. Try not to be frustrated. Continue listening to work out their meaning from context. For example, the speaker might use synonyms of the new word that you already know (e.g. *stadium – arena*). They might give an example that will help you understand the new word (e.g. *I was just jumping up and down, hugging people – I was delighted*.). There might be other words that will give you a clue (e.g. *She seemed invincible. She hadn't lost in more than 20 games.*)

3 🎧 5.7 Look at the Listening skill box. Then listen to an extract from the radio show. Write a definition for the words (1–3). Then discuss in pairs how you worked out the meaning.
   1 sponsorship   2 spectators   3 tournament

4 🎧 5.6 Listen to the radio show again. Complete the sentences with one word.
   1 Esports is a term used to describe video games when they are _____.
   2 Adam doesn't think they are sports because they don't involve _____ activity.
   3 Ji-Soo says professional gamers might practise for _____ hours every day.
   4 Adam believes the Olympics should encourage people to do _____.
   5 Ji-Soo doesn't agree that video games make people _____.

5 Work in pairs. Decide whose arguments you think are stronger, Ji-Soo's or Adam's. Should esports be featured in the Olympics? Do a class survey.

VOCABULARY

6 Complete the definitions with these words and phrases.

be determined to   beat your opponent
become a professional   compete against someone
participate in a tournament   perform poorly
require great skills   talented   win at all costs

   1 _____ do everything possible to succeed
   2 _____ defeat the other player
   3 _____ need to be good at something
   4 _____ try to win against another player
   5 _____ start being paid for doing sport
   6 _____ do badly
   7 _____ take part in a competition
   8 _____ having a natural ability for something
   9 _____ decide you will do something without letting anything stop you

7 Write sentences about your own experience of playing sports and games using some of the phrases from Exercise 6. Then share your sentences with a partner.

   Go to page 137 for the Vocabulary reference.

PRONUNCIATION

8 Look at the Clear voice box. Then underline the stressed syllables in these words. Decide which of the sounds in bold are long and which are short.

c**o**mpete   c**o**mpetitive   m**o**tivated
opp**o**nent   perf**o**rm   pr**o**fessi**o**nal
rec**o**rd the time   spectat**o**r

64

CLEAR VOICE
Saying 'o' in stressed syllables

The pronunciation of the letter 'o' in multisyllable words changes in stressed syllables, becoming longer than in unstressed ones. It is then often pronounced as /ɔː/ (perf**o**rm) or /əʊ/ (opp**o**nent) instead of /ɒ/ (c**o**mpetition) or /ə/ (spectat**o**r). It's important to pronounce these sounds as long.

9 🎧 **5.8** Listen to check your answers in Exercise 8. Practise saying the words.

GRAMMAR

10 Read the paragraph. Which of the phrases in bold are about:
1 a general past ability?
2 an ability to do with 'thinking' (two phr/ə/rases)?
3 an ability in a specific situation (two phrases)?

> It was amazing to be selected for the team. I'd only been playing Dota 2 for two years. Most players **could beat** me at the start, but by training hard I **was able to win** my first tournament. And I finally **managed to persuade** my parents that I wasn't 'wasting my time' by winning prize money. But I didn't expect to be part of a professional team in the World Cup. When I was invited, I **could understand** the words, but I **couldn't believe** it!

11 Read the Focus on box to check your answers from Exercise 10. In pairs talk about an achievement you are proud of.

> **FOCUS ON** Talking about past ability: *could*, *was able to* or *managed to*?
>
> Use *could* to talk about a general past ability.
> Most players **could** beat me.
> Use *could* with verbs of senses (e.g. *smell*) and thought processes (e.g. *believe*).
> I **could** understand the words.
> Use *was able to* or *managed to* to talk about past achievements in more specific situations.
> I **managed to** persuade my parents that ...

Go to page 146 for the Focus on reference.

SPEAKING

12 Work in pairs. Think about situations in which you compete. Use these ideas to help you. Then discuss the questions.

> going to the gym   an important exam   a job interview
> playing board/card/video games
> playing sports with friends   a (sports) tournament

1 How competitive are you?
2 Does being successful require great skill and talent or is it more about being determined?
3 How do you behave if you do not perform well?

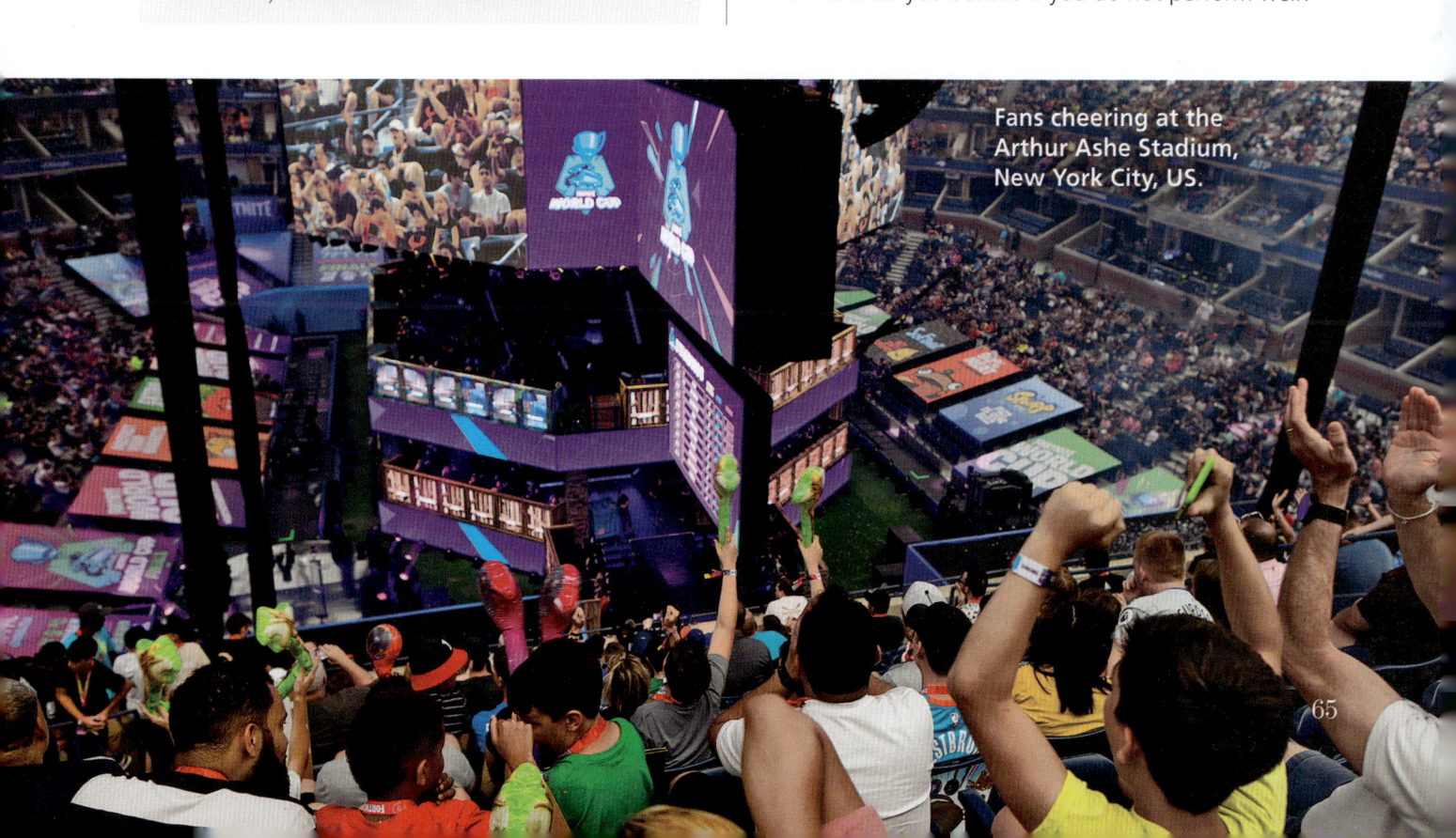

Fans cheering at the Arthur Ashe Stadium, New York City, US.

5D Communicating clearly in a group

LESSON GOALS
- Understand the illusion of transparency
- Communicate clearly in a group
- Practise communicating clearly and clarifying misunderstandings

SPEAKING

1 Work in pairs. Discuss the questions.
1 Think about teams that you are, or have been, a part of. How do the team members communicate with each other? Do they do this successfully?
2 Think of a situation where communicating with your partner(s) in a group or team did not go well. What happened? What could or should you have done differently?

MY VOICE ▶

2 ▶ 5.2 Watch the video about communicating clearly in a group. What problem about communicating is mentioned? Have you ever experienced it?

3 Work in groups of four. Repeat the experiment mentioned in the video.
- Think of a famous tune that you think the others will know. Don't tell them what it is.
- Tap out the tune with your finger.
- Can the others guess what it is?
- Change roles and repeat the experiment until everyone has tapped out a tune.
- How many times did someone correctly guess the tune?

4 ▶ 5.2 Watch the video again. Are the sentences true (T) or false (F)?
1 The project manager liked the poster.
2 The project manager wanted the poster to be made smaller.
3 It is important to make the right assumptions.
4 In international communication, it is more likely that false assumptions will be made.
5 If you're not sure if someone has understood what you mean, ask them questions to check their understanding.
6 When working in a group or team, we should talk to each other about how we typically communicate to avoid misunderstandings
7 The illusion of transparency cannot be avoided.

EXPLORE MORE!

Find out more about the 'illusion of transparency' and the experiments to show that it exists.

5 Read about the situations (1–3). Have you or someone you know experienced anything similar?

1. Makena, Dries and Margarita are discussing a project they're all working on together at work. Dries says 'I think it's time we send it to Paweł for review.' Margarita nods and Makena says 'Sure thing'. Two days later Dries asks Margarita and Makena whether they've heard back from Paweł. Margarita and Makena are confused why Dries expected *them* to send it.

2. Angela is working on a presentation with three other students. Her task is to send the presentation to the teacher before the class. The presentation has a lot of images, so Yu, another student in the group, says that it's probably too big to send via email, so she should just upload it to the cloud and share the link with the teacher. Angela doesn't know how she will send the presentation.

3. Oliver, Yuto and several other colleagues want to buy their manager a present for her birthday. They've all been working together on a big project and want to thank their manager for her help and support. Yuto says 'What about perfume?' There are a few quiet 'yeses' and 'maybes', but nobody continues the discussion. The next day, Oliver shows Yuto and his colleagues the perfume he has bought. They are a bit confused, because they thought the decision hadn't been made yet.

6 Work in pairs. Read the situations in Exercise 5 again and discuss the questions. Use the Communication skill box to help you.
 1 What problems does the 'illusion of transparency' lead to in each of the situations?
 2 What could and should the people have done to make communication clearer?

COMMUNICATION SKILL
Communicating clearly in a group

For groups to work well together, group members need to communicate clearly and avoid the illusion of transparency (when you assume people know exactly what you know, feel or believe).
- Ask questions to see if your assumptions might be wrong.
- If you're not sure if others understand what you mean, ask them to confirm.
- Check your own and others' assumptions more often in international situations.
- When working in a team, discuss communication preferences at the beginning.

7 🎧 5.9 Listen to a conversation at a basketball club. Then discuss the questions in pairs.
 1 Why doesn't Rudy know about the club tradition?
 2 What assumption do the other players make?
 3 Do you think the coach's solution to the problem of the missing cake is a good one? Why? / Why not? What else could he have done?

8 🎧 5.9 Look at the Useful language box. Then listen to the conversation from Exercise 7 again and underline the phrases you hear.

Useful language Clarifying misunderstandings

Expressing confusion
Would you mind explaining that to me again? I don't think I understood.
Sorry, but I'm not sure if you mean … or …

Clarifying
Just to confirm, I thought I should explain …
When you say … I guess you mean …?
Just to clarify, are you telling me that …?

SPEAKING

9 **OWN IT!** Work in pairs. Roleplay the situations from Exercise 5, using the Communication skill box and the Useful language to help you communicate clearly.

10 Work with another pair. Did you clarify the misunderstandings in the same way?

5E Are sports stars overpaid?

LESSON GOALS
- Organize a formal paragraph
- Link opposing points of view in formal writing
- Write an opinion essay

An ice hockey match between Medvescak Zagreb and KAC in Zagreb, Croatia.

SPEAKING

1 Work in pairs. Read the opinions (1–3) and discuss which you agree or disagree with. Give reasons.
   1 Some sports stars earn too much money.
   2 Male and female sports stars should earn the same salary.
   3 There should be a limit on how much a sports star can earn.

READING FOR WRITING

2 Read the opinion essay. Answer the questions.
   1 What is the writer's opinion? Which arguments do they use to support their opinion?
   2 What phrases does the writer use to express their opinion?

3 Read the essay again. Match the paragraphs (1–5) with the functions (a–d). There is one function that can be matched with two paragraphs.
   a Present the opposing point of view and show why it is not true
   b Introduce the main topic and the writer's opinion
   c Present arguments to support the writer's opinion
   d Summarize the essay topic and the writer's opinion

---

1 Top football or basketball stars earn more in a month than many of us might earn in a lifetime. While no doubt they are incredibly talented and hard-working, it is argued here that such high salaries cannot be justified.

2 First, it is not true that sports stars work more than other people. Although it is true that they spend several hours a day training and might play matches at the weekends, they do not even work 40 hours a week. Therefore, it would be difficult to argue they should earn so much more than others.

3 In addition, even though top sportspeople are very talented, there are also many highly gifted people in other professions who do not earn anywhere near as much. For example, it cannot be argued that a university professor is less talented. Nevertheless, they earn far less than most sports stars.

4 Finally, some might claim that the high salaries can be justified by the profits that top football or basketball players generate through advertising contracts, TV broadcasts or ticket sales. However, it cannot be said that they produce anything that directly benefits society. In contrast, bus drivers help us get to work, teachers educate future generations and doctors save lives; yet they all earn far less than sports stars.

5 All in all, it seems clear that top sports stars earn too much. Their salaries should reflect the number of hours they work or the benefits they offer to society.

4 Read paragraphs 2–4 from the essay and answer the questions. Then read the Writing skill box to check.

1 How many sentences does each paragraph have?
2 In which sentence does the writer present the main idea of the paragraph?
3 How is the main idea then developed?

WRITING SKILL
Organizing a paragraph in a formal text

Paragraphs in a formal text are often made up of three to four sentences. They begin with a 'topic sentence', which introduces the main topic of the paragraph. This is then developed by explaining, adding more information, showing opposing points of view, presenting causes or effects, and by giving examples. Well-organized paragraphs help the reader follow the writer's argument.

5 Put the sentences in order to make a paragraph.

1 Therefore, it cannot be said that every sports star is overpaid.
2 Their earnings can vary a great deal depending on the sport or the country.
3 For example, while a top football player in Spanish *La Liga* might earn tens of thousands of euros a week, a top volleyball player will not even make a tenth of this amount.
4 First, it is not true that all top sports stars earn very high salaries.

6 Look at the Useful language box. Then connect the opposing ideas (1–3) using the linking word in brackets. Sometimes you will need to connect the ideas into one sentence and sometimes you will need to keep the sentences separate.

> **Useful language** Linking opposing points of view in a formal essay
>
> **While** no doubt …, it is argued here that …
> **Although** it is true that …, they do not …
> **Even though** top sportspeople are talented …
> … is less talented. **Nevertheless**, they earn far less than …
> … TV broadcasts or ticket sales. **However**, it cannot be said that …
> … directly benefits society. **In contrast**, bus drivers help us … **yet** they earn far less.

1 Some people might argue that top sports stars are paid too much. Their salaries reflect their popularity. (although)
2 The health benefits of sports are clear. Many people around the world do not practise any sport regularly. (however)
3 Sports are often connected with physical activity. Some sports, such as chess, are far less active. (while)

7 Choose one of the topics. Write five sentences, using linking words to connect opposing ideas. Share your ideas with a partner.

1 Success in sports is mainly due to hard work and much less to talent.
2 Chess or esports should not be seen as sports because they do not involve any physical activity.
3 Children should be able to choose if they want to do physical education classes in school or not.

WRITING TASK

8 WRITE Write an opinion essay on the topic you chose in Exercise 7. Use the Writing skill box and Useful language to help you.

9 CHECK Use the checklist. I have …
☐ introduced the topic and presented my opinion in the introduction.
☐ written at least two paragraphs giving arguments for my opinion.
☐ included paragraphs of about three or four sentences with a clear topic sentence in each.
☐ presented an opposing point of view and shown why it is not true.
☐ summarized the essay and restated my opinion in the conclusion.

10 REVIEW Work in pairs. Read your partner's essay. Do you agree with their opinion? Which arguments do you find the strongest and the weakest?

Go to page 132 for the Reflect and review.

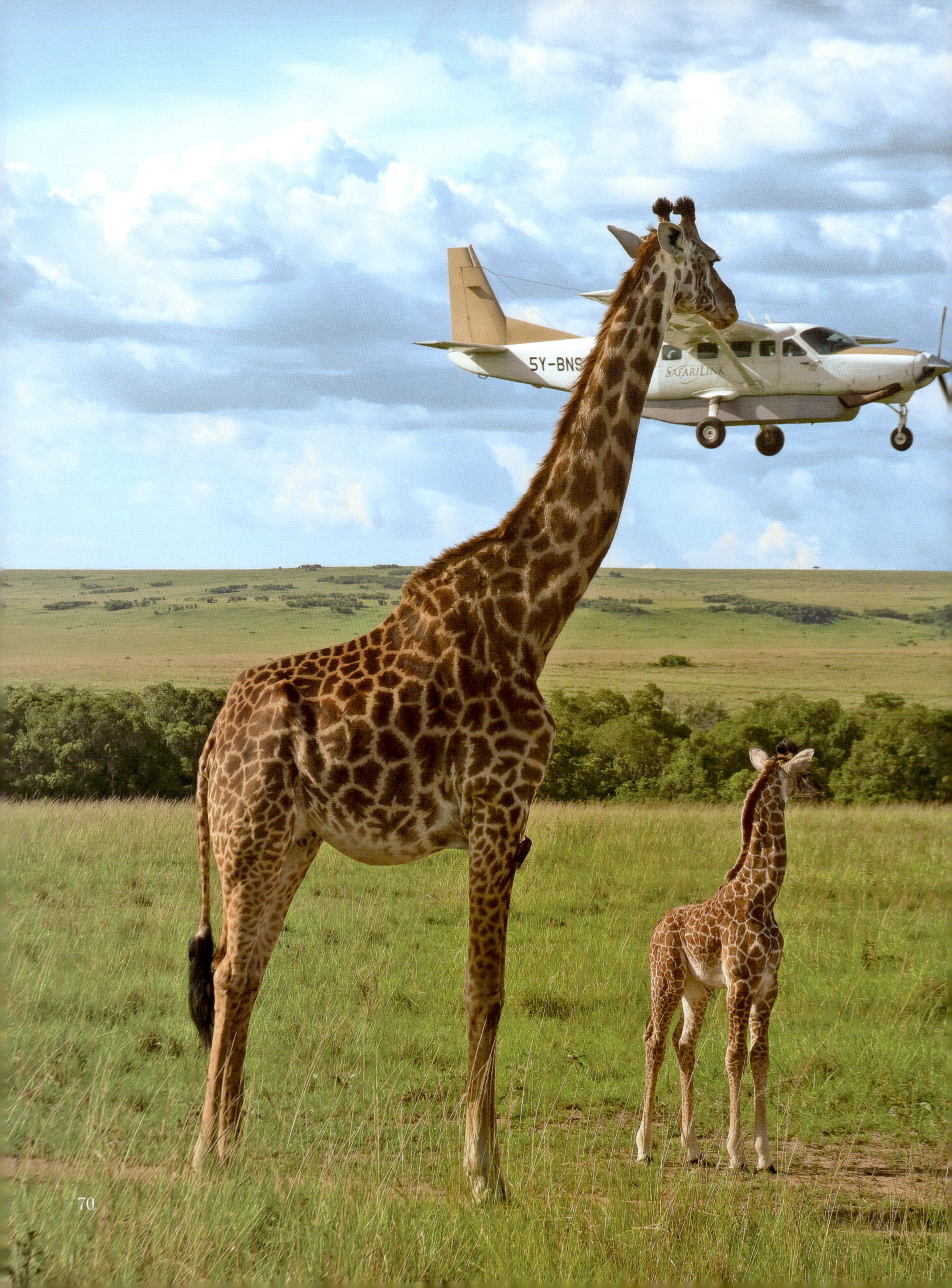
5Y-BNS
SafariLink

6
Accidents and incidents

GOALS
- Activate prior knowledge before reading
- Report what people say
- Understand a sequence of events in a story
- Talk about accidents and injuries
- Understand how to balance fluency and accuracy
- Write a formal email of complaint

1 Work in pairs. Look at the photo and discuss the questions.
  1 What's happening? What's the joke?
  2 Do you think the photo was deliberate, or was it a lucky accident? Why?

WATCH ▶

2 ▶ 6.1 Watch the video. Which explorer, Paola (P) or Joe (J) …

NATIONAL GEOGRAPHIC EXPLORERS

PAOLA RODRÍGUEZ   JOE CUTLER

  1 had a trick played on him/her?
  2 has a funny photo?
  3 might have the same joke done to him/her?

3 Make connections. Discuss the questions.
  1 Have you ever taken or been in a funny photo or video? What happened?
  2 Can you remember any funny accidents that happened to you or to others?

Giraffes in the Masai Mara, Kenya.

6A Accidental inventions

LESSON GOALS
- Activate prior knowledge before reading
- Analyse conclusions to find the best one for a text
- Discuss unusual dishes or food combinations

READING

1 Work in pairs. Discuss the questions.

1 Look at the quotes about cooking (a–c). How much do you agree or disagree with them?

   a 'Cooking requires … improvisation … dealing with failure and uncertainty in a creative way.' (Paul Theroux, writer)

   b 'Cooking is like painting or writing a song. Just as there are only so many notes or colours, there are only so many flavours — it's how you combine them that sets you apart.' (Wolfgang Puck, chef)

   c 'The discovery of a new dish does more for the happiness of the human race than the discovery of a star.' (Jean Anthelme Brillat-Savarin, lawyer, politician and food writer)

2 Do you ever try to experiment in the kitchen and be creative? Why? / Why not?

2 Look at the Reading skill box. Then look at the title, photos and headings of the article on page 73. Tell your partner about what comes to mind when you think about the topic. Then read the article to check your ideas.

READING SKILL
Activating prior knowledge before reading

Before you read a text, thinking about the topic first can help you predict what the text is about and understand it more easily. Look at the title, photos and headings and consider what you already know about the topic and what you expect to find in the text.

3 Read the article again. Are the sentences true (T) or false (F)?

1 We are sure about how coffee was invented.
2 Tofu can be used to replace meat.
3 Percy was curious why the chocolate and peanut bar had melted.
4 Stéphanie Tatin used the wrong ingredients to cook the tarte.

EXPLORE MORE!

Find a dish from your country that was invented by chance.

4 Look at the Critical thinking skill box. Then read the conclusions (1–3). Which one would be the most suitable for the article? Give reasons.

CRITICAL THINKING SKILL
Analysing conclusions

The conclusion is a very important element of any text because it summarizes all the ideas and gives the final take-away message to the reader. To decide what a good conclusion for a text might be, consider:
- what the writer's main message is.
- which arguments or examples are used in the text to support the main message.
- how the text began (the conclusion often restates part of the introduction).

1 Of course, cooking does need some planning. For example, you might need to buy the right ingredients. But it should also be about fun and creativity.

2 Many inventions in our kitchens happened completely by accident. From tofu in China, to coffee in Ethiopia, to microwaves in an American lab – they are all products of chance.

3 Inventing a new dish is often a product of chance. You start by following the recipe, but end up making something new by accident.

SPEAKING

5 Think about an unusual dish or combination of food that you eat. Make some notes on:
- what the food is and why you enjoy it.
- why it is unusual and how you 'invented' it.
- what others might think about this food.

6 Work in groups of three. Tell each other about the food. React to what your classmates say. Whose dish sounds the most:
1 delicious?
2 unusual?
3 disgusting?

A: I love toast with honey and peanut butter.
B: That sounds really tasty!

I DIDN'T PLAN TO INVENT IT!

1 The preparation of food often involves science and careful planning. But sometimes, the best dishes and the things we use to cook them are invented completely by accident. Let's look at some examples.

COFFEE

Coffee's origins are still a mystery, but the most well-known legend told in Ethiopia, where coffee was discovered, involves a 9th-century farmer named Kaldi and his goats. One day, Kaldi noticed that after eating berries from a certain plant, his goats became so energetic, they didn't go to sleep at night. He started chewing on the berries himself, and told a local wise man about it, who decided to make a drink from the berries. The drink became popular, and knowledge of the berries spread. By the 15th century, coffee was being grown on the Arabian Peninsula, most likely having been introduced there through trade. From there, it was introduced to Persia, North Africa, Turkey, India and Europe.

TOFU

This popular vegan alternative to meat was invented by chance in ancient China, over 2,000 years ago. No one is sure exactly how, but one theory is that a cook accidentally dropped a special type of salt into a pot of soya milk. The salt caused the soya milk to gel and become what we now know as tofu. The cook must have tried it, and realized that he could use this to make some delicious new dishes. We might never know exactly how tofu was invented, but I'm very glad that the cook didn't just throw the 'gel' away.

MICROWAVE

In 1945, Percy Spencer, an American engineer, was working on a project that involved microwaves, very short waves that are invisible to the human eye. During one of his experiments, he noticed that the chocolate and peanut bar he had in his pocket had melted. This intrigued him, so Percy started to aim the microwaves at other food. He successfully cooked popcorn and then an egg, which actually exploded. He realized he'd accidentally invented a new way of cooking. Nowadays, many of us can't even imagine our kitchens without this accidental invention.

TARTE TATIN

Since meals often end with desserts, let's finish by talking about one. Tarte Tatin is basically very thin pastry with caramelized apples on top of it. Delicious! But completely accidental too. The story is that two sisters, Stéphanie and Caroline Tatin, ran a hotel in France. One day Stéphanie was rather overworked and tired. She was making an apple pie, but left the apples cooking in a pan of sugar and butter for too long. Rather than throw it out, she put the base of the pie on top of the caramelized apples and put the pan in the oven. When it finished cooking, she turned the 'pie' upside down and *voilà*: tarte Tatin was born!

GLOSSARY:
caramelize – to cook food, e.g. fruit, with sugar
gel – to thicken and become more solid
intrigue – to cause someone to become interested and to want to find out more about something
pastry – the mixture of flour, butter and milk/water that is used to bake the bottom/top of a pie

6B
What a coincidence!

LESSON GOALS
- Understand stories about coincidences
- Report what people say
- Say auxiliary verbs at the end of sentence

LISTENING AND GRAMMAR

1 Work in pairs. Look at the photos. Each one relates to a story about coincidences. Discuss what you think each story might be about. Then compare your ideas with another pair.

2 ∩ 6.1 Work in pairs. Listen to the stories. Match the stories (1–3) with the photos (A–C). How do you think each story ends?

3 ∩ 6.1 Who said these sentences? Listen again and write the exact words that were said. Then read the Grammar box to check.
  1 'Have you ever been to London?' ➔ Amy asked Kyle _____.
  2 'I've been there twice.' ➔ He said _____.
  3 'Ask me about it later.' ➔ She told him _____.
  4 'Whoever gives me this dollar bill will be the man I marry.' ➔ She had told herself _____.
  5 'Is the last number 8?' ➔ Lucas asked her _____.
  6 'That can't be your phone number.' ➔ He told her _____.

> **GRAMMAR** Reporting what people say
>
> Use a past tense to report what people said.
> present tenses ➔ past tenses
> 'I **think** the boy **looks** like you.' ➔ *She said that she **thought** the boy **looked** like him.*
> past tenses / present perfect ➔ past perfect
> 'I **wrote** my name.' ➔ *She told him that she **had written** her name.*
> will, can ➔ would, could
> 'I**'ll** give it to her …' ➔ *He said he **would** give it to her in a frame.*
> Reference words and pronouns may change, e.g. *this, that, I,* etc.
> 'by now' ➔ *by then*
> 'my name' ➔ *her name*
> Use *ask* to report *wh-* and *yes/no* questions. Add *if/whether* for *yes/no* questions.
> '**Why is this** not my number?' ➔ *She **asked why it was** not her number.*
>
> **Go to page 146 for the Grammar reference.**

4 Rewrite the sentences using reported speech.

1 'I knew that we were going to be married that day.'
   Esther said that _____.
2 'The reason I'm asking is because I found some pictures.'
   She explained that _____.
3 'I'll bring it in.'
   She told him _____.
4 'It can't be your phone number.'
   Lucas told her _____.
5 'The number you just made up is my phone number.'
   He said that _____.

5 Work in groups of three. Student A: Ask Student B a question. Student B: Answer the question. Student C: Listen and write Student B's response using reported speech. Then change roles.

A: What will you do after class today?
B: I will go for a coffee.
C: She said that she would go for a coffee after class today.

PRONUNCIATION

6 🎧 6.2 Listen and underline the verbs that are stressed.

1 'What was the problem?'
   He asked her what the problem was.
2 A: Have you got any shopping bags?
   B: Yes, I have.

7 Look at the Clear voice box to check your answers to Exercise 6. Practise saying the sentences with the correct stress.

CLEAR VOICE
Saying auxiliary verbs at the end of sentences

Auxiliary verbs and the verb *be* are usually pronounced with a weak form, e.g. *has* = /əz/. However, when auxiliary verbs or the verb *be* are at the end of a sentence, such as in short answers and some reported questions, it is important to pronounce them in the strong form, e.g. *has* = /hæz/.
What was /wəz/ the problem? (weak form of *was*)
He asked her what the problem **was** /wɒz/. (strong form of *was*)

LISTENING AND SPEAKING

8 🎧 6.3 Listen to two friends talking about a trip. What is the coincidence?

9 🎧 6.3 Look at the Useful language box. Underline the expressions that could be used by someone telling a story. Circle the expressions that could be used by the listener. Listen again to check.

> **Useful language** Talking about surprising information
>
> You're not going to believe this, but …
> No way!
> That is such a coincidence!
> I swear it's true.
> You'll never guess what …
> That's weird/incredible/amazing!
> What are the chances of that happening?
> You're joking!

10 You are going to tell a story about a coincidence that has happened to you or to someone you know. Use these topics to help you. If you can't remember any situations, you can invent one.

accidentally meeting someone in a strange place
doing the same thing as someone else at the same time
finding something you lost
sharing something in common with a stranger

11 Follow the instructions. Then share your stories in small groups.

1 Decide on the most dramatic points in the story.
2 Think about the things people said. How will you report what they said?
3 Use expressions from the Useful language box to help you.

A: You'll never guess what happened! I had lost my favourite hat, but then one day, I was walking to school and I saw it hanging on a tree!
B: No way! That's amazing!

6C
It was an accident!

Joe falling off his raft in Gabon.

LESSON GOALS
- Talk about accidents and injuries
- Say /ʃ/, /dʒ/ and /tʃ/ clearly
- Understand a sequence of events in a story
- Discuss present habits

VOCABULARY

1 Work in pairs. Look at the photo of Joe Cutler. What do you think happened?

2 Read the stories. Have you ever been in similar situations? What happened?

Kamala

I once **ripped** my brand new trousers from my foot all the way to my waist when jumping over a fence. Fortunately, I didn't **get seriously injured**, but I did **get a few scratches** and **bruises**. My parents were absolutely furious!

Nam

I once **spilled** coffee all over myself and my boss! I was walking into the meeting room and I **tripped**. I'd just made the coffee, so it was pretty hot, and my boss **got a bit burnt**. And I **ruined** the new shirt I'd only just bought. Fortunately, my boss just started laughing and made a joke out of it.

Ashley

My partner tends to be quite **clumsy**. I mean, he'll often drop things, especially his phone. The poor thing is **in pretty bad shape** now. I'm just waiting for the screen to **smash** into a million pieces next time it falls.

3 Complete the sentences with the correct form of these words.

| bruise | burn | clumsy | injure | rip |
| ruin | scratch | shape | smash | spill | trip |

1 I once _____ hot soup all over the table and _____ my mum's new tablecloth. Luckily nobody got _____!
2 My little brother often gets into fights and comes home with _____ and _____.
3 Once my best mate accidentally _____ his neighbour's window with a football.
4 Do you know anyone who's really _____ and tends to drop things on the floor?
5 Yesterday, my dad _____ over a toy. Fortunately, he didn't get seriously _____.
6 I accidentally _____ my favourite jeans and they're in pretty bad _____ now.

Go to page 137 for the Vocabulary reference.

PRONUNCIATION

4 🎧 6.4 Listen to the sentences. What is the difference between the underlined sounds? Look at the Clear voice box to check.

1 I had scra<u>tch</u>es everywhere.
2 Fortunately, I didn't get seriously in<u>j</u>ured.
3 I sma<u>sh</u>ed the window completely.

CLEAR VOICE
Saying /ʃ/, /dʒ/ and /tʃ/

/ʃ/, /dʒ/ and /tʃ/ can be easy to confuse. When saying /ʃ/ (sma<u>sh</u>ed), the air flows from your mouth. For /tʃ/ (scra<u>tch</u>es) and /dʒ/ (in<u>j</u>ured), you stop the air coming out of your mouth. Put your hand on your throat. You will feel vibrations when saying /dʒ/, but not when saying /tʃ/.

5 🎧 **6.5** Look at the sounds in bold in the sentences (a–d) and complete the tasks (1–3). Then listen to check. Practise saying the sentences.

1 <u>Underline</u> the /ʃ/ sounds.
2 (Circle) the /dʒ/ sounds.
3 Tick ✓ the /tʃ/ sounds.

a My parents never allowed me to play with ma**tch**es.
b My **j**eans were ripped on my knee and I had a huge hole in my **sh**irt on my **ch**est.
c **Sh**e didn't want to **j**oin in, but one of us pu**sh**ed her into the water.
d He was very lucky the dama**g**e to our neighbour's car wasn't too serious: only a few scra**tch**es.

LISTENING

NATIONAL GEOGRAPHIC EXPLORERS

6 🎧 **6.6** Listen to Joe Cutler and Paola Rodríguez talk about accidents they've had. How would you have reacted if these things had happened to you? Tell your partner.

7 🎧 **6.7** Look at the Listening skill box. Then listen to the first and second stories again and put the events (a–c) in order. What helped you understand the sequence of events?

LISTENING SKILL
Understanding a sequence of events

When someone is telling a story, the events may not always be told in order. The speaker might talk about something that happened and then go back to an earlier event, for example. To help you understand a sequence of events, listen for words such as *while*, *after* or *before*. Also pay attention to the tenses the speaker uses. For example: *So this one time I twisted my ankle. I'd never been injured before.*

1 Story 1:
 a Joe slips and falls into the water head-first as he tries to do a backflip.
 b Megan starts filming Joe.
 c Megan and Joe start a competition.
2 Story 2:
 a Paola is carrying a tank for diving.
 b Paola buys new sandals.
 c Paola falls and fractures a bone in her hand.

GRAMMAR

8 🎧 **6.8** Listen to Paola talk about an accident that happens to her often. Complete the sentences with one word.

1 Often, when cooking, I <u>will get</u> _____.
2 My husband <u>likes</u> knives to be _____.
3 By not concentrating, I <u>tend to</u> _____ myself.

9 Look at the sentences in Exercise 8 again and answer the questions (1–3). Then read the Focus on box to check.

1 Are the sentences about the present or future?
2 Do they describe things that happen once or regularly?
3 Which of the underlined phrases are about actions or habits and which is about a state?

FOCUS ON Discussing present habits

To describe what people typically do, you can use the **present simple**.
She **has** really bad luck.
It's common to use **tend to** + **infinitive** to describe people's habits.
I **tend to dive** a lot.
You can also use **will** + **infinitive without to** to talk about habitual actions (but not states).
She **will** often **get** into funny situations.

Go to page 148 for the Focus on reference.

10 Complete the sentences about habits. Make some sentences true and some false. Then read the sentences to your partner and ask them to work out which are true.

1 My best friend will always _____.
2 I tend to _____.
3 My classmates _____.
4 My _____ will often _____.

SPEAKING

11 You are going to tell a story about someone who is clumsy: either someone you know or an imaginary person. Make notes on their habits and how they tend to have accidents. Use the language from Exercises 2 and 3 and the Focus on box to help you. Then share your story in groups.

6D Balancing fluency and accuracy

LESSON GOALS
- Discuss the importance of using correct English
- Understand how to balance fluency and accuracy
- Talk about situations when fluency or accuracy is more important

LISTENING AND SPEAKING

1 What's your attitude towards making mistakes in English? Decide on a scale of 1 (completely disagree) to 5 (completely agree) how much you agree/disagree with the sentences.
   1 Mistakes are bad because they show I haven't learned well.
   2 I think being understood is more important than using correct English.
   3 Mistakes are great opportunities for learning.
   4 It's important to get everything right in my head before I say something.
   5 If I realize I have made a mistake, I don't correct myself.
   6 I'm as worried about my spoken errors as I am about my written ones.

2 Work in pairs. Discuss your answers from Exercise 1. Who tends to worry more about their mistakes? Why?

3 ∩ 6.9 Listen to the two speakers. Discuss the questions in pairs.
   1 Who seems to pay more attention to being accurate or correct, and who to just being fluent and getting the message across?
   2 Which speaker is more like you when you speak English? Why?

4 Look at the text about language errors below. What is its main message? Does it change your mind about any of your responses from Exercise 1?

Language errors

EXAM	
Grammar and Vocabulary	2 /5
Fluency	4 /5
Pronunciation	3 /5
Interaction	5 /5 !

Many speaking exams test your **fluency** as well as **accuracy**.

She play the piano. *The girl which lives here.*

Many 'errors' have little impact on the message, especially when English is used as an international language.

I would of bought it if it was cheap.

I don't know nothing about that.

There were less people than last time.

Your going, aren't you?

This street is badly lighted. *This street is badly lit.*

First language users of English **make erors to**! The speech
                                       r   o
bubbles above show a few typical errors that Brits, Americans, Australians, etc. make.

Language changes ALL the time. What seems like an 'error' to us (*He builded this house.*) was correct not such a long time ago. And things people saw as 'bad' English in the past (*The street was badly lit.*) are now the correct form.

Are you more accurate or fluent in English?

accuracy   fluency

The see-saw.

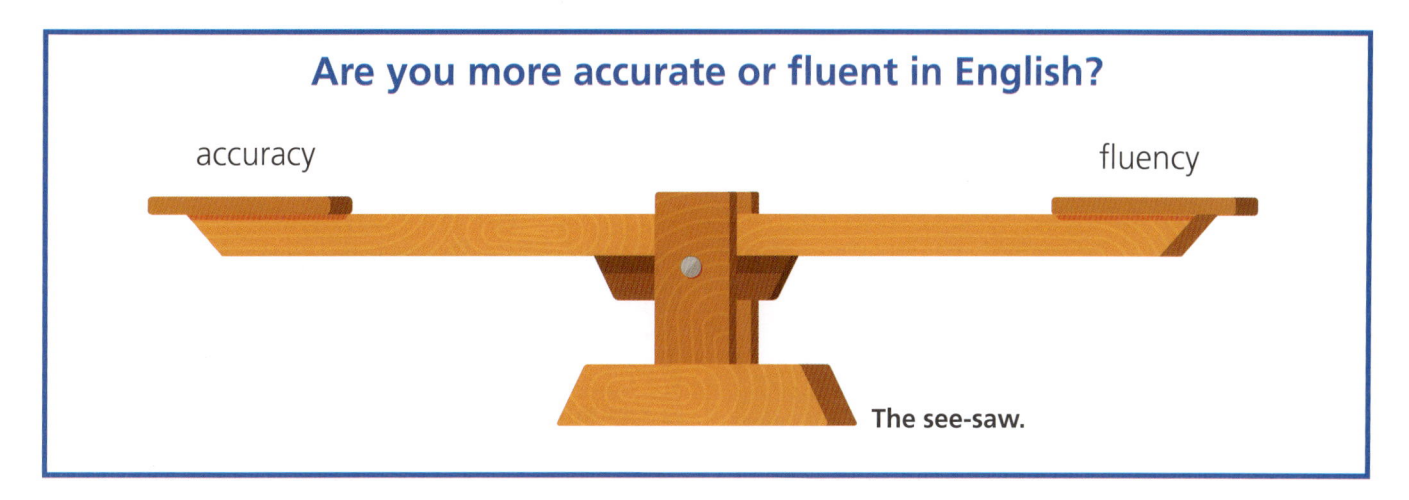

MY VOICE ▶

5 ▶ 6.2 Watch the video about fluency and accuracy. Then discuss the questions in pairs.
1. Why did Dani feel good in Venice?
2. Why did Eduardo feel bad in Jakarta?
3. Who is more focused on fluency and who on accuracy?
4. Which beliefs about fluency and accuracy do you share with Dani and Eduardo?

6 ▶ 6.2 Work in pairs. Watch the video again. Student A: write advice for Eduardo. Student B: write advice for Dani. Then share the advice.

7 Use the Communication skill box to check your notes from Exercise 6. In pairs, decide which advice you think is the most important.

COMMUNICATION SKILL
How to balance fluency and accuracy

Try to find a balance between being fluent and being accurate. If you tend to focus too much on accuracy:
- Remember most people won't judge your mistakes: they're interested in your message. Focus on that instead of the language.
- Remember everyone makes mistakes, even in their first language.
- Try to see mistakes as opportunities to improve.

If, on the other hand, you focus too much on fluency:
- Identify the situations when you need to pay more attention to accuracy.
- List some common mistakes you make and try to stop making them.
- Ask others to correct you.

SPEAKING

8 **OWN IT!** Are you more accurate or fluent in English? Put points on the see-saw above for these areas of English. Then compare with a partner. Do you think you have the balance right?

grammar   pronunciation   speaking   vocabulary   writing

9 Decide where on the see-saw you would put these English-language situations. How important are accuracy and fluency in each case?
1. chatting to a friend on a Friday evening
2. having a job interview to be a waiter
3. taking an English language speaking exam
4. texting cooking instructions to a friend
5. writing an essay for a geography course
6. complaining on the phone to the internet company about the bill

10 Work in groups. Discuss the questions.
1. What are your main goals in learning English?
2. How confident are you at speaking and writing? Where do your strengths lie – in fluency or in accuracy?
3. What do you need to focus more on: getting it right or saying what you want to say? How do you plan to do that?

EXPLORE MORE!

Make a list of common mistakes you make in English. Decide which ones are the most serious. How will you stop making them?

6E Formal complaint

LESSON GOALS
- Organize information in a formal complaint email
- Say what action you would like to be taken
- Write a formal email of complaint

SPEAKING

1 Work in pairs. Read the situations (1–3) and discuss the questions (a–c).

1 You are in a restaurant. One of the waiters accidentally spills coffee all over your shirt. Your shirt is almost brand new, but now it is completely ruined.
2 Your neighbour's child, who's only five, left their skateboard on the pavement. Your wife didn't notice it. She tripped over it, fell over and broke her arm.
3 You buy a bike. The first day, you go very fast downhill. The brakes don't work and you crash. Fortunately, you don't get seriously injured, but you are quite bruised and scratched.

a Would you complain? Who to?
b How would you complain (by telephone, email, etc.)? Why?
c What would you ask for in your complaint?

READING FOR WRITING

2 Read the complaint email. Answer the questions.
1 Which situation from Exercise 1 is it about and what exactly does the writer complain about?
2 What actions does the writer want the restaurant owner to take?
3 How would you respond if you received this email?

New Message

Dear Sir or Madam

I am writing to complain about the **poor** service I **received** in your restaurant.

After dinner, I ordered coffee, and one of the waiters spilled it over my shirt. Furthermore, rather than **apologize**, he left the table without a word and didn't return. I do not tend to complain, but this time the **negative** response caused me to ask for the manager.

However, when I told the manager about the situation, she said that it had been my fault because I had moved my cup while the waiter was pouring the coffee. I explained that this was not the case, but the manager refused to believe me.

Therefore, I would like to **request** a full **refund** for the meal as well as **compensation** for my shirt, which is ruined. Moreover, since the response by your staff to the incident was **unsatisfactory**, I would kindly ask you to share my feedback with them, to ensure that that this doesn't happen again.

I am looking forward to hearing from you.

Yours faithfully

Wafaa Amin

---

3 Read the email again. Answer the questions. Then read the Writing skill box to check.
1 How is the email organized? Put the topics (a–c) in the correct order.
   a request compensation
   b explain what the problem was
   c state why you are writing
2 <u>Underline</u> the words and phrases the writer uses to connect his ideas. Which of these words are used to:
   a add similar ideas?
   b show a result?
   c show reasons?
   d contrast two different ideas?

WRITING SKILL
Organizing information in a formal complaint email

Formal complaint emails follow a similar structure. Typically, you first explain why you are writing and then present the situation that caused the complaint. You end by asking for some action to be taken (e.g. money back). Each paragraph usually focuses on one idea. Ideas in the email should be linked using appropriate words/phrases to show:
- contrast: *even though, however, although, nevertheless*
- addition: *moreover, in addition, furthermore*
- cause: *since, because, as, due to*
- effect: *therefore, as a result, consequently*

4 Complete the sentences using linking words from the Writing skill box. Sometimes there is more than one possible answer.
1 The sunscreen was supposed to be waterproof. _____, I applied it before swimming.
2 The bike was new. _____, the brakes did not work.
3 _____ the accident, I was not able to go to work for two months.
4 I built the trampoline following the instructions carefully. _____, I then checked twice myself that it felt steady.

5 Read the email again. Match the formal words in bold in the email with the definitions (1–8).
1 ask for
2 money back
3 say sorry
4 opposite of positive
5 bad
6 not good enough
7 got
8 money given to someone due to injury, loss or damage

6 Rewrite the sentences using linking words and formal language.
1 So I want to first get an apology from you and also ask you for a new bike.
2 I was quite lucky I did not get bad injuries, but I'm super bruised and in pain.
3 So I couldn't brake and had an accident.
4 I'm writing 'coz I had an accident on the bike I bought in your store.
5 The bike was new, but the quality was bad and the brakes didn't work OK.

EXPLORE MORE!

Search online for 'funniest customer complaints ever'. Choose three that you find the funniest.

7 Put the sentences in Exercise 6 in the most appropriate order for an email of complaint.

WRITING TASK

8 Think about a situation when you or someone you know had a reason to complain about something. Make notes about what happened and what action you would like to be taken.

9 **WRITE** Write a formal email of complaint about the situation you chose in Exercise 8. Use the Writing skill box and the Useful language to help you.

> **Useful language** Saying what action you would like to be taken
> I would appreciate it if you could look into the matter.
> I trust that you will …
> As the service/product was below standard, I would like to request …
> I would kindly ask you to …
> I hope that you will take steps to prevent such situations from occurring in the future.

10 **CHECK** Use the checklist. I have …
☐ stated why I am writing in the first paragraph.
☐ explained what the problem is.
☐ asked for action to be taken.
☐ used formal vocabulary.
☐ used linking words to connect ideas.
☐ used some of the Useful language.

11 **REVIEW** Work in pairs. Read your partner's email of complaint. Tell your partner how you would respond if you received their email.

Go to page 132 for the Reflect and review.

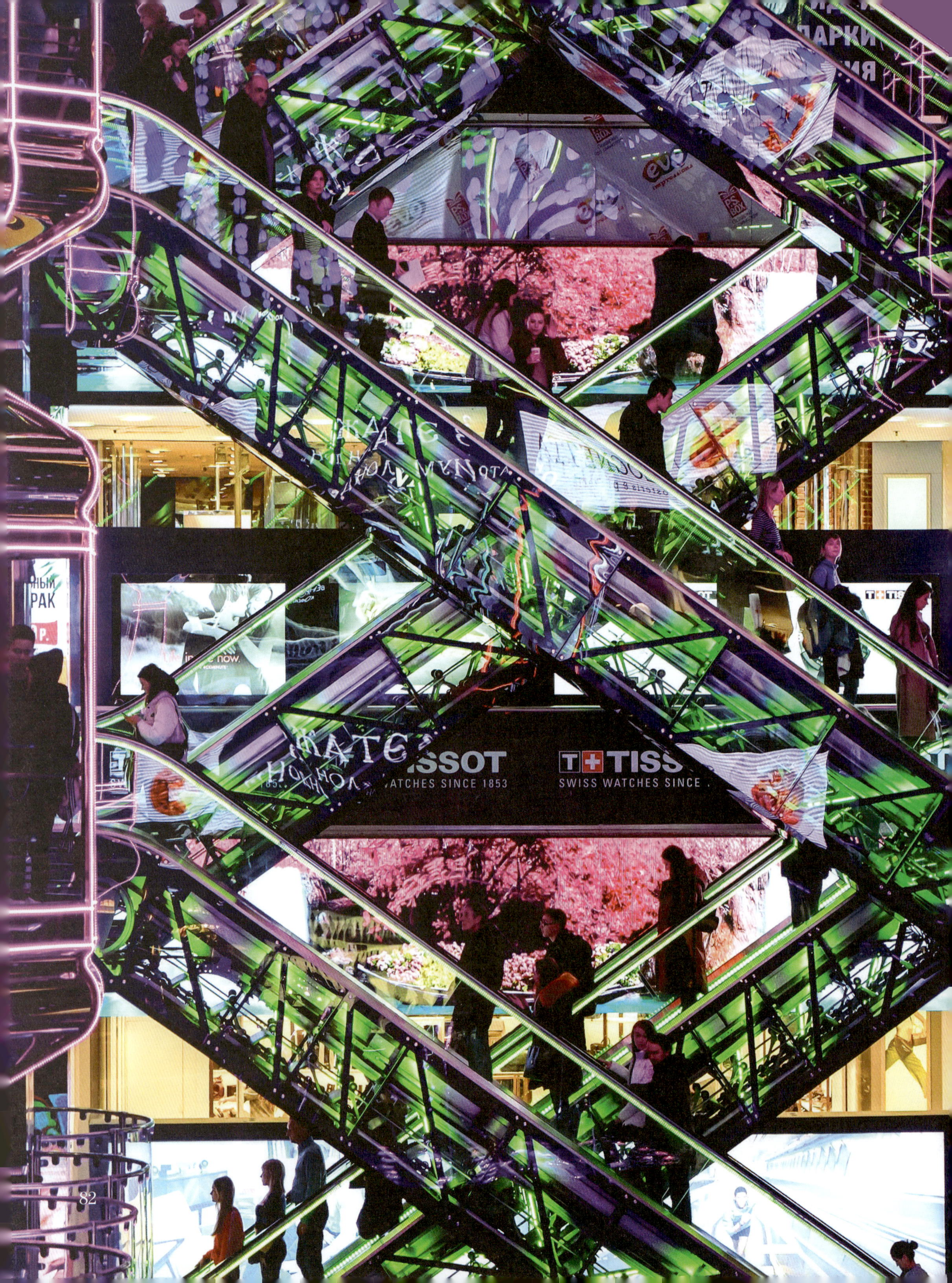
SWISS WATCHES SINCE

7

Going shopping

GOALS

- Identify fact and speculation in a text
- Talk about services you have done or get done
- Understand approximate numbers
- Talk about buying products and getting good deals
- Find solutions in negotiating situations
- Write an online advert for an item you want to sell

1 Work in pairs. Look at the photo and discuss the questions.

1 Do you ever shop in places similar to this? Why? / Why not?
2 Where do you prefer to shop and why:
   a small, local shops or big supermarkets?
   b online or offline?

WATCH ▶

2 ▶ 7.1 Watch the video. Answer the questions.

NATIONAL GEOGRAPHIC EXPLORER

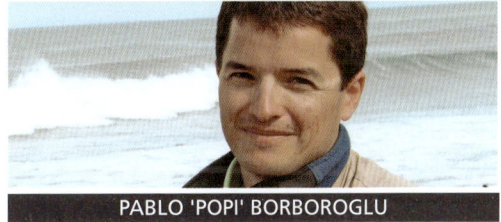

PABLO 'POPI' BORBOROGLU

1 Why does Popi prefer shopping offline?
2 How do Popi's shopping habits differ when he's at home and when he's travelling?
3 What second-hand products does Popi buy? Why?

3 Make connections.
   1 Are your shopping habits similar to Popi's?
   2 Have your shopping habits changed over the last few years?

Customers riding the escalators at a shopping mall in Moscow, Russia.

83

7A Secret lives of vending machines

LESSON GOALS
- Identify fact and speculation in a text
- Identify and evaluate the writer's purpose
- Design a vending machine

READING

1 Work in pairs. Discuss the questions.
1 Where can vending machines typically be found? Are there any near where you live?
2 Do you ever buy things from vending machines?

2 Read the infographic on page 85. Discuss the questions in pairs.
1 How have vending machines changed over the years?
2 Have you ever seen anything unusual in a vending machine?

3 Look at the Reading skill box. Then read the text on page 85 and decide which of the sentences (1–6) are facts (F) and which are speculation (S). In pairs discuss which words helped you decide.

READING SKILL
Identifying facts and speculation

In a text you might find a mixture of facts and speculation. Speculation is information the writer is either guessing or isn't 100% sure about, e.g. *It's also said to be the cheapest water in town!* To show speculation, the writer may use:
- adverbs such as *possibly*, *likely* or *probably*
- adjectives such as *possible* or *estimated*
- modal verbs such as *might*, *may* or *could*
- structures such as *X is said/reported to …*

1 The first vending machine was invented in London.
2 There are 15 million vending machines on the planet.
3 One third of all vending machines are in Japan.
4 The vending machine market has grown to $134 billion.
5 Japan has the most interesting vending machines in the world.
6 Only two in ten people bought the t-shirt from the German vending machine.

4 Work in pairs. Look at the Critical thinking skill box. Which of the reasons (1–3) best explains the writer's purpose? Use the questions in the Critical thinking skill box to evaluate whether the writer achieved their purpose.

CRITICAL THINKING SKILL
Identifying and evaluating the writer's purpose

A writer might have different reasons for writing their text, for example to provide information, argue their point of view, entertain, persuade, offer solutions to a problem, etc. The main aim typically becomes more and more visible in the final paragraphs and is restated in the conclusion. You can evaluate whether a writer has achieved their purpose by asking:
- Have they presented enough facts?
- Are their arguments logical and supported with examples?
- Were you persuaded by the arguments they used?

1 Present the history of vending machines.
2 Persuade you that vending machines can do much more than sell snacks.
3 Suggest a solution to the problem of too many vending machines.

5 Discuss the questions in pairs.
1 Which of the vending machines from the text did you think was the best idea? Why?
2 Do you think vending machines can replace human interaction in a shop? Why? / Why not?

SPEAKING

6 Work in groups of three. You are going to design a new vending machine. Think about:
- what the vending machine will sell and for how much.
- where you will place it.
- who your main audience will be and how you will attract them.
- how your vending machine will differ from the competition.

7 Present your ideas to another group. Do you think this machine would be popular where you live? Why? / Why not?

Our vending machine is completely unique. It's the first one ever to sell …

EXPLORE MORE!

Search online for 'unusual products sold in vending machines'. What is the strangest example you can find?

From **selling snacks** to **changing lives**

1 **Vending machines are everywhere: from airports, to shopping centres, office blocks and universities, to just your regular city street. They sell almost any product under the sun. Here are a few facts about vending machines you probably didn't know.**

5 You will likely find some of the most fascinating vending machines in Japan. They sell almost any item you need: toys, clothing, food, electronics – you name it. You can also buy a costume or a tie, depending on the occasion. And if your electronic devices are running out of power, you can charge them using a vending machine.

10 Need something for dinner? No problem! In Italy, you can find vending machines able to make 100 different pizzas completely from scratch. They even make the dough themselves. And if you're not up for a pizza, try a different vending machine. How about burritos in California, smoked salmon in Singapore, vegan food in Melbourne or noodles
15 in Japan?

There are also vending machines that help save lives. Lack of access to clean drinking water often leads to serious diseases. As a result, in Nairobi, Kenya, there are vending machines that sell up to 20 litres of clean water. It's also said to be the cheapest water in town!

20 Finally, vending machines have also been used to address social issues. A vending machine in Berlin was selling t-shirts for 2 euros, but buyers were first shown a video of the conditions in which such cheap clothes are made. Eighty percent of shoppers changed their minds about buying one.

25 Vending machines have come a long way from selling snacks to busy businesspeople. Now, they can not only cook for you, they are also being used to fight disease and raise awareness of social issues.

A pizza vending machine in Hiroshima, Japan.

1883 – the first ever vending machine was invented in London. It is reported to have mainly sold snacks to busy businesspeople.

The **2000s** saw the rise of vending machines selling a huge variety of products: from face masks, to caviar, to gold.

There are said to be about **15 million** vending machines around the world today.

Japan is reported to have over 30% of the world's vending machines: there is **one for every 23 people** there!

Around **30%** of vending machines are internet connected, and it is estimated that this figure will rise rapidly over the next few years.

$134 billion – this is the estimated size of the annual vending machine market around the world. That's roughly $15 for every person on the planet!

7B
Get your food delivered

LESSON GOALS
- Understand a conversation about services
- Talk about services you have done or get done
- Stress the object with *have/get something done*

SPEAKING

1 Work in pairs. Look at the photos (A–D) and discuss what services they might show. Then match the photos with the descriptions (1–4).
   1 apology service – get your apologies delivered
   2 goat rental – have your grass cut by goats
   3 alibi writer – have your excuses written by a professional
   4 queuing service – save time and have all your waiting done by a full-time queuer

2 Discuss the questions in pairs.
   1 Which service do you find the most unusual? Which seems the most useful? Why?
   2 Which of the services would you definitely/maybe/never pay for? Why?

LISTENING AND GRAMMAR

3 🎧 7.1 Listen to two people. Which of the services from Exercise 1 did they use? Why?

4 🎧 7.1 Listen again and complete the sentences with the words you hear.
   1 So I decided to _____ the tickets bought for me.
   2 My professional queuer got _____!
   3 The grass definitely needed _____.
   4 After days of searching on the internet, I finally had their garden _____.

5 Work in pairs. Discuss what kind of services you pay to have done for your hair, house, food, etc. How often do you get these things done?

6 Read the sentences in Exercise 4 again. Answer the questions. Then read the Grammar box to check.
   1 Who does the action: the speaker or someone else?
   2 Which sentences mention something you pay another person to do?
   3 Which sentence refers to something unpleasant that happened?
   4 Which sentence mentions something that should be done?

86

GRAMMAR have/get something done

You can use *have/get* + object + past participle to talk about actions you pay other people to do.
*So I **got the apology written** by a professional.*
You can also use *get* + past participle to talk about unpleasant things that happen by accident.
*A few weeks ago my friend's bike **got stolen**.*
Get something done is often seen as more informal than *have something done*.
You can use *need* + gerund to talk about things that should be done, often by someone else.
*The grass definitely **needed cutting**.*

Go to page 148 for the Grammar reference.

7 Complete the sentences with the correct form of the words in brackets.

1 I didn't feel like cooking, so I _____. (a curry / deliver)
2 My camera broke, so I needed to _____. (fix)
3 I left the window open in my car and it _____. (steal)
4 After a whole day of hiking my boots _____. (need / clean)
5 Do you ever _____ when they break or do you just buy new ones? (shoes / repair)
6 When was the last time you _____? (eyes / check)

8 Look at the before and after drawings. Write sentences about the things Julia had/got done.
Julia had her windows cleaned.

PRONUNCIATION

9 🎧 7.2 Look at the phrases. Will the main stress fall on *have/get*, the object (e.g. *curry*, *shoes*) or the past participle (e.g. *delivered*, *checked*)? Listen to check.

1 have a curry delivered
2 have your shoes repaired
3 get your eyes checked

10 Look at the Clear voice box. Then practise reading out your sentences from Exercise 8, paying attention to the main stress.

CLEAR VOICE
Stressing the object with *have/get something done*

In the structure *have/get* + object + past participle, the main stress of the phrase is usually on the object (*I got my **windows** cleaned*). Putting the main stress on the correct word is important for clear pronunciation.

SPEAKING

11 Work in pairs. Follow the instructions. Then change roles.

Student A: You have just moved to a new city. Ask Student B for recommendations about where to get things done. Try to think of some unusual services as well as more typical ones. Use the Useful language to help you.

Student B: You live in the city that Student A has just moved to. Give Student A advice about where to get things done. Use the Useful language to help you.

Useful language   Recommending where to get things done

Asking for recommendations
Which … would you recommend?
Where is the best place to get …?
What's the best … in town?

Giving recommendations
You must try …
You should definitely go to …
Their prices are really reasonable.
I'd highly recommend …

7C What a bargain!

LESSON GOALS
- Understand approximate numbers
- Talk about buying products and getting good or bad deals
- Say longer vowels before voiced consonants
- Talk about cost, price and worth

1 Work in pairs. Discuss the questions.
  1 Have you ever bought something you weren't happy with? What happened?
  2 What's the last thing that you bought that made you really happy?

LISTENING

NATIONAL GEOGRAPHIC EXPLORER

2 🎧 7.3 Listen to Popi Borboroglu talking about buying products. Was he happy or unhappy about each product he talks about? Why?

3 🎧 7.4 Listen and complete the extracts with the words you hear.
  1 … he asked for _____ 140 euros …
  2 … that was _____ 160 dollars …
  3 … I bought it for _____ 100 dollars.

4 Look at the extracts in Exercise 3 again. Which word/phrase does Popi use to mean:
  1 something was more or less that price?
  2 something was a bit more?
  3 something was a bit less?

5 🎧 7.5 Look at the Listening skill box and check your answers from Exercise 4. Then listen to an extract of Popi talking about why he thinks the arm guard was a good deal. Circle all the answers (1–4) that are correct.

LISTENING SKILL
Understanding approximate numbers

Sometimes a speaker might not say an exact number, either because they have forgotten it or because it is not important. You might hear phrases like *approximately*, *around*, *about*, *more or less*, etc. You're also likely to hear *just over/under* (to mean a bit more/less) or *well above/under* (to mean a lot more/less).

A similar piece in Portobello Market would have cost Popi:
1 approximately 1,000 pounds.
2 around 1,000 dollars.
3 much more than 1,000 dollars.
4 more or less 1,300 dollars.

VOCABULARY

6 Which of these phrases could be used to say:
  1 something cost less than the full price?
  2 you are happy with what you paid for something because the price was fair?
  3 you paid far too much for something?
  4 you talked to the seller to reduce the price of something?
  5 the amount you will have to pay for something?

a bargain   bargain with   be charged ($50)
be on sale   a complete rip-off   cost a fortune
get a discount on   get a good deal on
good value for money   a special offer   well worth it

Popi loves shopping for antiques.

The arm guard Popi bought.

7 Complete the sentences with two words from Exercise 6 in the correct form.

1 They had a _____ on laptops, so I decided to buy one.
2 Those things normally cost _____, but in the sales you can get some really _____.
3 They thought I was a tourist, so I _____ $60. I would have paid half that if I were local.
4 I know in some countries it's common practice, but I really don't feel comfortable _____ shop assistants.
5 I waited until the headphones were _____, so I only paid half the original price.
6 I tried to get a _____ the painting, but in the end I still had to pay the full price.

Go to page 138 for the Vocabulary reference.

PRONUNCIATION

8 🎧 7.6 Listen to sentences a and b in 1–2. In which sentence does the underlined word have a longer vowel? Look at the Clear voice box to check.

1 a It wasn't a good <u>prize</u> at all.
  b It wasn't a good <u>price</u> at all.
2 a I've seen plenty of <u>caps</u> over there.
  b I've seen plenty of <u>cabs</u> over there.

CLEAR VOICE
Saying longer vowels before voiced consonants

In words that are one syllable, the same vowel will be longer before a voiced consonant (e.g. b, d, g, z) than before a voiceless consonant (e.g. k, p, s, t). To be easily understood, it is important that you make this distinction.

9 Work in pairs. Say one of the sentences (a or b) from Exercise 8. Your partner listens and says a or b. If they can't decide, say the sentence again, making sure the vowel is shorter or longer, as appropriate.

GRAMMAR

10 Look at the Focus on box. Then complete the sentences with *cost*, *price* or *worth*.

> **FOCUS ON** *cost, price, worth*
>
> **Cost** is often used as a verb in questions with 'how much' or in sentences stating the amount:
> *How much did it **cost**? It **cost** 1,000 pesos.*
> As nouns, both **price** and **cost** refer to the amount of money, but only *price* is used about things in a shop.
> *The **cost/price** is £25 per person.*
> *They've lowered the **price**, so I'm going to buy it.*
> **Worth** is an adjective:
> *It cost $4, but it's only **worth** half that.*
> **Cost**, **price** and **worth** can also be used to talk about things other than money, e.g. *the environmental cost, It cost me a lot of time, a small price to pay, It's well worth a visit, nothing worth watching.*

Go to page 149 for the Focus on reference.

1 That bike only _____ you 24,000 yen? That's such a bargain! It must be _____ twice that much.
2 He looked after his mum for years, at great personal _____ to himself. He always said that you can't put a _____ on family.
3 One or two shops are _____ visiting. They sell fashionable clothes at reasonable _____.

SPEAKING

11 Think about two things you or someone you know have bought: one a good deal and one a rip-off. Prepare to tell your classmates about the experience. Use the questions to help you.

1 Where did you buy the item? Why did you buy it?
2 Did you get a good deal? Why? / Why not?
3 Would you recommend it to others? Why? / Why not?

12 Share your stories in groups of three. Whose purchase was the biggest rip-off? Who got the best deal?

EXPLORE MORE!

Search online for 'how to bargain over price in different countries'. What's the most useful tip you found?

7D Finding solutions when negotiating

LESSON GOALS
- Talk about negotiating
- Find solutions in negotiating situations
- Practise negotiating in order to reach an agreement

SPEAKING AND VOCABULARY

1 Work in pairs. Discuss the questions.
   1 When was the last time you negotiated over something at home, at work or in your studies?
   2 Do you usually get what you want in negotiations? Why? / Why not?

2 Match these words/phrases with the definitions (1–5). Then choose one of the words and think of a situation you've experienced that illustrates the word well. Tell your story to your partner. Can they work out which word it illustrates?

---
compromise   conflict   negotiation   priorities
satisfy the needs of
---

   1 a situation in which people change their opinion or accept less so that they can reach an agreement
   2 provide someone with what they need
   3 disagreement or fighting between people with different opinions
   4 things that are important and come before other things
   5 a discussion with someone to try to reach an agreement about something

3 Work in pairs. Read about Lian and Mei and discuss the questions.

> Lian and Mei want to buy a laptop to share. Lian wants to get good value for money by buying a second-hand computer. She thinks that new ones aren't worth it because they quickly lose value, and buying a second-hand computer is better for the environment. Mei wants a new one. She cares about the environment, but she's had bad experiences with second-hand laptops, and repairs have cost her a lot. Also, because a new laptop can last for years, she thinks in the long run it's worth it. And there are some good deals at the moment. Both Lian and Mei say they will be unhappy if they don't get what they want.

   1 What options are open to Lian and Mei? Are there any options that might satisfy both of their needs?
   2 How different are Lian's and Mei's priorities in making this decision?
   3 Have you ever had to negotiate with someone about a big decision? Did you manage to find a compromise? How?

MY VOICE ▶

4 ▶ 7.2 Watch the video and complete the sentence with the best ending: The story about the conflict over the laptop shows that …
1 the best solution to disagreement is compromise.
2 we can reach 100% satisfaction on both sides with greater information.
3 negotiations can only have one winner.

5 ▶ 7.2 Watch the video again. Then discuss the questions in pairs.
1 Why does Lian and Mei's conflict seem like it cannot be resolved at the beginning?
2 What two things do you need to know when entering any negotiation? Why?
3 How can asking questions help in negotiating?
4 What kind of solutions should you suggest when negotiating?

6 Look at the Communication skill box. In pairs discuss which suggestions:
1 you have already tried or would like to try?
2 would work really well for you?
3 might be difficult for you to apply? Why?

COMMUNICATION SKILL
Finding solutions when negotiating

In situations where two people are negotiating, it's natural to assume that one person's win is the other person's loss. But it's possible to find solutions that everyone is happy with.
- Before negotiating, identify your own priorities.
- Enter into the negotiation with a collaborative attitude – you can help each other.
- Find out what the other person wants – their priorities and interests.
- Suggest solutions that satisfy both of your needs.

7 Work in pairs. Read the situations. Identify each person's interests and suggest a solution that may satisfy everyone's needs.

1
> Ahmed and Carlos live in the same flat. They've decided to buy a new TV together. Ahmed wants the best and newest TV. Carlos is more concerned about the money. He wants a TV that works well and is big, but he thinks that the TV Ahmed is suggesting is just not worth the price.

2
> Four friends are looking forward to going away for a weekend break at the end of a busy academic year. Aidah has never been camping and really wants to go somewhere in the countryside away from the city. Kang has a bad back and is looking forward to going somewhere relaxing and comfortable. The important thing for Milly and Jack is that they all have a good time together.

3
> Miguel and Gabriela are brother and sister. It's their dad's 60th birthday soon, and they have agreed to get him something from both of them. Miguel wants to spend the money taking him out for a special meal. Gabriela wants to use the money to buy him a present that he can keep.

LISTENING AND SPEAKING

8 🎧 7.7 Listen to a conversation about one of the situations from Exercise 7. Answer the questions in pairs.
1 Which situation is it?
2 What solution do they reach and how?

9 Work in pairs. Look at the Useful language box. Which expressions can you use for …
1 asking about people's interests?
2 coming to an agreement?
3 offering suggestions?
4 showing you understand the other person's opinion?

Useful language Negotiating
I see where you're coming from.
How about we …?
What would you like to get out of this?
Can we agree on …?
That's understandable.
Can I suggest something?
What would need to change for you to say yes?
Are we both happy with …?

10 OWN IT! Work in pairs. Choose a situation from Exercise 7 and roleplay finding a solution. Try to come to an agreement where you are both happy.

7E I'm selling it

LESSON GOALS
- Talk about selling second-hand items online
- Omit words to shorten a text
- Write an online advert for an item you want to sell

SPEAKING

1 Work in pairs. Discuss the questions.
1 Have you ever bought second-hand items online?
2 Have you ever tried selling items you own online?
3 What are the advantages and disadvantages of buying and selling second-hand items online?

READING FOR WRITING

2 Read the adverts (1–4). Do you think the adverts are persuasive enough to attract buyers? Why? / Why not? Would you buy the items?

3 Look at the sentences (1–3). How did the writer of the first advert (1) shorten them?
1 Are you looking for an excellent phone?
2 It's still in excellent condition.
3 The battery still lasts a whole day.

4 Look at the Writing skill box. Then find other examples of sentences with omitted words in the adverts.

WRITING SKILL
Omitting words to shorten a text

In texts such as online adverts and informal messages it is common to omit certain words to make the message shorter. Typically, the words that will be omitted are:
- pronouns, e.g. *Will comfortably fit two people.*
- the verb *to be*, e.g. *Still in excellent condition.*
- auxiliary verbs in questions, e.g. *Looking for an excellent phone?*
- articles (*a*, *an*, *the*), e.g. *Battery still lasts a whole day.*

These are often combined, so more than one word is omitted, e.g. *(It has been) Recently washed.*

1
ZenX 360 Pro for sale
Dubai, United Arab Emirates – 5 hours ago
600 AED
Looking for an excellent phone? I'm selling my old ZenX 360 Pro. 512 GB memory. Fantastic camera. Still in excellent condition. Only a few scratches at the back. Battery still lasts a whole day. Comes with all original accessories, including charger and headphones. Interested? Send me a message here or email me.

SELLER INFORMATION

Ayesha

Send seller a message

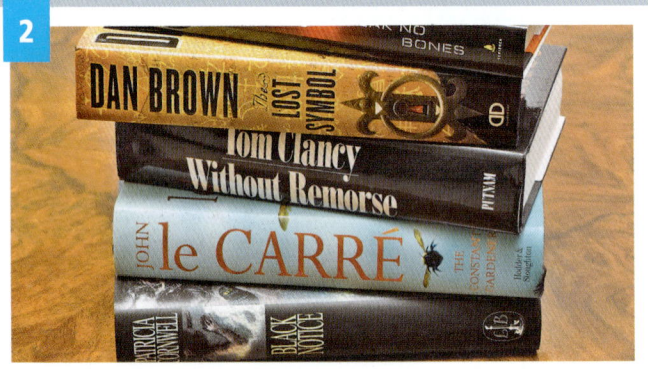

2
Collection of crime novels
Moscow, Russia – 15 hours ago
1,200 RUB (negotiable)
Enjoy thrillers? Like reading crime novels? You will love these books. Got a collection of five novels I need to sell as we're moving abroad. All like new, without any marks or bent corners – I take care of my books. Would prefer to sell all, but happy to negotiate. Will sell all five for 1,200 RUB or one for 300 RUB. Drop me a message if you're interested.

SELLER INFORMATION

Alexandr

Send seller a message

5 Rewrite the sentences to make them shorter.
1 Do you need new running shoes?
2 It comes with a brand new laptop case and a mouse.
3 It has got only a minor scratch at the back.
4 Are you looking for quality speakers?
5 I had it fixed last week.

6 You are going to write adverts for two items, either real or imaginary, that you would like to sell. Read the adverts again and look at the Useful language box. Underline any language that you could use in your adverts.

> **Useful language**   Selling items online
> Measures x cm in length/height/depth.
> Comes with (original case and instruction manual).
> In very good condition.
> Like new.
> (It's got only) a few minor scratches/marks.
> If interested, get in touch on …
> Free delivery. / Collection only.
> Price (non-)negotiable.

WRITING TASK

7 WRITE Write an advert for each of the two items you would like to sell. Use the Writing skill box and Useful language to help you.

8 CHECK Use the checklist. I have …
- [ ] described the item and its condition.
- [ ] omitted words when appropriate.
- [ ] used some of the Useful language.
- [ ] included the price.
- [ ] included delivery/collection details.

9 REVIEW Put your adverts on the classroom wall. Walk around and choose one advert you would like to respond to. Write a message to the owner expressing your interest and asking at least one question.

Go to page 133 for the Reflect and review.

3

Sofa bed
Rio de Janeiro, Brazil – 2 hours ago
515 BRL
Need a new sofa or a bed? Got an excellent offer for you. Selling this sofa bed for only 515 reais (bought it originally for 1500). Measures 220 cm by 180 cm. Will comfortably fit two people. Excellent condition. Collection only, no delivery. Needs to be sold by the end of the week. Discount if you buy today. Call or message me if interested.

SELLER INFORMATION

Fernanda

Send seller a message

4

Gear 10 Extreme Mountain Bike
Sydney, Australia – 10 hours ago
150 AUD
Enjoy mountain biking? Selling this Gear 10 Extreme mountain bike. Still in very good condition, though brakes might need fixing. Recently had the tyres changed to 27.5". Comes with 18-speed gears and front suspension. Had the gears checked a week ago too. Super lightweight – easily carry it up the stairs to my flat every day. Want this great bike for a good price? Send me a message or give me a call.

SELLER INFORMATION

Chris

Send seller a message

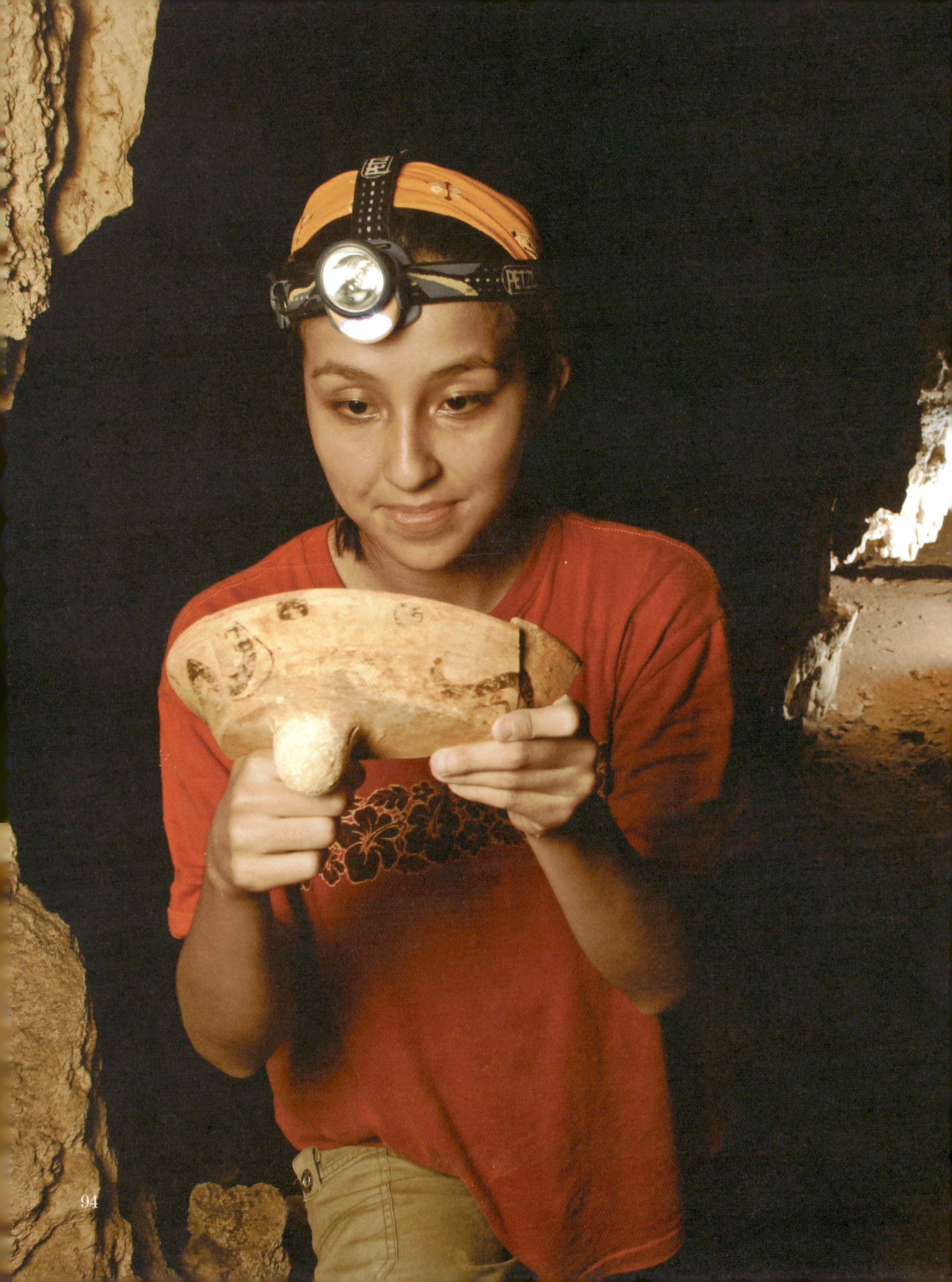
PETZL

8
Working life

GOALS

- Take notes using symbols and abbreviations
- Talk about jobs using noun phrases
- Synthesize ideas across listening passages
- Talk about employment and describe jobs
- Deal with different working styles in teams
- Write a professional profile

1 Work in pairs. Look at the photo and discuss the questions.
   1 What is the person's job? What skills do you think you need to do a job like this?
   2 Would you like to do a job like this? Why? / Why not?

WATCH ▶

2 ▶ 8.1 Watch the video. Answer the questions.

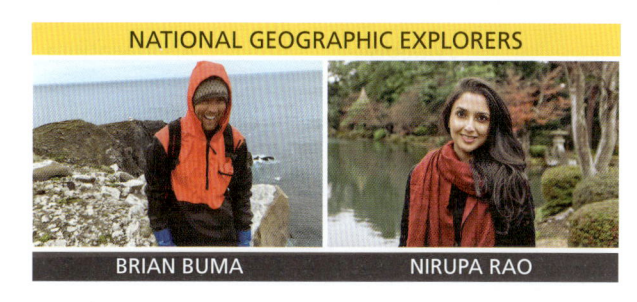

NATIONAL GEOGRAPHIC EXPLORERS

BRIAN BUMA   NIRUPA RAO

   1 What is one job Nirupa and Brian have each done? Did they enjoy it?
   2 What are Nirupa's and Brian's jobs now?
   3 What do they each enjoy about their jobs?

3 Make connections. What is your ideal job? What skills are needed to be good at it?

An archaeologist looks at some Maya pottery in the Illuminada Cave, Guatemala.

8A Breaking the glass ceiling

LESSON GOALS
- Take notes using symbols and abbreviations
- Evaluate a writer's statements
- Talk about the glass ceiling

READING

1 Work in pairs. Look at the title of the article and the illustration on page 97. Discuss the questions.
  1 What do you think 'the glass ceiling' is? Why is it described as made of glass?
  2 What do you think it means to 'break the glass ceiling'?

2 Read the article on page 97 to check your ideas from Exercise 1. What is the aim of the article?
  1 to give examples of women who have broken the glass ceiling
  2 to show different ways of breaking the glass ceiling
  3 to define what the glass ceiling is

3 Look at the Reading skill box. Are there any other symbols or abbreviations that you already use?

READING SKILL
Taking notes using symbols and abbreviations

While reading a text, you might want to take notes to remember it better, for example to tell someone else about it or to write a summary. To take notes more quickly and efficiently, only write key words and use symbols and abbreviations. Here are some common ones.

Symbols		Abbreviations	
+ / −	also, positive, more / minus, without	b/c	because
= / ≠	equals, means / does not equal / mean	def.	definition
> <	greater / smaller than	e.g.	for example
↑↓	increase / decrease	expl.	explanation
→	lead to, change	min. / max.	minimum / maximum

You can also invent your own symbols and abbreviations that work for you.

4 Choose a paragraph from the article and take notes using symbols and abbreviations.

5 Read the article again. Are the sentences true (T) or false (F)?
  1 Because of the glass ceiling, many people cannot achieve their goals.
  2 It is illegal for employers in Iceland to pay a man more than a woman for doing the same job.
  3 Recruitment in orchestras in the US was not fair and, as a result, blind auditions were introduced.
  4 Blind recruitment is not very common.

6 Work in pairs. Look at the Critical thinking skill box. Then use the questions from the box to give the arguments (1–3) a score from 1 (weak) to 5 (strong). Give reasons.

CRITICAL THINKING SKILL
Evaluating a writer's statements

After reading a text where the writer presents a certain point of view, it is important to look at the statements they make in more detail. This can help you decide if you should believe the writer's opinion. Consider if the statements made are:
- objective or subjective?
- based on science or personal stories?
- likely to be true globally or only locally?
- supported by facts/statistics?

1 Women are very likely to earn less than men.
2 Introducing new laws is a good way of achieving greater equality.
3 Equality for women in Rwanda has not yet been achieved.

SPEAKING

7 Discuss the questions in groups.
  1 Can you think of jobs in your country that have a glass ceiling?
  2 Are there jobs where there are now more women in senior positions than before?
  3 In your opinion, are laws that ensure a minimum number of women get certain jobs and equal pay a good idea?

EXPLORE MORE!

Read more about one of the women mentioned in the article, or another woman who has broken the glass ceiling.

EDITORIAL

Beyond the glass ceiling

In the summer of 1968, in England, a group of female factory workers had had enough of their lower 'women's rate' of pay. Instead of accepting it, they went on strike and were successful in achieving equal pay. This inspired similar strikes as women throughout the country started to stand up for their rights.

Although this victory was over 50 years ago, the glass ceiling, the barrier that prevents women from achieving their career goals, is still there, and remains largely invisible. That is, until you see someone break it, like Jane Fraser, who in 2018 became the first woman to lead a Wall Street bank. But even when a woman manages to break this glass ceiling, she is still very likely to earn less than a man. For example, in the EU men earn on average 16% more than women.

> In Iceland it is not the responsibility of the woman to prove she is paid less, but of the employer to prove all employees are paid equally.

So how can greater equality be achieved? One solution is new laws. In Iceland, it is a criminal offence to pay a woman less than a man for doing the same job. Jóhanna Sigurðardóttir, former Prime Minister of Iceland, compared differences in pay to theft. While most countries have equal pay laws, in Iceland it is not the responsibility of the woman to prove she is paid less, but of the employer to prove all employees are paid equally. The result: Iceland now has the smallest gender pay gap in the world.

Another solution is to set a minimum quota of women for certain positions. Since 2004, 30% of elected offices in Rwanda must be held by women. The result? Fast forward to now, and more than 60% of members of parliament are women, more than in any other country. However, 'mindset changing is not something that happens overnight,' says politician Emma Furaha Rubagumya. According to Mary Balikungeri, founder and director of the Rwanda Women's Network, addressing 'how we transform our own families, our own husbands' is the next step. It is hoped that through education and by making sure that men are brought into the dialogue, attitudes will change in time. So while Rwanda's future looks hopeful, the journey is not finished.

Some might argue that quotas should not be necessary because in a fair recruitment process, if a woman is a better fit for the job, she should be selected over a male candidate. Unfortunately, this isn't always the case. For example, in the 1970s, top orchestras in the US had approximately 5% female musicians. Today, they have over 30%. What happened? In the 1980s, blind auditions were introduced. This meant that the judges could no longer see the candidate, nor know their name, skin colour or gender. They could only hear their music. Similar 'blind' recruitment happens in many companies, such as the BBC, HSBC and Deloitte, whereby no personal attributes (gender, name, etc.) are admitted on CVs. Such practices can lead to fairer hiring and, as Katherine McNamee from the Society for Human Resource Management observes, it can change an organization's whole mindset and make people 'more aware of hiring biases'.

Change might seem slow, but the examples above prove that it can and does happen. The important first steps towards living in a world beyond the glass ceiling have been taken.

GLOSSARY:
mindset – the attitudes or ideas someone has, which don't change easily

strike – when a group of employees refuse to work for a certain amount of time because of something they are unhappy about, e.g. their pay

8B
A job for the brave

LESSON GOALS
- Understand a conversation about unusual jobs
- Talk about jobs using noun phrases
- Say /ɜː/ and /ɑː/ clearly

LISTENING AND GRAMMAR

1 Work in pairs. Look at these job titles and discuss the questions (1–3).

> colour expert   dream watcher   flavourist
> golf ball diver   gravity bed sleeper for NASA
> line stander   nail polish namer   robot trainer

1 What do you think the job might involve?
2 What skills might be needed?
3 Only six of the jobs are real. Which two do you think aren't real? Why?

2 🎧 8.1 Listen to a conversation about some of the jobs in Exercise 1. Answer the questions.
1 Which jobs do they mention and what skills are needed for them?
2 Which job does Samira decide to apply for? Why?

3 🎧 8.1 Which jobs are the sentences about? Listen to the conversation again to check and complete the sentences with one word.
1 But look, it says it's **a job for** _____ lovers. And **someone who** has a good _____ of language.
2 They're looking for **someone with** a passion for _____.
3 And **knowledge of** current _____ trends.
4 They're looking for **someone who** _____ diving and being outdoors.
5 You'll take part in **an experiment to research** sleeping in _____.
6 If it's **a job that** requires you to _____ all day, then you're the perfect candidate!

Andy Taylor makes money by diving for golf balls at golf clubs in England.

4 Look at the Grammar box to learn more about noun phrases. Then match the three types of noun phrases (1–3) from the box with the phrases in bold in the sentences in Exercise 3.

> **GRAMMAR** Noun phrases
>
> You can add more information to a noun to make a noun phrase by adding:
> 1 a preposition: *a job **for** energetic people; a job **with** a large bank*
> 2 the infinitive with *to*: *a job **to be** jealous of; colleagues **to chat** with*
> 3 a relative clause: *a job **which/that** I can't stand; someone **who/that** has good communication skills; the building **where** I work*
>
> If the noun is the object of the clause, you can leave out the relative pronoun:
> *It's a job (**which/that**) I can't stand.*

Go to page 149 for the Grammar reference.

5 Write sentences with noun phrases. Which jobs from Exercise 1 do you think they are about?
1 We need someone / degree / Chemistry.
  We need someone with a degree in Chemistry.
2 We're looking for someone / stand / queues.
3 It's a job / requires knowledge / technology applications.
4 Experience / field / food tasting is not necessary.
5 Only candidates / have / necessary knowledge / design techniques will be contacted.
6 This is a job / you will love if you have a passion / sleeping and science.
7 It's a job / someone / loves diving.

6 Choose two of these jobs and write sentences about them using noun phrases. Then work in groups of three to work out which jobs your classmates are describing.

> art historian   babysitter   engineer   fisherman
> hairdresser   landscape gardener   librarian
> mechanic   nurse   politician   receptionist
> swimming instructor   town planner

It's a job for people who enjoy meeting the public.
People who have a passion for books will love this job.

PRONUNCIATION

7 🎧 **8.2** Look at the Clear voice box. Then listen to these words. Do they have the /ɜː/ or /ɑː/ sound? Practise saying the words.

> architect   barber   be in charge   farmer
> learn   research   university   work

CLEAR VOICE
Saying /ɜː/ and /ɑː/

The /ɜː/ sound as in h*ear*d is pronounced in the centre of your mouth with your lips only slightly open. However, the /ɑː/ sound as in h*ar*d is said at the back of your mouth with your lips more open and slightly rounded. In order to be easily understood, it's important you do not confuse these two sounds, and that you say both as long vowels.

8 Complete the sentences so that they are true for you. Then read them to your partner, paying attention to the /ɜː/ and /ɑː/ sounds.
1 My [member of your family] w*or*ks as a(n) _____.
2 I am det*er*mined to _____.
3 I'd like f*ur*ther experience of _____.
4 My personal t*ar*get is to _____.

SPEAKING

9 Work in pairs. Choose an interesting or unusual job and use noun phrases to write a description of the job, as if you were an employer. Give the job an attractive-sounding title.

Children's party entertainer
We are looking for someone with excellent people skills who loves children to join our team …

10 Now present your job to the class and try to find as many job candidates as you can. Ask each candidate why they would be the best person for the job. Then decide on the best candidate and say why.

EXPLORE MORE!

Find out more about one of the unusual jobs in Exercise 1 or another unusual job, including what qualifications and experience you need.

8C Changing jobs

LESSON GOALS
- Talk about employment and describe jobs
- Say /r/ at the end of syllables clearly
- Synthesize ideas across listening passages
- Use compound words

SPEAKING

1 Work in pairs. Look at the photo and answer the questions. Then go to page 156 to check your answers.
  1 What do you think Kunal is doing?
  2 What objects and equipment is he using?
  3 Why do you think he needs to do it this way?

2 Discuss the questions in pairs.
  1 Do you think Kunal got good results?
  2 What skills and qualities does Kunal show?
  3 Have you ever had to change the way you work or study? Why? What did you do?

Photographer Kunal Kelhar gets creative.

VOCABULARY

3 Read the advert from an employment agency. Answer the questions.
  1 How can the employment agency help jobseekers?
  2 What, according to the advert, will help jobseekers stand out from others?

> Are you **unemployed** and looking to get back to work? Are you looking for work in a **competitive** industry? Do you want to **work 9 to 5** on a **permanent contract**? Or can you be **flexible** and accept that you may have to **work long hours**? Perhaps you would prefer to work from home. Our **employment agency** can help you find fantastic **job opportunities**! Developing your **transferable skills** (skills you can use in more than one job) will help you **stand out** from other jobseekers. Visit our website for ways we can help you achieve **job satisfaction**.

4 Complete the sentences with these words. Use the advert in Exercise 3 to help you.

competitive   contract   employment
flexible   hours   opportunities   out
satisfaction   skills   unemployed   work

  1 Joining an _____ agency will give you greater job _____.
  2 If you're currently _____ and looking for work, be _____. You might not get a permanent _____ to begin with.
  3 If you're working from home, you don't have to _____ 9 to 5. You can work when it is convenient and avoid working long _____.
  4 Job _____ is about more than money. Make sure the hours aren't too long, you get enough days off, etc.
  5 To stand _____ from other jobseekers in more _____ industries, take courses to develop your transferable _____.

Go to page 138 for the Vocabulary reference.

PRONUNCIATION

5 🎧 **8.3** Look at the Clear voice box. Listen to three people say sentences 1–5. How do they say 'r'? Which accents do you find easiest to understand? Practise saying the sentences.

CLEAR VOICE
Saying /r/ at the end of syllables

The /r/ sound can sound different across different accents. In some accents, /r/ is not pronounced when it is at the end of a word (e.g. *retire*) or after a vowel (e.g. *work*), which can make it harder to understand the word. To be easily understood, you might want to always pronounce the /r/ sound.

1 He's a commercial photographer.
2 She's a retired teacher.
3 Fair working conditions are important.
4 What's your other job?
5 These are hard times.

LISTENING

NATIONAL GEOGRAPHIC EXPLORERS

6 🎧 **8.4** Listen to Nirupa Rao and Brian Buma talking about their work and how their field is changing. Tick (✓) the topics they discuss.

	Brian	Nirupa
communication with colleagues and other people	☐	☐
job satisfaction	☐	☐
job security	☐	☐
place of work	☐	☐
the skills people need in their field	☐	☐
their working hours	☐	☐
effects of working practice on the environment	☐	☐
work-life balance	☐	☐

7 🎧 **8.4** Listen again. Find two things Brian and Nirupa have in common with each other and one difference.

Both Brian and Nirupa have been working from home more recently.

8 🎧 **8.5** Look at the Listening skill box. Then listen to the extract and compare what Brian and Nirupa say about working from home.

LISTENING SKILL
Synthesizing ideas across listening passages

One person's opinion or one information source is not enough to offer a complete picture of a topic. Listening to more than one source helps get a better idea of the topic. By comparing information, you can get new ideas and insights into a topic. When presented with different perspectives of a topic, compare them and decide what you believe: the same as one of the speakers or a combination of them all.

9 🎧 **8.6** Listen and decide which is the best synthesis of Brian's and Nirupa's opinions about working from home.

GRAMMAR AND SPEAKING

10 Look at the Focus on box. Then match a word from column A with a word from column B to form compound words about jobs and working.

FOCUS ON Compound words

Compound words are created when two words are used together so they function as one word. They are either written as one word (*firefighter*), hyphenated (*part-time*), or two separate words (*employment agency*). Many job titles are compound nouns.

Go to page 150 for the Focus on reference.

A	B
1 swimming	a assistant
2 working	b skills
3 people	c paid
4 shop	d hours
5 well	e instructor

11 Discuss the questions in pairs.
1 Have you ever had to travel for work or study?
2 When you work or study at home, are you easily distracted? How do you try to stay focused?
3 How do you think technology will change the way we work and learn in the future?

8D Working in a team

LESSON GOALS
- Talk about working as part of a team
- Deal with different working styles in teams
- Practise adapting to different working styles within a team

SPEAKING AND LISTENING

1 Work in pairs. Look at the photos and answer the questions.
   1 What are the people doing? What is their relationship?
   2 Do you think it is a good idea to spend time getting to know your colleagues or classmates? Why? / Why not?
   3 When you are working in a team, do you think it is more important to achieve results or to develop good working relationships?

2 🎧 8.7 Listen to a conversation between two colleagues, Carlos and Lek. Which of them is focusing more on their relationship? Which is focusing more on work?

MY VOICE ▶

3 ▶ 8.2 Watch the video about working in a team. Then use these words to complete the text about Carlos and Lek's conversation in Exercise 2.

identity   long-term   motivation   people
relationship   task   team

Carlos' and Lek's attitudes to working relationships are very different. Lek is focused on the ¹_____. He feels that his ²_____ with Carlos and other colleagues will develop as they work together. For him, you show you are professional and dedicated to the ³_____ by getting tasks done. Carlos is more concerned with his ⁴_____ relationships with Lek and the rest of the staff. He believes that if you focus on the ⁵_____, then the tasks will get done by working as a team. The team is important to his own sense of ⁶_____. Both completing tasks and doing the best for the team can give people ⁷_____ to work.

4 Discuss the questions in pairs.
   1 Are you more like Lek or Carlos? Provide examples.
   2 Think of different groups you are in, e.g. classes, your company or clubs. Are the team members more focused on the tasks or the relationships within the team?
   3 What are the advantages and disadvantages of each approach to working in teams?

5 ▶ 8.2 Watch the video again. Why might people adapt from focusing on the task to focusing on relationships and vice versa?

6 Look at the Communication skill box. Decide whether each tip is for people who focus more on relationships (R), people who focus more on the task (T), or both (B).

COMMUNICATION SKILL
Dealing with different working styles in teams

1 Make an effort to get to know people, but also trust that these relationships will develop over time.
2 Check with people individually if deadlines or meeting times are possible for them if you know there are different preferences.
3 Remember to plan extra time for relationship-building.
4 Try to see the positive intentions behind people's actions. If they don't want to spend time socializing, it may be that they value efficiency over relationship-building.
5 See social activities as a positive investment in time if the relationships you are developing will last a long time.
6 If you want to suggest a social activity to the group, explain the benefits and find out if other people agree.

SPEAKING

7 OWN IT! Work in pairs. Read about the situations and discuss what each person could do to be more flexible. Use the advice in the Communication skills box to help you. Then answer the questions for each situation.

1
> Zaid wants to organize an excursion for his politics study group. There is a lot of pressure on everyone to pass the end-of-year exam and this is making the atmosphere in the classroom very serious and, in his opinion, unfriendly. He thinks a trip to a museum or similar will be fun and a good way to improve the atmosphere. He speaks to a couple of classmates and mentions it to their tutor, but nobody seems interested.

Have you ever been in a group in which you wanted to be more friendly? What did you do?

2
> Marta starts a new job at a supermarket next week. The manager has asked her to attend a day's training this week, and she has to finish her current job a day early to attend. She is disappointed to learn that they will spend most of the time doing getting-to-know-you activities. She sees this as a waste of time. She decides to speak to the manager about it.

Do you ever get frustrated when you have to do things that seem like a waste of time? What is your approach in situations like these?

3
> Henri wants to build his own website but doesn't know how. He's just found out that a classmate, Lottie, has helped several of her friends design their sites for free. He's keen to get started soon but feels uncomfortable asking her for help because he doesn't know her well.

Would you be comfortable asking someone you didn't know well for a big favour like this?

8 Look at the Useful language box. Which expressions show the greatest willingness to adapt?

Useful language Adapting to different working styles within a team

We could do it that way, no problem.
If that's complicated for everyone, I'm willing to look at alternatives.
If everyone feels the same, then please don't let me get in the way.
I could definitely be persuaded.
It's not how I normally do things, but I'm willing to give it a go.
I'm up for that, sure!

9 Work in pairs. Roleplay conversations between Zaid and one of his classmates, Marta and her manager, and Henri and Lottie from Exercise 7. Try to adapt your approach to find a solution that satisfies everyone. Use the Useful language to help you.

8E Your online professional profile

LESSON GOALS
- Discuss applying for jobs online
- Use the -ing form to turn verbs into nouns
- Write the 'About me' section of a professional profile

SPEAKING

1 Work in pairs. Look at the infographic. Do you think professional networking sites are a good way for employers to find candidates?

FINDING JOBS AND CANDIDATES ONLINE

More than **122 million** people have got a job interview thanks to professional networking sites.

59% of LinkedIn users in the US are aged between 25 and 34.

87% of employers use LinkedIn to check candidates.

72% of recruiters will reject a candidate whose online profile has typos.

For each corporate job vacancy, there are on average 250 CVs, 4–6 people interviewed, and only **1 person hired.**

READING FOR WRITING

NATIONAL GEOGRAPHIC EXPLORER

2 Read the 'About me' section of Brian Buma's profile. Discuss the questions in pairs.
1 Which of these positions would Brian be a good candidate for? Why?

> ecologist   landscape gardener   nature photographer
> plant biologist   summer camp organizer

2 What sort of employee do you think Brian is?

3 Put the things Brian writes about in the order they appear in his profile.
a his work experience
b his personal interests and hobbies
c his professional interests
d what he is currently doing
e how he discovered his passion

4 Look at the Writing skill box. Find three uses of the -ing form in Brian's profile.

WRITING SKILL
Using the -ing form to turn verbs into nouns

The first thing an employer will see on your online profile is the headline and 'About' section, so make sure it clearly shows what you do. Noun phrases can state a lot of information with fewer words, but to describe what you do, you need verbs. You can turn verbs into nouns using the gerund, or -ing form.

*I love **solving** customer problems with a friendly smile.*
*I believe in **learning** new skills from others.*
***Helping** ordinary people with modern technological applications is my passion.*

5 Rewrite the sentences using the -ing form of the underlined verbs.
1 It is important that I <u>work</u> in a friendly and productive team.
   I value _____.
2 I have spent a great deal of energy on the <u>development</u> of my web design skills.
   I have worked hard at _____.
3 In particular, I want to <u>protect</u> the living planet.
   I'm particularly interested in _____.
4 In my free time, I <u>learn</u> languages and <u>make</u> my own clothes.
   My personal interests include _____.

Brian Buma
Lecturer and Explorer. I help people recognize the importance of the environment.
Juneau, Alaska, United States

● University of Alaska
● University of Colorado

MESSAGE   Email • More …

About me

I grew up in the woods, and I am passionate about the environment. When I was a child, I would spend most of my day running around and discovering the hidden caves, creeks and wilderness of my hometown. This drive to explore led me to the sciences, where I gained substantial experience as a wilderness research guide in the mountains of Washington and as a conservation specialist in the wild parts of Hawaii. I have always been good at maps and orienteering; at one point I remember having to find research locations in the Alaskan wilderness that had been lost for 100 years, which I was able to do with compasses and old charts. This love of science and the wilderness led me back to school, and I graduated from the University of Colorado with a PhD in ecological science. My first job as a PhD scientist was at the University of Alaska, where I worked and taught for five years.

I am currently working back in Colorado where I teach ecology and continue to do research in areas around the world. Last year I went to both Nepal and Chile to research ecological change, and I have recently started research projects on wildfires and landslides in the Colorado mountains. I continue to be particularly interested in research and exploration, and I am always looking to expand my experiences and research network around the world.

When not working, I spend most of my time snowboarding, downhill mountain biking, hiking, fishing and exploring. Recently I started raising chickens and building a large garden as well!

---

6 Look at the Useful language box. Which expressions does Brian use in the 'About me' section of his profile? Add the expressions in bold from Exercise 5 to the correct section of the Useful language box.

> **Useful language**   Your professional profile
>
> **Talking about experience**
> I have always been (good at / passionate about) …
> I'm currently working at/in …
> To date, I have …
>
> **Talking about strengths, interests and goals**
> I'm particularly interested in / passionate about …
> I've always wanted to …
> This love of (the environment) led me to …

7 Choose 3–5 expressions from the Useful language box and write sentences about your experience, strengths, interests and goals. Share them in pairs. Ask each other questions to find out more.

WRITING TASK

8 WRITE Write the 'About me' section of your professional profile. Use the Writing skill box and Useful language to help you.

9 CHECK Use the checklist. I have …
☐ included a headline that shows who I am and what I do.
☐ shown what I'm passionate about professionally and personally.
☐ used some of the Useful language.
☐ presented my current and previous work experience and skills.

10 REVIEW Work in pairs. Read your partner's profile. Share with them one thing you liked about it and one thing that could be improved.

Go to page 133 for the Reflect and review.

EXPLORE MORE!

Search online for 'top LinkedIn profile tips'. Which could you apply to the profile you wrote in class?

People on the beach in Norderney, Germany, between 1890 and 1900.

9

History revisited

GOALS
- Understand reference words
- Talk about interesting moments in history
- Take notes when listening
- Talk about periods in history
- Adapt your argument to suit your listener
- Write a biography of an historical figure

1 Look at the photo and answer the questions.
  1 Apart from the caption, what clues are there that this photo was taken more than 100 years ago?
  2 How can restoring old photographs and other objects from the past help people understand history better?

WATCH ▶

2 ▶ 9.1 Watch the video. Where and when in history would Francisco go? Why?

NATIONAL GEOGRAPHIC EXPLORER

FRANCISCO ESTRADA-BELLI

3 Make connections. If you could go back to any time and place for one day, where and when would you go and what would you do? Why?

107

9A Inspired by the past

LESSON GOALS
- Understand reference words
- Synthesize from multiple sources
- Invent an imaginary world

READING

1 Work in pairs. Look at the illustrations on page 109 and answer the questions.
1. What kind of story do you think these illustrations come from?
2. Do you enjoy stories like this? What kinds of stories do you like to read or watch?

2 Read about 'world building', then match the definitions (1–7) with the words in bold.

> 'World building' is when writers invent an **imaginary** place for their story. It might be a **fantasy**, like *Lord of the Rings*, or science fiction like *Star Wars*. Writers must consider various **elements** when building worlds: the physical landscape, the architecture of the buildings, the **politics** of the **society** in which the **characters** live, the level of **technology** and whether things that are impossible can happen.

1. the people in a story
2. only existing in the mind
3. the way a country is ruled and decisions are made
4. the use of scientific discoveries
5. a story that describes events, people and places very different from real life
6. the parts that make something
7. a group of people who live and work near each other and organize themselves

3 Read the extract from *Path of a Novice*, by R K Lander, at the bottom of page 109. With your partner, identify three elements from Exercise 2 that help create the world of the story.

4 Now read the interview with R K Lander at the top of page 109. Match the questions (a–e) with the spaces in the text (1–5).
a Does that mean you have to do lots of research?
b Have you got more books planned? And if so, where – and when – are you thinking of going?
c What are the elements of world building, and how are they inspired by history?
d When in history is the world of the *Silvan* novels?
e Why is it that world building in fantasy is so often based on certain periods of history?

5 Read the Reading skill box. Then look for the reference words (1–4) in the first paragraph of the interview and decide what each word refers to.

READING SKILL
Understanding reference words

Reference words such as *he*, *this*, *which*, *there* and *them* refer to people, things, places or ideas that are normally mentioned earlier.
- Look for nouns that match the gender of the pronoun.
- Writers avoid repetition by leaving out certain words when referring to things, e.g. *The cities were smaller than* **today's** *[cities]*.
- Some reference words refer to ideas, e.g. *It's useful for a writer to have* **this starting point**.

1 they (line 6)   3 that (line 9)
2 it's (line 6)   4 this one (line 11)

6 Read the Critical thinking skill box. Then look at the illustrations, the extract and the interview again and discuss the questions in groups.

CRITICAL THINKING SKILL
Synthesizing from multiple sources

When you have various sources, such as texts and images, think critically about what each source is communicating in order to form fuller, more reliable opinions about the topic. Think about:
- the purpose of each source.
- what the person is trying to achieve.
- how the sources work together. Do they support each other's arguments or contradict them?

1. Do the illustrations and the texts support the argument that fantasy is inspired by history?
2. Why do you think the author has agreed to talk about this topic here? Do you think she has succeeded in her aim?

SPEAKING

7 Work in small groups to 'build' a world. Use the questions on page 156 to help you.

History or fantasy?

1 R K Lander is the author of the *Silvan* fantasy novels, which have sold over 60,000 copies. She talks to us about world building and how history helps.

1 _____?

I think it's impossible to separate the writer from their knowledge, so it's just much easier to create a world that's similar to a period of history they know about. I'd say it's one of the hardest things to get right, so it's useful for a writer to have this starting point. It means you don't have to explain *everything* about the world – that would take too long. And it allows the reader to already understand a lot about it. And then slowly you reveal the differences, why it's *not* the same as this one. But it's not the only source of inspiration, or even the main one – I get my ideas from all sorts of places.

2 _____?

There are so many questions you need to answer, like where do the characters live? What are their politics? In fantasy there's nearly always a king or queen, or some sort of ruler. That's a sign that we're looking back into the days before democracy. Also, people tend to live in villages; cities are nearly always smaller than today's. What about technology, or the lack of it? If our hero rides a horse and fights with a sword we assume that motorized transport and modern weapons don't exist yet.

3 _____?

Yes, it does! I spent a lot of time investigating soldiers' clothes – what would their armour look like? What is it made out of? How is it made? And again, the technology doesn't let me dress them in modern materials, they have to be natural ones like leather or wool.

4 _____?

It's pre oil and gas, so no cars or plastics. But there are cities, and trade between countries, and complicated objects. If this was Europe it might be around the 15th or 16th centuries. But it's not as simple as that, because there are other aspects of the world that are much more modern, such as the fact that women can be fighters.

5 _____?

There are still two more books to go in the *Silvan* saga series. After that, the next one may be a modern fantasy, and not necessarily an invented world. It could be in our world, but with added elements that don't exist, such as paths to other universes. You'll have to wait!

The three friends rode in silence, each thinking of what lay ahead of them. The more they thought, the more nervous they became. It was Fel'annár who broke the silence. Before their disbelieving eyes, on the horizon, Thargodén's city fortress climbed into the sky.

Mighty towers of stone rose to the clouds, tall and pointed. Colourful domes shone in the sun, and platforms hung off the side of the rock. It was a strange sight within the forest landscape, a massive structure that stood proudly among the trees of Ea Uaré.

Fel'annár suddenly wanted to be closer, to see the detail he knew decorated the stairways, walls and halls of rock and wood. He had seen it in books: the gardens and fountains, fine men and women in expensive clothing; soldiers in skilfully made armour. It was strange, he thought, because the architecture was artificial, so different from their Silvan homes in the Deep Forest that tried to copy nature. These structures seemed designed to achieve the opposite. Despite the contrast, the trees protected it, embracing it in their caring, green arms.

EXPLORE MORE!

Analyse the world of a fantasy or science fiction film or book that you know. Make a list of the different elements that make it what it is, and decide how close to the real world it is.

9B At the same moment in history

LESSON GOALS
- Understand an infographic about interesting moments in history
- Use and stress pronouns correctly
- Discuss important events in your life

SPEAKING

1 Work in pairs. Look at these events in history and try to work out when they happened.
- paper invented
- Eiffel tower built
- European lions die out
- mammoths die out
- Nintendo company founded
- pyramids at Giza built

2 Look at the infographic. Were your predictions from Exercise 1 correct?

LISTENING AND GRAMMAR

3 🎧 9.1 Listen to two conversations. What were the speakers doing at the same time? When?

4 🎧 9.1 Look at the extracts (1–5). What are the underlined pronouns referring to? Match the pronouns with these nouns. Then listen again to check.

a piece of news   Fran   Fran's phone
the photo of Fran   the photographer

1 Did you take it <u>yourself</u>?
2 <u>Someone</u> else took it.
3 I dropped <u>mine</u>.
4 I know <u>they</u> sent <u>it</u> to <u>me</u> …
5 A happy <u>one</u>?

THEY HAPPENED AT THE SAME TIME!

2500 BCE

The last woolly mammoths are still living on Wrangel Island in the Arctic.

The ancient Egyptians are building the Pyramids at Giza.

~100 CE

Cai Lun from China invents a cheaper form of paper, making it available to the general population.

The last European lions die in the Balkans.

1889

The Eiffel Tower is officially inaugurated in Paris. At 300 metres tall, it was by far the tallest structure in the world.

The Nintendo company is founded in Japan. At first it produced playing cards, not video games!

5 Look at the Grammar box. Match the types of pronouns from the box with the underlined pronouns in Exercise 4.

> **GRAMMAR** Pronouns
>
> *I, you, they*, etc. are **subject pronouns**. *Me, you, her, them* etc. are **object pronouns**.
>
> **Possessive pronouns** such as *mine*, *yours* or *theirs* replace the noun.
> *What happened to **yours**?*
>
> **Reflexive pronouns** such as *myself, herself* or *themselves* are used when the subject and the object of the verb are the same. They are also used for emphasis.
> *The Egyptians built the Pyramids **themselves**.*
>
> **Indefinite pronouns** are formed by adding *some-* or *no-* (used in positive sentences), and *any-* (used in negative sentences and questions) to *-body/one, -thing*, or *-where*.
> ***Nobody** had ever been to Madeira before.*
>
> **One**(s) can be used to replace nouns. It often follows an adjective.
> *Chinese ships were much bigger than European **ones**.*

Go to page 150 for the Grammar reference.

6 🎧 9.2 Complete the sentences with a pronoun. Then listen to check.
1 Cai Lun didn't invent paper _____. He just improved it.
2 Has _____ ever climbed the outside of the Eiffel Tower? _____ must be either very brave or very crazy!
3 The Aztecs called _____ 'Mexica', which is where Mexico gets _____ name.
4 I spent most of my teenage years playing video games. What did you do in _____?
5 She never went to university because not a single _____ offered _____ a place.
6 I'm sure I've seen you _____ before. Did _____ work at the supermarket together?
7 Although Juliya and Liza were in chess clubs at the same time, they went to different _____.

7 Work in pairs. Tell your partner about …
1 someone who is very important to you.
2 somewhere you would like to visit.
3 something you should be able to do by yourself, but can't.

PRONUNCIATION

8 🎧 9.3 Look at the Clear voice box. Then listen to the first four sentences from Exercise 6. Tick (✓) the ones where the pronoun is stressed.

> **CLEAR VOICE**
> **Stressing pronouns**
>
> Most subject and object pronouns are not stressed, unless you want to add extra emphasis. However, reflexive and indefinite pronouns are typically stressed. Possessive pronouns and *one* are also stressed when they replace nouns (e.g. *It's **mine**, I'll have just **one**, thanks*). But when *one* follows an adjective, it is not usually stressed. Instead the adjective before it is stressed (e.g. *She was the **first** one*).

9 Practise saying the sentences in Exercise 6, stressing the pronouns when appropriate.

SPEAKING

10 Think about five important events in your life. Put when they happened on a timeline. Then talk to as many people in class as you can. Find out what they were doing at the same time.

11 Share your findings in pairs. Whose life events would you like to know more about?

While I was taking my driving test, Yu was on holiday in Thailand. Lucky her!

EXPLORE MORE!

Find out what important events around the world happened at the same time as the important events in your life.

9C This is how they lived

LESSON GOALS
- Take notes when listening
- Talk about periods in history
- Say /ɜː/ with and without 'r'
- Use the passive voice with *by*

SPEAKING

1 Work in pairs. Discuss the questions.
  1 Which periods or events in history do you find interesting? Why?
  2 How do you think people's lives were different 3,000 years ago? Can you think of any similarities?

LISTENING

NATIONAL GEOGRAPHIC EXPLORER

2 ∩ 9.4 Listen to an interview with Francisco Estrada-Belli. Which period in history does he discuss? What is an interesting thing that you learned about it? Tell your partner.

3 Work in pairs. When might you need to take notes when listening? What advice for taking notes can you think of? Look at the Listening skill box to check.

LISTENING SKILL
Taking notes when listening

To take notes effectively when listening to an interview or lecture, use symbols (e.g. = or >) and abbreviations (e.g. *b/c* or *def.*). See page 96 for examples. Focus on key words because you won't have time to write everything down. Write short phrases instead of whole sentences.

4 ∩ 9.4 Listen to the interview again. Use the tips in the Listening skill box to take notes on:
  1 how scientists get information about the Maya.
  2 what we can learn from the Maya.
  3 how our lives are similar to the Maya.

5 Compare notes with your partner. Add any information you missed. Then discuss the questions.
  1 Who was able to write down more information?
  2 What could you do better next time?

VOCABULARY

6 Can you remember how Francisco used these words and phrases in the interview? Try to add some of them to your notes from Exercise 4.

be ruled by	(advanced) civilization	date from/back to
a historic site	inhabitants	period
the rise and fall of	(ancient) ruins	rural to settle

Francisco next to a giant Maya portrait, dating to 200 BCE, in northern Guatemala.

7 Complete the sentences with one word.
1 My favourite _____ is the time of the ancient Egyptian empire. They were such an advanced _____.
2 The rise and _____ of the Roman empire is a fascinating story. There are many ancient Roman _____ you can visit.
3 New evidence shows that the first people _____ in South America almost 20,000 years ago.
4 Athens was probably the first city to be _____ by the people themselves instead of a king or a queen.
5 Most people in the past used to live in _____ areas rather than cities.
6 The first _____ of Australia left us incredible cave paintings, some of which are 40,000 years old.
7 The ancient temples of Angkor Wat, which _____ from the 12th century, are one of the most important _____.

Go to page 139 for the Vocabulary reference.

PRONUNCIATION

8 🎧 9.5 Look at the Clear voice box. Then listen to these words and underline the ones that have the /ɜː/ sound. Do both speakers pronounce the 'r' after /ɜː/?

| early first historic research rural university world |

CLEAR VOICE
Saying /ɜː/ with and without 'r'

Many words with -ir, -ear, -ur, a few with -or, and those with -er in stressed syllables will have the /ɜː/ sound. Most speakers pronounce the 'r', so /ɜː/ will sound like /ɜ˞ː/ or /ɜːr/. Make sure you pronounce /ɜː/ as long.

9 Practise saying /ɜː/ with and without 'r'. Which do you prefer?

GRAMMAR

10 Look at the sentence, paying attention to the underlined passive form. Answer the questions. Then read the Focus on box to check.
They were ruled by powerful kings.
1 How is the passive formed?
2 Who does the action? (Who is the agent?)
3 What preposition introduces the agent?

> **FOCUS ON** The passive voice with *by*
>
> It is common to use the passive voice when you don't know the agent of the action, or when it is unimportant or obvious.
> *The first pyramids **were built** 3,000 years ago.*
> However, if the agent is important, use **by** to add this information.
> *Tikal was built when the Maya were ruled **by** Yik'in Chan K'awiil.*

Go to page 152 for the Focus on reference.

11 Rewrite the sentences using the passive form. Only include the agent if it is important.
1 People invented vehicles with wheels about 5,500 years ago.
   Vehicles with wheels were invented about 5,500 years ago.
2 The caliph Al-Mansur founded Baghdad in 762.
3 Scientists have discovered the ruins of large cities in the Cambodian jungle.
4 People designed the first writing systems in three places around the same time: Egypt, Mesopotamia and the Indus valley.

SPEAKING

12 Work in pairs. Choose one historic period or different ones. Write ten sentences using the passive form about your chosen historic period(s). Make half of the sentences true and the other half false.

13 Work with another pair. Take turns to read each other your sentences. Can they work out which sentences are true and which are false?
A: Coins were first made by the Lydians in 600 BCE.
B: I think that's true.

EXPLORE MORE!

Choose a period in the history of your country or another country you are interested in. Learn more about how people used to live then.

9D Adapting your argument

LESSON GOALS
- Adapt your argument to suit your listener
- Reflect on your own influencing style
- Practise persuading others

READING AND SPEAKING

1 Work in pairs. Look at the photos and answer the questions.
   1 What different aspects of history do the photos show?
   2 Are you interested in history? Why? / Why not?
   3 What can help us feel more connected to history?

2 Work in pairs. Read two texts about *change* in history and answer the questions.
   1 What is each text's main argument? Are the texts arguing the same thing or different things?
   2 How does each text try to convince the reader of the argument?
   3 Which text convinces you more, 1 or 2? Why?

MY VOICE ▶

3 ▶ 9.2 Watch the video. Which text in Exercise 2 follows each approach? Choose the correct options.
   Text *1 / 2* follows an examples-first approach.
   Text *1 / 2* follows a theory-first approach.

1

The study of history has benefits for individuals and society as a whole. You could argue that knowing about the past has no practical use. But despite its reputation of being dull, history is popular: recent figures show that it is a more popular university course than maths or languages. And for good reason: although we live in the present and plan for the future, it is the past which allows us to evaluate our current decisions and can teach us to avoid past mistakes. Without a clear vision of history, we would be unable to see patterns over time and to be able to predict what direction events might take.

2

I remember a classmate asking our teacher: 'Why do we have to study history?' To me, it was always clear: it's so fascinating! Not only are the stories exciting, history has also given me a greater perspective on current events and my country's place in the world. Knowing how different life was long ago frees me from feeling that our lifestyle is the only one possible. It helps me imagine a very different society from the one we live in now. On a different note, a friend who studied history told me how the experience helped her find work, because the skill of evaluating evidence has practical applications in a range of professions.

4 ▶ 9.2 Watch the video again. Are the sentences true (T) or false (F)?
1 You are more likely to hear evidence if the person takes a theory-first approach.
2 Personal stories are a good way to influence someone who prefers a theory-first approach.
3 If you are not sure of someone's preferred style, the best approach is to use the way that works for you because you are likely to do that better.
4 You must choose one approach and stay with it; changing halfway through doesn't work.

5 Look at the Communication skill box. Are the statements (1–3) more likely to be said by someone who prefers an examples-first approach (E) or by someone who prefers a theory-first approach (T)?

COMMUNICATION SKILL
Adapting your argument to suit your listener

Here are two different ways you can persuade people. You can follow one approach or use a combination of both, depending on your listeners' preferences.

Examples-first approach
EXAMPLES → APPLICATIONS → CONCLUSION
Some people are persuaded by hearing about real-life examples and practical applications for ideas. An examples-first approach begins with specific examples to persuade people of a more general truth.

Theory-first approach
THEORY → EVIDENCE → CONCLUSION
Others are persuaded by hearing a logical theory being tested through questions and evidence. A theory-first approach starts with a general theory and moves to a specific conclusion.

1 'Do we need to know all this theory? No wonder people think history is boring!'
2 'Is it a good idea to reach a conclusion based on only one or two examples? The situation here is different from the examples they gave.'
3 'There's no evidence to prove that what she's saying is true.'

6 Discuss the questions in pairs.
1 Can you think of a time you a) successfully and b) unsuccessfully tried to persuade someone? What happened?
2 Would you say you are good at persuading people? How could you improve?

SPEAKING

7 Look at the Useful language box. Which expressions are better suited to an examples-first approach (E) and which to a theory-first approach (T)?

Useful language Persuading people
If that's the case, it makes sense to …
If it works for them, it probably works for you too.
If you look at the facts, you'll see that …
In the same way, you might find that …
Lots of people I know use this and they don't have a problem.
The numbers clearly suggest that …

8 **OWN IT!** Read the three situations. Follow the instructions.
1 For each situation, think of different ways that A could persuade B to do what he/she wants. Think of personal stories, theories and evidence (you can invent this).
2 Organize your argument either for someone who prefers an examples-first approach or for someone who prefers a theory-first approach.
3 Find expressions in the Useful language box to help you.

Situation 1
A is a keen rock climber. B wants to take up a new sport. Rock climbing interests them, but they are worried that they might get hurt. A would love it if B started rock climbing.

Situation 2
A and B are siblings. A has noticed that B has been going to bed later and later and this is affecting their ability to do things and even their behaviour. A thinks B should work on getting earlier nights. B is unconvinced that this is a problem.

Situation 3
B throws all their rubbish in the bin and doesn't recycle plastic, paper or glass. They are not sure that recycling helps. A hates to see B not being responsible with their rubbish and would like to change their mind about it.

9 Work in pairs. Roleplay the situations in Exercise 8. Student A: Try to convince Student B. Then change roles.

9E Voices from the past

LESSON GOALS
- Paraphrase a text
- Describe historical figures and their achievements
- Write a biography of an historical figure

SPEAKING

1 Work in pairs. Match these historical figures with the images (a–f). Then read the quotes about three of the figures (1–3). Who do you think they are about?

Abū Rayhān al-Bīrunī   Indira Gandhi   Nelson Mandela
Rosa Parks   Sun Tzu   Wolfgang Amadeus Mozart

1 'His was a life filled with purpose and hope; hope for himself, his country and the world.'
2 'Her courage, determination and tenacity continue to be an inspiration to all those committed to non-violent protest and change.'
3 'What a picture of a better world you have given us!'

2 Think about a historical figure that is important to you. Think about some basic facts you know about their life, personality and achievements. Tell your partner about them.

READING FOR WRITING

3 Read the biography of Abū Rayhān al-Bīrunī. Why might someone choose to write about him? Are any of the reasons similar to your reasons for your choice in Exercise 2?

4 Look at the Writing skill box. Then find the paraphrased sentences 1–3 in the text. Did the author paraphrase them well? Why? / Why not?

How big is the Earth?

If you don't know, you can google it. But back in the 11th century, no one knew what the size of the Earth might be, or how to calculate it. That is, until Abū Rayhān al-Bīrunī came on the scene.

Al-Bīrunī was born in 973 near the city of Kath in Khwārizm (modern-day Uzbekistan) into a family of modest means. However, thanks to his mathematical talents, he managed to get important positions with different local rulers as the court scientist.

Al-Bīrunī is said to have been very confident, perhaps even arrogant, and determined. He dedicated his entire life to science. When the sultan gave him an elephant loaded with silver as a gift, al-Bīrunī sent it back, explaining he did not need such wealth.

He insisted on observation and experiments, and made great contributions to astronomy, physics, history, geometry, geography and mathematics. In his most famous work, the *Mas'ūdi Canon*, he developed the basics of calculus 600 years before Newton. He also opposed the idea of the Earth being the centre of the universe and argued that the sun was at the centre of the solar system, 400 years before the Polish astronomer Mikołaj Kopernik (Nicolaus Copernicus) proved it.

But he's probably best known for calculating the size of the Earth. Using basic geometric principles with incredible skill, al-Bīrunī established that the Earth is 39,700 km in circumference: only 1% higher than the actual figure!

As the historian George Sarton put it, the first half of the 11th century was without doubt the age of Abū Rayhān al-Bīrunī.

WRITING SKILL
Paraphrasing sources

To write a good biography of an historical figure, you will first need to research information about them in books and on the internet. You will then need to put this information into your own words and cite your source to avoid plagiarism. To do this, make sure you use different words to the original text (e.g. *famous – best-known*). You should also change the structure of the sentence (e.g. *His parents were relatively poor – He was born into a relatively poor family*). Try to take notes from the sources using your own words, and then use these notes to write your text.

1. 'Like Ibn Sīna, he never married or had a family, but he did not seek power or wealth, and was single-mindedly devoted to his research.'
(Al Khalili, 2012, p.177)

2. 'We know that he was born near the city of Kath in Khwārizm (modern-day Uzbekistan) in a family of modest means.'
(Al Khalili, 2012, p.175)

3. '… which gives a value for the circumference of the earth that is within 1 per cent of the modern value – just under 25 000 miles.'
(Al Khalili, 2012, p.186)

5 Rewrite the sentences in your own words.

1. 'Nelson Mandela studied law at the University of Witwatersrand in Johannesburg and opened the nation's first black law firm in the city in 1952.'
(CNN, 2013)

2. 'Indira Gandhi was India's third prime minister and the only woman prime minister of India till date. She is considered by many to be the strongest Prime Minister India has ever seen.'
(Business Standard)

3. 'Rosa Parks is most famous for refusing to give up her seat on a bus so that a white person could sit down. Her protest was supported by many other African Americans and sparked the civil rights movement.'
(History Extra)

4. 'Two main principles that defined Luís Alberto Monge's presidency were born from his early life in the countryside: love for and defence of Costa Rica's working classes.'
(Baeza Flores, 1981)

6 Look at the introduction to the text about Abū Rayhān al-Bīrunī. How did the writer try to make it interesting? Write a short introduction to a text about the historical figure you chose in Exercise 2.

7 Look at the Useful language box. Find three phrases to describe your chosen historical figure.

> **Useful language** Describing historical figures and their achievements
>
> She is said to (have been the first female president).
> She is best-known / most famous for …
> Thanks to his (mathematical) talents, he …
> She made great contributions to …
> He devoted his entire life to …
> She was ahead of her time.
> One of his major achievements was …

WRITING TASK

8 WRITE Write a biography of the historical figure you chose. Use the Writing skill box and Useful language to help you.

9 CHECK Use the checklist. I have …
- [ ] researched the topic before beginning to write.
- [ ] divided my text into paragraphs.
- [ ] paraphrased the original texts.
- [ ] cited my sources.
- [ ] explained the person's achievements using the Useful language.

10 REVIEW Work in pairs. Read your partner's text. What was the most interesting thing that you learned about their historical figure?

Go to page 134 for the Reflect and review.

An underwater lagoon in Mauritius that creates the illusion of a waterfall.

10

Believe your eyes!

GOALS

- Scan a text to interpret visual information
- Talk about adverts using quantifiers
- Understand reference when listening
- Talk about truth and lies
- Learn techniques to save face in international situations
- Write and respond to formal and informal invitations

1 Work in pairs. Look at the photo and answer the questions.
   1 What can you see in the photo? Why might this be described as an 'illusion'?
   2 What places of great beauty or interest that you have seen would you recommend? What's special about them?

WATCH ▶

2 ▶ 10.1 Watch the video. Which two amazing sights does Jeff describe? Why are they very different?

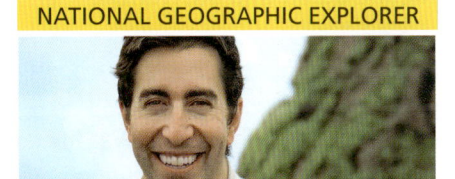

NATIONAL GEOGRAPHIC EXPLORER

JEFF MARLOW

3 Make connections. Which of Jeff's experiences would you most like to experience? Why? If you could see one amazing sight in the world, what would it be?

119

10A Tricking the eye

LESSON GOALS
- Scan a text to interpret visual information
- Apply knowledge to new situations
- Talk about illusions

READING

1 Work in pairs. Look at the images on this page and on page 121, which all show 'optical illusions'. Answer the questions.
   1 Which of these images have you seen before?
   2 Why do you think these images are called 'optical illusions'?
   3 What other optical illusions do you know? Describe them to your partner.

2 Look at the Reading skill box. Then scan the timeline on page 121 quickly to find out which of the images are examples of illusions:
   1 that play with perspective.
   2 that you have to look at in a certain way.
   3 to do with movement.
   4 that were not deliberately designed to be illusions.
   5 that work because of the way people interpret shades of light.

READING SKILL
Scanning to interpret visual information

In order to make sense of photos, diagrams and other visual information, you often have to read an accompanying text. Visual information can also help you understand a text, so when reading a text accompanied by images it is helpful to:
- look at the images to work out what the text is about.
- scan the text for clues about the images: why do they accompany the text? What do they illustrate?

3 Read the timeline again and answer the questions.
   1 What is the reason to doubt that the mammoth-bison painting is an illusion?
   2 Why does the writer describe the skull as 'hidden' even though you can see it in the painting?
   3 Why do people think the second line is longer than the first in the Müller-Lyer illusion?
   4 Why did people disagree about the colour of the dress?

4 Work in pairs. Decide which of these statements about optical illusions you agree with the most.
   Optical illusions teach us that:
   1 we can't trust our eyes to tell us the truth.
   2 our brains have developed to see the real world, not man-made pictures.
   3 what the eyes see and what the brain sees are not the same thing.

5 Work in pairs. Look at the Critical thinking skill box. Then look at illusions a–c. Discuss how you think they work.

CRITICAL THINKING SKILL
Applying knowledge to new situations

It is important to apply the knowledge you have to new situations. This can help you think about it in new ways and evaluate situations from a new perspective. For example, learning how the Müller-Lyer illusion works may help you explain how other illusions of perspective work.

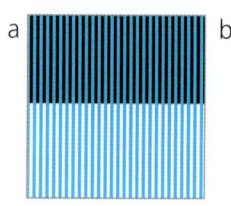

a The blue appears lighter against the white background than against the black.

b The image appears to move.

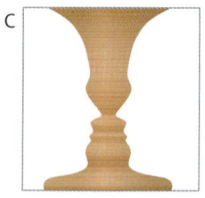

c There are two interpretations of this image.

6 Choose your favourite optical illusion. Say why you like it.

SPEAKING

7 Work in groups of six. Divide your group into three pairs. Pair A: Go to page 156. Pair B: Go to page 157. Pair C: Go to page 157. Look at the optical illusion and discuss the questions. Then tell the other pairs about the optical illusion. Discuss how you think each illusion is achieved.

Illusion evolution

We now mostly understand how optical illusions work on our brains, but just because the science was unknown in the past, it doesn't mean that clever artists couldn't confuse their friends with tricks of the eye. Here are some of the important stages in the evolution of illusions …

… starting 14,000 years ago! You'll have seen drawings that can be viewed two ways, like the classic duck-rabbit drawing (*'It's a duck.' 'No! It's a rabbit.'*). Well, that wasn't the first optical illusion. Cave art in France features this puzzling piece: concentrate on the eye-shaped mark on the left, and a mammoth's tusk curves below it; but look instead at the eye lower down and you might see a sad bison looking down (the tusk becomes the bison's horn). However, just because the cave painting might look like two animals does not mean it was intended to deceive. Another explanation is that we see it as an illusion but those who painted it did not.

Playing with perspective is nothing new. In 1533, Hans Holbein painted this portrait of two men, but the real star of the painting is the third figure hidden on the floor. Look at the picture from a particular angle and you should be able to make out the spooky image of a skull.

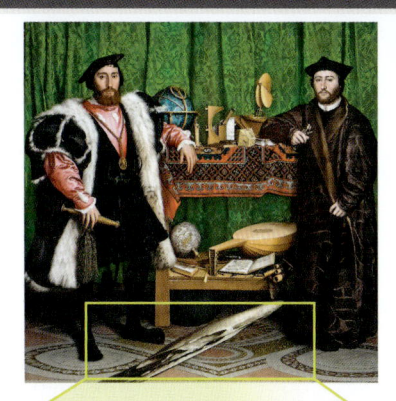

Speaking of perspective, it wasn't until the 19th century that people started studying the science of illusions. German psychologist Franz Carl Müller-Lyer described this, the well-known Müller-Lyer illusion, to show how our eyes can deceive us. But have you ever wondered *why* you see the second line as longer than the first? It's actually a good thing! It means that your brain is interpreting what it sees on paper based on what it normally sees in reality, and it's to do with how we see perspective. It's the same reason we don't believe a person gets smaller when they walk away from us!

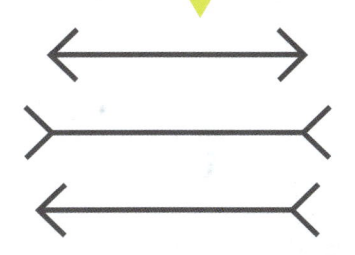

No history of illusions would be complete without moving pictures, or cinema, which is one huge optical illusion. What we perceive as movement is in fact thousands of still images shown one after the other so quickly that we don't notice. The zoetrope was an early machine that created the illusion of movement as long as you looked at it through the holes in the sides. Images can also appear to move and bend for other reasons to do with the way lines and blocks of colour go together.

One or two illusions have almost broken the internet! Recognize this dress from 2015? If you do, you'll remember that no one could agree: was it blue and black or white and gold? The problem lay in how people interpreted the light in the photo. If you thought the dress was in shadow, you might perceive it as being white and gold even though it was in fact blue and black!

EXPLORE MORE!

Show some of the illusions from today's class to a friend or relative and explain how they work.

10B
Advertising tricks

LESSON GOALS
- Understand a radio show about advertising
- Talk about adverts using quantifiers
- Understand vowels across accents

SPEAKING

1 Work in pairs. Answer the questions.
1 Do you tend to enjoy adverts or do you get annoyed by them?
2 What kind of adverts do you like? What don't you like?

2 Look at the adverts below (1–7). Find an example of each of these advertising techniques.

appeal to emotions   celebrity endorsement
compliment the customer   facts and statistics
offers and discounts   'others like it'
positive lifestyle associations

3 Discuss the questions in pairs.
1 Which of these advertising techniques have you seen? Can you give examples?
2 Which of them works best in your opinion? Why?

LISTENING AND GRAMMAR

4 🎧 10.1 Listen to a radio show about advertising. Answer the questions.
1 Which advertising techniques from the infographic are mentioned?
2 What does the expert say about celebrity endorsement?
3 Which advertising technique is the most effective according to the expert?

5 🎧 10.1 Listen again and complete the sentences with the words you hear.
1 Would you agree that **all** adverts are just trying to make you _____ the product?
2 It's true that the main _____ of **most** of the adverts that you'll see is to sell a product.
3 I'm sure **everyone** who uses _____ media has seen posts by celebrities or influencers endorsing a product.
4 I think it's important that as a _____ you are aware that **none** of these celebrities or influencers do those posts for free.
5 That's not to say that **no** celebrity actually likes **any** of the products they _____.
6 I'd also say that **neither of them** on its own will give you great _____.

6 Work in pairs. Look at the words in bold in Exercise 5 and discuss the questions. Then read the Grammar box to check.
1 In which sentences do the underlined words refer to things or people in general and in which to a specific group? What is the difference in form?
2 Which of the underlined words mean *all* or *nothing*, i.e. 0% or 100%? Which word means somewhere in between, i.e. 1–99%?
3 Look at sentences 1 and 3. What is the difference in form between *everyone* and *all*?
4 What form of noun follows *no*? What form of noun follows *none of*?

MOST COMMON ADVERTISING TRICKS

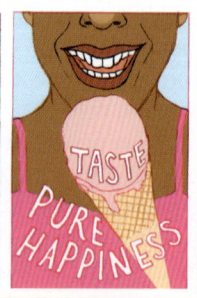

1 2 3 4 5 6 7

GRAMMAR Quantifiers

Use **some** to express the idea of 1–99% of the total and **any** to express *all* or *nothing*, i.e. 0% or 100%.
*Why not treat yourself to **some** relaxation?*
*We will beat **any** other supermarket price!*
Use **no/all/most** + uncountable/plural noun to mean everything/nothing in general.
*Almost **all** adverts are …*
Use **none/all/most of the** + uncountable/plural noun to mean everyone/everything in a specific group.
***Most of the** adverts that you'll see …*
Do not use **all** without a noun as the subject. Instead use **everything/everyone** or **every** + singular noun.
*I'm sure **everyone** who uses …*
Use **both/either/neither of** with object pronouns, e.g. *both of **them** / neither of **us***.

Go to page 152 for the Grammar reference.

7 Choose the correct option to complete the text. Then in pairs discuss what your opinion is about photos in adverts that do not reflect reality.

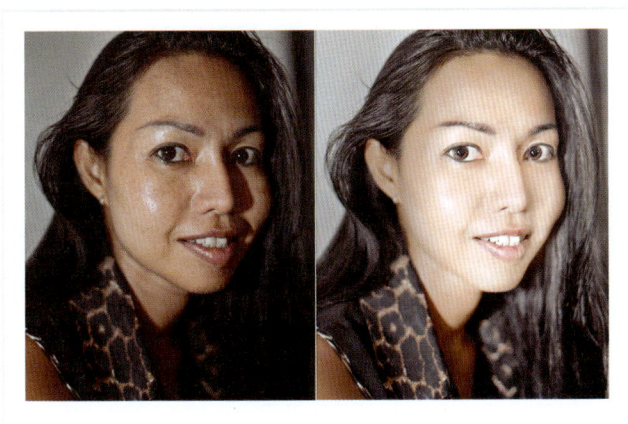

Look at the two images. ¹*Both / Neither* show the same person. But only one is true to life, and it would probably never appear in ²*some / any* advert. Why? Almost ³*none of / no* image in an advert will be published without changes. This means that ⁴*most / most of* advert images do not actually reflect reality. ⁵*Some / Any* psychologists point out that this can have negative effects on ⁶*all / many* people. For example, such adverts create an image of beauty that ⁷*most / no* people could never achieve.

PRONUNCIATION

8 🎧 10.2 Complete the sentences so they are true for you and share with your partner. Then listen to different people finish the sentences. Whose were the most similar to yours?
1 I enjoy some adv**er**tisements, for example …
2 N**o**ne of the adverts I've seen on social media …
3 When the adverts come on TV, I **ei**ther … or …

9 🎧 10.3 Listen again to the sentences in Exercise 8, this time said by two different speakers. Pay attention to the underlined words. How do the sounds in bold change?

10 Look at the Clear voice box to check your answers to Exercise 9. Then practise saying the sentences in Exercise 8 using the pronunciation you prefer.

CLEAR VOICE
Understanding vowels across accents

Some words can be pronounced differently depending on the speaker's accent. For example, the 'o' in n**o**ne or s**o**me can either sound like /ʌ/ (c**u**p) or /ʊ/ (g**oo**d). Some words have more than one pronunciation, e.g. *advertisement* can sound like /əd'vɜːtɪsmənt/ or /ˌædvərˈtaɪzmənt/. Also, **ei**ther and n**ei**ther can have the long /iː/ or the diphthong /aɪ/. None of these versions are better or worse. Paying attention to these changes can help you understand various accents.

SPEAKING

11 Work in groups. Think of a product and plan an advert for it. Decide:
- the type of advert you will use (TV, social media, magazine, street poster, etc.).
- which advertising techniques you will use.
- what images you want to show.
- the words you will use, and how you can make them sound positive.

12 Share your ideas with another group. Would they buy the product? Do they have any suggestions for how to make the advert more convincing?

EXPLORE MORE!

Search online for 'best (e.g. sports) adverts' to find the best adverts for a topic that interests you. What makes these adverts effective?

10C
That sounds like an excuse

LESSON GOALS
- Talk about truth and lies
- Understand reference when listening
- Describe your impressions using verbs of the senses
- Change meaning by stressing different words

> Sorry I'm late, Mr Price! I had to help my mum catch an ENORMOUS spider in the bathroom.

Fifteen years later ...

> See, there was a cat outside my flat, and it looked as if it was in trouble, so I had to catch it to take it to the vet. So that's why I'm going to be late for work.

The skills you learn at school … are the skills you need at work! 😂

SPEAKING AND VOCABULARY

1 Work in pairs. Tell your partner about excuses you've made up in the past, or excuses people gave to you that may not have been true.

2 Read the sentences. Which are true for you? Compare your answers in pairs.
   1 I'm good at **making up excuses** for being late.
   2 I find it easy to **hide my emotions** and **pretend** that something doesn't bother me.
   3 I'm **suspicious** of social media posts as they often **spread lies**.
   4 If I make a mistake, I sometimes **blame** it on someone else.
   5 I would never **cheat** at a game or sport. I think that's **dishonest**.
   6 I don't always give an **honest** answer when a friend asks for my opinion on their appearance. I sometimes **tell a white lie** instead.

Go to page 139 for the Vocabulary reference.

LISTENING

NATIONAL GEOGRAPHIC EXPLORER

3 🎧 10.4 Listen to Jeff Marlow talking about three situations that happened to him. In which one …
   a did a friend lie to him?
   b did he make up a story in a difficult situation?
   c did he tell the truth but wasn't believed?

4 🎧 10.4 Listen again. Rewrite the sentences so that they are true.
   1 Jeff was travelling to go on an expedition.
      Jeff was returning from an expedition.
   2 The officers finally believed Jeff when he showed them photos of his research ship.
   3 The ice had been strong enough to have a snowball fight on it earlier that day.
   4 Jeff felt bad because he had risked his friend's life.
   5 Jeff and his friends were looking for a lost map.
   6 The woman was angry that they had lied to her.

5 🎧 10.5 Work in pairs. Look at the Listening skill box. Then listen to two conversations and answer the questions.

LISTENING SKILL
Understanding reference

When people talk about things you can't see or don't know about, you can use clues to work out what they are referring to. For example, in the following dialogue, you can work out that *that* is something to eat, and that *she* is someone the speaker is pointing to:

A: What's **that** in your hand?
B: This? **She** gave it to me. I was hungry.

When listening, imagine where the speakers are, what they are doing and looking at, and who else might be there. Try to work out what is being referred to to from what you already understand.

1 Conversation 1
   a How do the speakers know each other?
   b What are *these*?
2 Conversation 2
   a Who is *he* in relation to the other speakers?
   b What is *he* late for?

6 🎧 10.6 Listen to people answering some difficult questions. For each question, give the speaker a score to decide how honest they are being, with 0 for very dishonest and 3 for very honest. Then compare your scores in pairs.

7 🎧 10.6 Listen again. What are the speakers referring to when they say the words in bold?
1 'I chose a different **one**. So yeah, I'd do **the same** again.'
2 'It isn't **his** fault the food's bad. **He**'s just doing **his** job.'
3 'But then what if **they** catch you doing **it**?'
4 'But then it's going to be obvious that something happened while I had **it**.'
5 'Yeah, it's not like **it**'s a big lie, is it?'
6 'If I told him **the truth, he**'d understand.'

GRAMMAR

8 Look at the Focus on box. Then complete the sentences with your own ideas.

> **FOCUS ON** Verbs of the senses: *looks, sounds, smells, feels, seems*
>
> The verbs *look, sound, smell, feel* and *seem* can be used to suggest that the impression you have of something may not be the truth. The verbs can be followed by:
> • an adjective:
> *He **seems** honest, but how do we know?*
> *She's eighteen, but she **looks** much younger.*
> • *like* + a noun:
> *That **sounds like** rubbish to me.*
> *It **smells like** coffee, but it looks more like tea.*
> • *as if / like* + a verb phrase:
> *It **looks as if** it's been photoshopped.*
> *It **feels like** it's made of leather, but I'm not sure.*

Go to page 153 for the Focus on reference.

1 This band is terrible! They don't sound …
2 Don't all leave at the same time. It will look …
3 What's that smell? It smells …
4 When we stepped inside the old building, it felt …
5 The house was completely silent and very cold. It seemed …
6 What's that noise? It sounds …

PRONUNCIATION

9 🎧 10.7 Look at the Clear voice box. Then listen carefully to the sentences said twice. Which time, a or b, does the speaker sound suspicious?

CLEAR VOICE
Changing meaning by stressing different words

The words you stress in a sentence can change the meaning of the sentence. For example, if you said: '*He seems **honest**'*, then you clearly think the person is honest. But if you said '*He **seems** honest*', i.e. stressing *seems* instead of *honest*, you are showing uncertainty. Practise stressing sentences in different ways to see how the meaning changes.

1 She looks as if she's happy with him.
2 This one feels expensive.
3 It seems like a good idea.

10 Work in pairs. Take turns saying the sentences in Exercise 9, using different stress to change the meaning. Can your partner work out the meaning?

SPEAKING

11 Play the game 'The Unbelievable Truth' in pairs. Follow the instructions.
1 Prepare five questions to ask your partner.
2 Take turns to ask each other your questions. The other person must answer all the questions untruthfully except one.
3 Ask follow-up questions to test the truth of your partner's answers.
4 Decide which of your partner's answers you think is true.

A: *What's one food you don't like?*
B: *Pineapple.*
A: *Why don't you like it?*
B: *I had a bad experience when I was little.*

EXPLORE MORE!

Search online for 'the funniest excuses for missing work'. Choose your favourite!

10D Saving face

LESSON GOALS
- Identify situations that may cause someone to lose face
- Learn techniques to save face in international communication situations
- Discuss how to save face in sensitive situations

SPEAKING

1 Work in pairs. Read about the situations (a–d) and discuss the questions (1–3).

  a Juana once told her grandmother that she liked her horrible vegetable soup. Now, every time she visits, her grandmother makes it for her and she has to eat a big bowl of it.

  b Kevin is getting to know a new colleague. He isn't at all sure that they will be friends, but he says: 'Perhaps you could come over for dinner some time.' Secretly, he has no intention of inviting them to his house.

  c Neera receives a present from a friend. She decides that it is awful, and as soon as her friend is gone she will hide it in a cupboard. But she smiles and pretends to be happy: 'It's what I've always wanted. Thank you so much!'

  d Kyung-Ja has been invited to a friend's party, but she has no intention of going. A few days before the party she tells her friend how much she is looking forward to it.

1 Why do Juana, Kevin, Neera and Kyung-Ja say the things they say?
2 Do you think these 'white lies' are necessary?
3 If you were the other people in the situations, would you be happier if you were told the truth? Why? / Why not?

MY VOICE ▶

2 ▶ 10.2 Watch the video. Put the questions in the order that they are answered.
  a What different factors do you need to consider?
  b What makes it harder to avoid losing face with people from other places?
  c What is 'face'?
  d Why is it important to 'save face'?

3 Work in pairs. Discuss the answers to the questions in Exercise 2.

4 ▶ 10.2 Watch the video again. Complete the sentences with one word.

1 If you are made to feel embarrassed in front of others, they may lose _____ for you.
2 By being tactful when you speak, you can _____ face in sensitive situations.
3 If you need to challenge someone's opinion or disagree with them, don't do it in _____.
4 Try to avoid asking difficult questions that others aren't likely to _____.
5 If you have to say no, then make sure you give a _____.
6 Three topics you should avoid in many situations are people's age, their _____ and politics.

5 Work in pairs. Look at the Communication skill box. Then discuss the questions (1–3).

COMMUNICATION SKILL
Saving face

'Face' is about your social position among friends, family and colleagues. It is how you see yourself and how other people see you in terms of respect and importance. It is important to understand the idea of 'face' when you are with people from other cultures because different situations can cause people to 'lose face'.

1 Be tactful: try to avoid saying anything that is likely to upset someone.
2 If you need to tell someone something sensitive, such as pointing out a mistake they have made, do this in private.
3 Ask yourself if you really *have* to disagree with someone. If you do, you should do this privately or quietly.
4 Avoid using difficult language or asking difficult questions that others may not understand.
5 If you have to say no, do so with a reason, and try to be genuine.
6 Avoid sensitive topics such as money, politics, etc.

1 Do you think you are particularly sensitive to face issues? Why? / Why not?
2 What subjects do you tend to avoid asking or talking about?
3 How can you learn about 'face issues' of people from other places?

SPEAKING

6 Look at the Useful language box. Which phrases can be used for:
1 asking difficult questions?
2 disagreeing politely?
3 saying no?

> **Useful language** Being tactful in sensitive situations
>
> That's a lovely offer, and I'd normally say yes, but …
> Do you mind if I ask you …
> Are you sure that's correct? It's just that …
> I'd love to come, but the thing is …
> That's a very good point, but …
> I may be wrong, but I think that actually …
> … or would you prefer it if we didn't talk about that?
> Excuse me, but I'm afraid I need to ask you …

7 OWN IT! Work in pairs. Discuss how in each situation the people involved could save face. Decide what you would say and how you would say it. Use the Useful language to help you.

Situation 1
William keeps calling a new friend 'Pamela' even though her real name is 'Patricia'. She didn't correct him the first time, but now she feels embarrassed about correcting him. Now he wants to introduce her to some of his friends.

Situation 2
On the train, an older man in a suit has fallen asleep next to Min. His head is now resting on her shoulder. She is getting off at the next stop.

Situation 3
Yuan is listening to a classmate present a report that Yuan and she wrote together to their team. However, she has made an important mistake in one of the statistics.

Situation 4
Petr and Gabi are celebrating the end of exams with their classmates. Someone has suggested they go out for a meal. But Gabi recently told Petr that she is having money problems at the moment. Petr wants to help her by paying for her meal.

10E
I'd love to come!

LESSON GOALS
- Discuss accepting and declining invitations
- Practise inviting people, accepting and declining invitations
- Write and respond to formal and informal invitations

SPEAKING

1 Work in pairs. Read about the situations (a–b) and discuss the questions (1–2).

a A classmate invites you to his astronomy club to watch a meteor shower. He promises it will be amazing, but you aren't interested in space.

b You invite a good friend of yours to go go-karting with you. She tells you that she doesn't want to go because she isn't interested in go-karting.

1 How likely would you be to accept an invitation to an event that you aren't interested in?
2 When declining an invitation, do you think it is better to tell the truth or make up an excuse? Why?

READING FOR WRITING

2 Work in pairs. Read the invitations (1–3). Discuss how easy it would be for the readers to say no. If they decided not to accept, what excuse could they give?

3 Read the Writing skill box. Which of the messages in Exercise 2 is formal? Which are informal? Why are they written in that style?

WRITING SKILL
Writing formal and informal invitations

Informal invitations are used when the recipient is someone you know well. Formal invitations are used for people you don't know so well, e.g. in work or study situations.

- Informal invitations begin by asking how the person is. Formal invitations are often more direct, though they may begin *I hope/trust that you are well*.
- Explain why you are writing: *Just a quick message to let you know that/about …* (informal); *I am writing to invite you to …* (formal).
- If the invitation is to an event, give details about where and when.
- Finish by saying you hope they can come: *It would be great to see you.* (informal); *I look forward to seeing you there.* (formal)

---

1 Marianna *last seen today at 17:06*

Hey Jorge, how are things? Hope you're doing well. Just a quick text to see if you'd be up for a coffee later this week. I know I haven't been in touch lately and didn't get back to your last message – really sorry about that. But I'd love to catch up soon. Let me know when you're free!

---

2 New Message

To: to me & other undisclosed recipients
From: Mohammad
Subject: Leaving party

Hi everyone

How are you doing? This is just a quick message to remind you about my leaving do this Thursday. We're meeting at the 'Golden Dragon' at 6pm.

I hope you can make it. Please get back to me so that I know how many tables to book. Really looking forward to seeing you there!

Mohammad

---

3 GOING GREEN

Dear colleagues

We are pleased to invite you to an exciting webinar about our new 'Going Green' initiative by Abena, our Sustainability Officer. She will explain the details of our transition to a low-carbon workplace and you will have the opportunity to ask questions.

The webinar will be held on Zoom next Tuesday at 10.30am. Please confirm your attendance as soon as possible.

Yours, with warm regards

Caitlin

4 Read the invitations again and underline other useful phrases you can use:
1 to begin an invitation.
2 to say why you are writing.
3 to give details about an event.
4 to end a message.

5 Match the responses (a–c) with the invitations in Exercise 2 (1–3). Which are not written in an appropriate style?

a Thanks for that invitation – sounds interesting, but I'm busy that morning (hairdresser's appointment), so I can't make it. Is it going to be recorded? Could I watch it later?

b It was a nice surprise to receive your kind message. It has been a long time since we saw each other. I'd like to join you for a drink and a chat, but I'm afraid I'm not available this week. Would next week suit you?

c Thanks for the reminder and sorry for not confirming earlier. You can definitely count me in. I wouldn't miss it for the world! I will be sad to see you go, though … Anyway, looking forward to Thursday already. See you then!

6 Rewrite the responses from Exercise 5 that are not in an appropriate style.

7 Look at the Useful language box. Follow the instructions.
1 Put the expressions in two groups: Accepting invitations and Declining invitations.
2 Decide if the expressions are formal or informal.

> **Useful language** Accepting and declining invitations
>
> I can't wait!
> I won't be able to attend, unfortunately, because …
> I'd love to, but I've already made other plans.
> I'd normally be up for it, but …
> I'll be there!
> That's a great idea! Let's do it!
> That's a lovely offer, but unfortunately …
> Thursday doesn't work for me, I'm afraid.
>   I have to …

WRITING TASK

8 Imagine you are organizing an event. Decide what the event is and whether the invitation will be formal or informal. Use one of these ideas or your own idea.

| a birthday party | a class trip | dinner with friends |
| lunch with colleagues | | a work event |

9 WRITE Write your invitation. Use the Writing skill box and the Useful language to help you.

10 CHECK Use the checklist. I have …
☐ asked how the other person is doing.
☐ explained why I'm writing.
☐ said why it would be good to see them.
☐ written it in a suitable style.
☐ used some of the Useful language.

11 Exchange invitations with a classmate. Decide if you're going to accept or decline. Write your response in a suitable style. Use the Useful language to help you.

12 REVIEW Share the replies with each other. Are you happy or disappointed with your partner's reply? Why? What would you write in response?

Go to page 134 for the Reflect and review.

Reflect and review

1 Your life Pages 10–21

1 Look at the goals from Unit 1. Tick (✓) the three you feel most confident about.
 - [ ] Skim an article to identify the main ideas
 - [ ] Practise asking questions and giving short answers
 - [ ] Talk about education at different ages
 - [ ] Understand different accents
 - [ ] Establish good rapport with people of all ages
 - [ ] Write a description of an influential person

2 Work in pairs. Discuss the questions.
 1 What do you think you did well in this unit?
 2 Which goal is the most difficult for you? What can you do to work on it?
 3 Which goal is the most important for outside of class? Why?

3 Read the ideas for working on the Unit 1 goals. Choose three ideas and add one more. Then share your ideas with a partner.
 - Find an online article in English and skim it to get the main idea
 - Write questions in English to ask my friends about people who have influenced them
 - Learn one new word or phrase per day to talk about education
 - Watch online videos of people from around the world speaking English
 - Use the tips for establishing rapport and useful phrases to keep a conversation going
 - Listen to a podcast about an influential person then write an article about them

My idea: _____
_____
_____

2 Breaking the rules Pages 22–33

1 Look at the goals from Unit 2. How confident do you feel about them? Rate the goals from 1 (very confident) to 4 (not confident at all).
 - [ ] Understand the meaning of new words from context
 - [ ] Tell stories and talk about the past
 - [ ] Understand fast speech
 - [ ] Talk about crime and punishment
 - [ ] Understand power distance
 - [ ] Write a story

2 Work in pairs. Write down:
 - the names of two past tenses and two example sentences.
 - three adverbs often used with past tenses.
 - five words or phrases about crime.

3 Choose one of the Unit 1 goals that you want to work on. Write three ways you can do this. Use these ideas or your own ideas.
_____
find new collocations related to crime
listen to the news in English
read news stories in English
subscribe to a podcast in English
tell a friend about a crime story I've read
watch a crime documentary
write a crime story
write a paragraph about power distance in my country
_____

I want to work on:
_____

Some ways to work on this goal are:
_____
_____
_____

3 Imagining the future *Pages 34–45*

1. Look at the goals from Unit 3. How confident do you feel about them? Write the letters (a–f) in the table.
   a Scan a text for specific information
   b Talk about predictions
   c Discuss future trends
   d Understand fillers in conversations
   e Give constructive feedback
   f Write a personal development plan

Goals I feel confident about	Goals I need more practice on

2. What do you think your life will be like in the future? Write a short paragraph, using the grammar and vocabulary you have learned in this unit. Then share your answers with a partner.

3. Look at the goals in Exercise 1. Choose two goals that you want to work on. Then look at the example and make your own plan for how you will achieve your goals.

   Goal: Discuss future trends in learning English

   Today – Review the grammar and language from the unit

   This week – Read articles about the future of learning English and make notes on new words or phrases

   This month – Write an article on future trends using ten new words/phrases I have learned

4 Good taste *Pages 46–57*

1. Look at the goals from Unit 4. Tick (✓) the goals you feel you have achieved.
   ☐ Identify supporting stories
   ☐ Compare different types of food
   ☐ Talk about good and bad table manners
   ☐ Understand assimilation in fast speech
   ☐ Recognize different ways of saying 'no'
   ☐ Write a review of a restaurant

2. Choose a topic and write a short paragraph.
   - a bad dinner or restaurant experience
   - a delicious meal you've had
   - an unusual meal or food you've tried
   - a time you've found it difficult to say 'no'

3. Read the ideas for working on the Unit 4 goals. Choose two ideas and add one more. Then share your ideas with a partner.
   - Revise this unit and make notes
   - Read online blogs and identify stories that support the writer's argument
   - Watch shows and documentaries about food and travel
   - Watch online videos to help with understanding
   - Tell a friend different strategies for saying 'no'
   - Look online for other words and phrases for saying 'no'
   - Read online reviews and note down new language
   - Write reviews of other experiences I've had

   My idea: _____
   _____
   _____

Reflect and review

5 Let's play Pages 58–69

1 Look at the goals from Unit 5. How confident do you feel about them? Write the letters (a–f) on the scale.
   a Read to identify examples supporting an argument
   b Talk about past regrets and possibilities
   c Use context to understand new words when listening
   d Talk about being competitive
   e Communicate clearly in a group
   f Write an opinion essay

Not confident ←——————————→ Very confident

2 Complete the sentences. Then compare your ideas with a partner.
   1 To talk about past regrets, I can use … and for past results I'm certain of I can use …
   2 To talk about possibility in the past, I can use …
   3 Three words/phrases to talk about being competitive are …
   4 Three words/phrases to link opposing points of view in a formal essay are …

3 Think about the goals in Exercise 1. Complete the sentences with your own ideas.
   1 I want to improve … and …
   2 To work on the first goal, I can …
   3 To work on the second goal, I can …
   4 Some useful websites and apps I can use are …

6 Accidents and incidents Pages 70–81

1 Look at the goals from Unit 6. Tick (✓) the goals you feel confident about. Underline the goals you want to work on.
   ☐ Activate prior knowledge before reading
   ☐ Report what people say
   ☐ Understand a sequence of events in a story
   ☐ Talk about accidents and injuries
   ☐ Understand how to balance fluency and accuracy
   ☐ Write a formal email of complaint

2 Write one true sentence about yourself and one false sentence. Choose one of these topics:
   • a coincidence
   • an accident or injury
   • a complaint you've made

Now share your sentences with a partner. Can they guess which sentence is true and which is false?

3 Work in pairs. Look at the goals you underlined in Exercise 1. Discuss one way to work on each goal.
To understand a sequence of events in a story, I can listen to stories online and pay attention to the tenses and time words the speaker uses …

7 Going shopping
Pages 82–93

1 Look at the goals from Unit 7. Work in pairs. Use these words and phrases or your own words to say how you feel about each goal.

important   more practice   not so confident
not useful   useful   very confident

- Identify fact and speculation in a text
- Talk about services you have done or get done
- Understand approximate numbers
- Talk about buying products and getting good deals
- Find solutions in negotiating situations
- Write an online advert for an item you want to sell

2 Work in pairs. Discuss the questions.
1 What is something you have done or get done regularly?
2 What is the difference between cost, price and worth?
3 What types of words can often be omitted when shortening a text?

3 Read the ideas for working on the Unit 7 goals. Choose two ideas and add two more. Then share your ideas with a partner.
- Read online articles and look for facts and speculation
- Ask a friend about the things they have done or get done
- Roleplay shopping scenarios with a classmate
- Practise writing about my shopping experiences
- Watch online videos about negotiation
- Read other people's online adverts
- Write my own online adverts

My ideas: _____

8 Working life
Pages 94–105

1 Look at the goals from Unit 8. Work in pairs. Tell your partner if you agree or disagree with each statement and why.
After studying Unit 8, I can:
- take notes using symbols and abbreviations.
- talk about jobs using noun phrases.
- synthesize ideas across listening passages.
- talk about employment and describe jobs.
- deal with different working styles in teams.
- write a professional profile.

2 Write a short paragraph describing your dream job and why you would like to do it. Use the grammar and vocabulary you have learned in this unit. Then share your ideas with a partner.

3 Complete the sentences with these ideas or your own ideas.

identify noun phrases in texts I read
look online for suggested abbreviations
make flashcards
read people's online professional profiles
review the unit and take notes
watch online videos about teamwork
write a list of my own symbols and abbreviations
write a paragraph about different jobs and skills needed

1 To help myself feel more confident about the goals from Unit 8, I can …
2 To remember grammar and vocabulary from the lesson, I can …
3 To practise my reading skills, I can …

Reflect and review

9 History revisited   Pages 106–117

1 Look at the goals from Unit 9. How confident do you feel about them? Rate the goals from 1 (very confident) to 4 (not confident at all).
   - Understand reference words
   - Talk about interesting moments in history
   - Take notes when listening
   - Talk about periods in history
   - Adapt your argument to suit your listener
   - Write a biography of an historical figure

2 Work in pairs. Discuss the questions.
   1 What do you think you did well in this unit?
   2 What are three useful things you learned?
   3 Which goals do you want to work on? Why?

3 Choose one of the Unit 9 goals that you want to work on. Choose two ideas and add one more. Then share your ideas with a partner.
   - Read online articles and identify reference words
   - Write a short biography of someone I know
   - Watch online history videos and write down new vocabulary
   - Research a period in history and describe it in English to a friend
   - Make a list of symbols and abbreviations to use when taking notes
   - Listen to interviews of people I admire
   - Read stories about different periods in history
   - Roleplay situations for persuading someone with a classmate and adapt my argument if necessary

   My idea: _____

10 Believe your eyes!   Pages 118–129

1 Look at the goals from Unit 10. How confident do you feel about them? Write the letters (a–f) in the table.
   a Scan a text to interpret visual information
   b Talk about adverts using quantifiers
   c Understand reference when listening
   d Talk about truth and lies
   e Learn techniques to save face in international situations
   f Write and respond to formal and informal invitations

Goals I feel confident about	Goals I need more practice on

2 Complete the sentences. Then compare your ideas with a partner.
   1 Five words or phrases to talk about truth and lies are …
   2 Verbs of the senses can be followed by …
   3 Two techniques for saving face are …
   4 When writing an informal invitation, you could start by saying …

3 Look at the goals you need more practice on in Exercise 1. Answer the questions. Then share your answers with a partner.
   1 What are some ways to work on this/these goal(s)?
   _____
   _____
   2 How will this/these goal(s) be useful outside of the classroom?
   _____
   _____

Vocabulary reference

UNIT 1

do evening classes (phr) /duː ˈiːvnɪŋ ˈklɑːsɪz/   There are a lot of older people doing evening classes at my college.
education system (n) /ˌedʒuˈkeɪʃn ˈsɪstɪm/   What's the education system like in your country?
get a degree (phr) /ɡet ə dɪˈɡriː/   If I want to become an engineer, I'll need to get a degree.
get good/bad grades (phr) /ɡet ɡʊd/bæd ˈɡreɪdz/   If I get good grades, I'll be accepted onto the course.
graduate (v) /ˈɡrædjʊeɪt/   Which university did you graduate from?
memorize (v) /ˈmeməraɪz/   My teacher says I shouldn't memorize sentences to use in the speaking exam.
pay attention (phr) /peɪ əˈtenʃ(ə)n/   I find it hard to pay attention in Mr Williams' class – his lessons are so boring.
revise for exams (phr) /rɪˈvaɪz fər ɪɡˈzæmz/   Shall we revise for the science exam together?
stay focused (phr) /steɪ ˈfəʊkəst/   Going for a walk at lunchtime helps me stay focused on my work later on.

1 Complete the sentences with the correct form of the words or phrases from the word list.
  1 We are looking for someone who has recently _____ from university.
  2 My mum is _____ at the local school to improve her Spanish.
  3 It's important to _____ these important historical dates for next week's exam.
  4 Unless you start _____, I don't want you in this class, Jakub.
  5 The Finnish _____ is supposed to be one of the best in the world.
  6 I find it hard to _____ on my own, so I usually go to my friend Mei's house to study with her.
  7 When I go to university, I want to _____ in history.
  8 If you _____ this term, we can go on that camping trip you always talk about.
  9 I usually work for two hours then take a 30-minute break. It helps me _____.

2 Complete the sentences with your own ideas. Then compare with a partner.
  1 Some jobs you don't need to get a degree for are …
  2 To help me stay focused, I …
  3 If I did evening classes, I would study …
  4 I find it hard to pay attention when …

UNIT 2

be/get caught (phr) /biː/get ˈkɔːt/   The man was caught trying to steal bikes from the school.
be sentenced to (phr) /biː ˈsentənst tə/   The hackers were sentenced to three years in prison.
break into (phr v) /breɪk ˈɪntuː/   My house was broken into and most of my jewellery was stolen.
break the law (phr) /breɪk ðə ˈlɔː/   I would never break the law!
a fine (n) /ə faɪn/   In some countries, you have to pay a fine if you use your phone when driving.
guilty (adj) /ˈɡɪlti/   His story doesn't make sense. I think he's guilty.
innocent (adj) /ˈɪnəsənt/   The woman was found innocent of all her crimes.
rob (v) /rɒb/   Did you see the news about that bank being robbed last night?
robber (n) /ˈrɒbə(r)/   The robbers got in through the window.
victim (n) /ˈvɪktɪm/   The victim gave a statement to the police about what happened.
a warning (n) /ə ˈwɔːnɪŋ/   The police let me go with a warning for not wearing a seatbelt in the car.

1 Choose the correct option to complete the sentences.
  1 Did you watch that series about the *victims / robbers* that printed millions of euros in a bank?
  2 If he's found *guilty / innocent*, he might be *sentenced to / caught* up to ten years in prison.
  3 In your country, if you drive too fast and get *caught / sentenced to*, do you have to *pay a fine / break the law* or do you get a warning?
  4 Where's my bag? It's gone! I've been *caught / robbed*!
  5 What's that noise? I think someone's *being sentenced to / breaking into* our house!
  6 She was the *victim / robber* of a cyberattack. All her personal information was stolen.
  7 I accidentally *broke the law / robbed* once when I drove the wrong way down a one-way street! I got a *warning / fine*. I didn't have to pay anything.

2 Write a short story using the prompt or your own idea. Try to use at least five words or phrases from the word list.
  The police arrived at the scene of the crime to find broken glass everywhere and money all over the floor …

135

Vocabulary reference

UNIT 3

continue rising gradually (phr) /kən'tɪnju 'raɪzɪŋ 'grædjuəli/   *The number of first-time house buyers is expected to continue rising gradually.*

estimate (v) /'estɪmeɪt/   *We estimate that it'll take around three months to do the research.*

is set to (phr) /ɪz 'set tə/   *Global temperatures are set to increase year on year.*

it's only a rough estimate (phr) /ɪts 'əʊnli ə rʌf 'estɪmət/   *It's only a rough estimate, but I think we'll sell around 150 tickets.*

it's unlikely (phr) /ɪts ʌn'laɪkli/   *It's unlikely we'll know who won until all the votes have been counted.*

look at the data (phr) /'lʊk ət ðə 'deɪtə/   *If you look at the data, you'll see that more people are shopping online.*

remain unchanged (phr) /rɪ'meɪn ʌn'tʃeɪndʒd/   *Over the last few years, house prices have remained unchanged.*

see a sharp growth (phr) /si: ə ʃɑ:p 'grəʊθ/   *We've recently seen a sharp growth in the number of people using our service.*

steady drop (phr) /'stedi drɒp/   *There's been a steady drop in unemployment across the country this year.*

1 Match the beginnings of the sentences (1–7) with the endings (a–g).
  1 The number of people studying English will …
  2 Plastic takes over 400 years to break down, so …
  3 It's very difficult to estimate …
  4 The work will cost around £250, but …
  5 Since the rise of podcasts, there has been a …
  6 If you look at the data, you will see that …
  7 This area has remained …
  a continue rising gradually, as more employers use it to conduct business.
  b that's only a rough estimate. It could be more.
  c steady drop in the number of radio listeners.
  d unchanged since I lived here 50 years ago!
  e we have seen a sharp growth in the number of companies developing alternative materials.
  f how many trees were destroyed in the forest fire.
  g more people are now working from home.

2 Work in pairs. Say if you agree or disagree with the statements and why.
  1 It's unlikely we'll ever have flying cars.
  2 We'll see a sharp growth over the next five years in the number of people with university degrees.
  3 The way people communicate with each other will remain unchanged for years to come.

UNIT 4

appropriate (adj) /ə'prəʊpriət/   *This isn't the appropriate time or place to be having this argument.*

guest (n) /gest/   *You're our guest – please just sit down and relax. You don't need to do the washing up.*

host (n) /həʊst/   *João is such a good host. He made us all feel very welcome in his home.*

impolite (adj) /ˌɪmpə'laɪt/   *I think it's impolite to refuse their invitation.*

offended (adj) /ə'fendɪd/   *I think Asha was offended when you didn't finish your food.*

a sign of good manners (phr) /ə saɪn əv gʊd 'mænəz/   *In some countries, it's a sign of good manners to wait until everyone has their meal before eating.*

show some respect (phr) /ʃəʊ sʌm rɪs'pekt/   *Can you show some respect and listen to your mother?*

socially acceptable (phr) /'səʊʃəli ək'septəbl/   *I don't think it's socially acceptable to talk loudly on the phone.*

typical behaviour (phr) /'tɪpɪkl bɪ'heɪvjə/   *People using their phones during dinner has become typical behaviour.*

1 Complete the conversation with the correct form of the words or phrases from the word list. There is one you do not need to use.

  Beyza: Can you believe how ¹_____ Jake was at dinner tonight? No manners at all!
  Helena: I know, I was quite ²_____ when he told me he didn't like any of the food.
  Beyza: He shouldn't have said that. It wasn't ³_____. He was a ⁴_____ in our home, and he should have ⁵_____. He should be happy we even invited him!
  Helena: Well, we know not to again. He can be the ⁶_____ next time.
  Beyza: I think it's a ⁷_____ to say you like the food someone cooks you, even if you don't.
  Helena: Yeah … well that's just his ⁸_____. He always says mean things!

2 Work in pairs. Discuss the questions.
  1 What behaviour do you think is a sign of good table manners? Why?
  2 What do you think is impolite behaviour in a restaurant? Why?
  3 Do you think it's socially acceptable to use your phone at the table? Why / Why not?
  4 Have you ever been a host and had guests over for dinner? What happened?

UNIT 5

be determined to (phr) /biː dɪˈtɜːmɪnd tə/   *I'm determined to become a manager one day!*
beat your opponent (phr) /biːt jər əˈpəʊnənt/   *To beat your opponent, you must use all your skills and knowledge of the game.*
become a professional (phr) /bɪˈkʌm ə prəˈfeʃənl/   *He'd like to become a professional actor one day.*
compete against someone (phr) /kəmˈpiːt əˈgenst ˈsʌmwʌn/   *In the spelling competition final, Alek had to compete against his best friend.*
participate in a tournament (phr) /pɑːˈtɪsɪpeɪt ɪn ə ˈtʊənəmənt/   *Last year, our club participated in a gymnastics tournament and we came second.*
perform poorly (phr) /pəˈfɔːm ˈpʊəli/   *I performed really poorly in that exam. I just know I've failed.*
require great skills (phr) /rɪˈkwaɪə greɪt ˈskɪlz/   *Studying kung fu at the Shaolin Temple requires great skills.*
talented (adj) /ˈtæləntɪd/   *My daughter is such a talented singer.*
win at all costs (phr) /wɪn ət ɔːl ˈkɒsts/   *Our team is very competitive. We'll win at all costs!*

1 Complete the sentences with the correct form of the words or phrases from the word list.
   1 You're really good at dancing. Would you like to _____ one day?
   2 I feel uncomfortable when I have to _____ I know in a race.
   3 You're quite a _____ writer. Have you ever thought about writing a book?
   4 Camila, you _____ in your last French exam, and I know you could have done better.
   5 Dimitri easily _____ and became class president.
   6 Our basketball team are _____ where the winning team gets to go to a real NBA match.
   7 Becoming a company director _____ such as problem solving and teamwork.
   8 Adaku _____ be successful in her new job.

2 Work in pairs. Discuss the questions.
   1 Do you think you're talented? What are you talented at?
   2 What are you determined to achieve in the future?
   3 Have you ever participated in a tournament? What happened?
   4 What hobby could someone turn into a job, and become a professional at?

UNIT 6

bruise (n) /bruːz/   *I fell off my bike and now I've got a huge bruise on my leg.*
clumsy (adj) /ˈklʌmzi/   *My sister is so clumsy. She dropped her phone down the toilet!*
get a few scratches (phr) /get ə fjuː ˈskrætʃɪz/   *Kasem got a few scratches on his arm from climbing a tree.*
get burnt (phr) /get ˈbɜːnt/   *Stay away from the candles – I don't want you to get burnt.*
get seriously injured (phr) /get ˈsɪərɪəsli ˈɪndʒəd/   *If you don't wear a seatbelt, you could get seriously injured.*
in pretty bad shape (phr) /ɪn ˈprɪti bæd ˈʃeɪp/   *My laptop's in pretty bad shape. I dropped it, and now it's really slow.*
rip (v) /rɪp/   *I've ripped my jeans! How embarrassing!*
ruin (v) /ruːɪn/   *If the guests don't arrive on time, the surprise party will be ruined!*
smash (v) /smæʃ/   *Gaia smashed a glass when she was opening the cupboard.*
spill (v) /spɪl/   *I can't believe I spilt coffee all over their white carpet!*
trip (v) /trɪp/   *Be careful – don't trip over that step.*

1 Choose the correct option to complete the sentences.
   1 I *got burnt / spilt* on my hand when I was taking the pizza out of the oven. I'm so *ruined / clumsy*!
   2 I was running too fast, and I *tripped / smashed* up the steps and fell on my face. That's why I've got this *burnt / bruise* on my chin.
   3 Dao fell over in the playground this morning. He's fine, he's just got *seriously injured / a few scratches* on his knee.
   4 The boat is *clumsy / in pretty bad shape* after last night's storm.
   5 My sister got angry with me and *smashed / ripped* pages out of my favourite book.
   6 Matias and Drew accidentally *spilt / smashed* the kitchen window with their football.
   7 You've *ruined / smashed* my new top! Did you *spill / trip* your drink on me on purpose?
   8 A player got *seriously injured / a few scratches* so couldn't play for the rest of the season.

2 Work in pairs. What would you do or say in these situations?
   1 You spill a drink in your sister's new car.
   2 You trip on the carpet in front of your whole class.
   3 You accidentally smash your friend's expensive vase.
   4 You tell your friend you're excited for their party. They don't know about it, and you ruin the surprise for them.

Vocabulary reference

UNIT 7

a bargain (n) /ə ˈbɑːgɪn/ *This bag was a bargain. I got it for half the price I expected to pay!*
bargain with (phr) /ˈbɑːgɪn wɪð/ *Do you bargain with the shop assistants in your country?*
be charged (phr) /bi ˈtʃɑːdʒd/ *I think we were charged too much for this meal. Let's check the receipt.*
be on sale (phr) /bi ɒn ˈseɪl/ *These shoes are on sale for £20. Shall I get them?*
a complete rip-off (phr) /ə kəmˈpliːt ˈrɪp-ɒf/ *This wallet was a complete rip-off. It's falling apart already!*
cost a fortune (phr) /kɒst ə ˈfɔːtʃən/ *Things in this shop cost a fortune because everything's a designer brand.*
get a discount on (phr) /get ə ˈdɪskaʊnt ɒn/ *You get a 10% discount on these towels if you buy two.*
get a good deal on (phr) /get ə gʊd ˈdiːl ɒn/ *I'm so pleased we got a good deal on that car.*
good value for money (phr) /gʊd ˈvæljuː fə ˈmʌni/ *This airline gives good value for money. Food and drink are included in the ticket price.*
a special offer (phr) /ə ˈspeʃəl ˈɒfə/ *There's a special offer at this hotel – children stay for free.*
well worth it (phr) /wel ˈwɜːθ ɪt/ *Climbing the mountain is well worth it for the amazing view.*

1 Complete the conversations with the correct form of the words or phrases from the word list.
  1 A: We have ¹_____ on today. If you buy one pair of sunglasses you get one free. Also, all our bags ²_____ for today only.
     B: Excellent. Usually these bags ³_____, so I'm happy I can afford one today!
  2 A: You can ⁴_____ this laptop of £50, because it's the only one left and it was our display model.
     B: That's ⁵_____! Thanks for telling me.
  3 A: I'm happy with the gifts we bought today. I think we ⁶_____ the perfume, after we ⁷_____ the shop assistant to get a discount.
     B: Yes! Our shopping trip was ⁸_____.
  4 A: Do you think that meal was ⁹_____? It was expensive, and it wasn't even nice.
     B: I think it was a ¹⁰_____. I'm so annoyed. We should've known from last time, when we ¹¹_____ too much for our food! We won't be going back there again.

2 Work in pairs. Tell your partner about a time:
  1 you got a discount on something.
  2 you bought something that was a rip-off.
  3 you got a bargain.

UNIT 8

competitive (adj) /kəmˈpetɪtɪv/ *Athletes need to be competitive in order to win.*
employment agency (n) /ɪmˈplɔɪmənt ˈeɪdʒənsi/ *An employment agency can help you find a job.*
flexible (adj) /ˈfleksəbl/ *You need to be flexible to be able to adapt to different situations.*
job opportunity (n) /dʒɒb ˌɒpəˈtjuːnɪti/ *I'm looking for a job opportunity in marketing.*
job satisfaction (phr) /dʒɒb ˌsætɪsˈfækʃən/ *Is job satisfaction more important than earning a high salary?*
permanent contract (phr) /ˈpɜːmənənt ˈkɒntrækt/ *The role is for six months, so it isn't a permanent contract.*
stand out (phr v) /stænd ˈaʊt/ *We are looking for a candidate that stands out from everyone else.*
transferable skill (phr) /trænsˈfɜːrəbl ˈskɪl/ *Time management is a transferable skill.*
unemployed (adj) /ˌʌnɪmˈplɔɪd/ *I've been unemployed since the restaurant I worked at closed down.*
work long hours (phr) /wɜːk lɒŋ ˈaʊəz/ *I'll be working long hours while the sale is on in the shop.*
work 9 to 5 (phr) /wɜːk naɪn tə ˈfaɪv/ *I work 9 to 5, Monday to Friday, as a secretary.*

1 Complete the definitions with the correct form of the words or phrases from the word list. There are two you do not need to use.
  1 A(n) _____ is a place you go to find work.
  2 Someone who wants to win or be more successful than other people is _____.
  3 A(n) _____ is an ability which can be used in a variety of different job roles.
  4 If someone _____ from the rest of a group, it means they are better than the others.
  5 When someone doesn't have a job, they are _____.
  6 A(n) _____ is an open position at work or for a company.
  7 Something that offers employees regular hours and consistent pay is a(n) _____.
  8 _____ is feeling happy in your job.
  9 Someone who is _____ is able to change easily to fit a new situation.

2 Work in pairs. Say if you agree or disagree with the statements and why.
  1 If I love my job, I don't mind working long hours.
  2 If I saw a job opportunity that meant working in a different country, I'd apply for it.
  3 I'm a very competitive person.

UNIT 9

(advanced) civilization (n) /(əd'vɑːnst) ˌsɪvɪlaɪ'zeɪʃən/ *Sumer was an advanced civilization that had one of the earliest known forms of writing.*
(ancient) ruins (n) /('eɪnʃ(ə)nt) 'ruːɪnz/ *Did you visit any ancient ruins while you were in Peru?*
date from/back to (phr) /deɪt frɒm/bæk tə/ *This coin dates back to the 16th century.*
a historic site (phr) /ə hɪs'tɒrɪk 'saɪt/ *Ephesus is a historic site in Turkey.*
inhabitant (n) /ɪn'hæbɪtənt/ *It was a city of only 10,000 inhabitants.*
period (n) /'pɪərɪəd/ *The Dark Ages refers to a period in history between the 5th and 14th centuries.*
be ruled by (phr) /biː 'ruːld baɪ/ *The country used to be ruled by a fearless leader.*
rural (adj) /'rʊərəl/ *We want to get out of the city and move to a rural area.*
the rise and fall of (phr) /ðə 'raɪz ən 'fɔːl əv/ *It was shocking to see the rise and fall of a once well-loved actor.*
to settle (v) /tə 'setl/ *After travelling for years, the couple decided to settle in Singapore.*

1 Match the beginnings of the sentences (1–8) with the endings (a–h).
  1 Your family tree says your great-grandfather settled …
  2 I don't think I could live in a rural …
  3 Adam's Calendar in South Africa are ancient …
  4 The ancient Egyptian empire was an advanced …
  5 The kingdom was ruled …
  6 The state of New York has almost 20 million …
  7 Ayutthaya is a historical …
  8 Did you watch that documentary about the …
  a ruins, which are around 75,000 years old.
  b by a powerful queen.
  c civilization that survived for almost 30 centuries.
  d inhabitants, and the number is growing.
  e rise and fall of that famous CEO?
  f in Australia in 1921.
  g site in Thailand that dates from the 14th century.
  h area because I'd miss city life too much.

2 Choose a topic. Do some research and write five interesting facts. Then share with a partner.
  • something discovered which dates back more than 200 years
  • an advanced civilization that invented something
  • a historic site you have visited
  • ancient ruins in your country or another country

UNIT 10

blame (v) /bleɪm/ *No one will know I broke the chair – I'll just blame it on someone else.*
cheat (v) /'tʃiːt/ *He always cheats at board games.*
dishonest (adj) /dɪs'ɒnɪst/ *Some companies have been dishonest about the quality of their products.*
hide my emotions (phr) /haɪd maɪ ɪ'məʊʃənz/ *I tend to hide my emotions and not show if I'm upset.*
honest (adj) /'ɒnɪst/ *I'm not always honest, but I try to tell the truth if I know it won't hurt anyone.*
make up an excuse (phr) /meɪk 'ʌp ən ɪks'kjuːs/ *Do you ever make up an excuse if you are late?*
pretend (v) /prɪ'tend/ *I think Pablo's pretending to be ill. He sounded fine on the phone.*
spread lies (phr) /spred 'laɪz/ *That website spreads lies and makes up false stories about people.*
suspicious (adj) /səs'pɪʃəs/ *The police are looking for a suspicious man in a blue jacket and sunglasses.*
tell a white lie (phr) /tel ə waɪt 'laɪ/ *Do you ever tell a white lie if you think the truth will hurt someone?*

1 Complete the conversations with the correct form of the words or phrases from the word list.
  1 A: Do you think Karl was ¹_____ his car broke down, or do you think he was being ²_____ and telling the truth?
    B: I'm not sure, but it was a bit ³_____ that it sounded like he was in bed!
  2 A: You definitely ⁴_____ at that game. You shouldn't have won!
    B: I'm not a ⁵_____ person, so I'd never do that. You're just ⁶_____ for why you lost so you don't look bad!
  3 A: Monica ⁷_____ so I never know how she's feeling.
    B: She told me some people at school had ⁸_____ about her.
  4 A: Today a student broke one of the computers and tried to ⁹_____ it on me!
    B: That's awful! I ¹⁰_____ today. My friend asked me if I liked his new shirt and I said I did, but it was horrible!

2 Work in pairs. Say if you agree or disagree with the statements and why.
  1 It's never OK to lie, even if you tell a white lie.
  2 It's better to show your emotions than pretend you're OK if you're not.
  3 It's fine to cheat at something if no one finds out.

Grammar reference

UNIT 1

1B Grammar: Auxiliary verbs in questions and short answers

Positive questions
- Use positive questions to ask for information.
- Form positive questions with auxiliary verb + subject + main verb. You can use positive questions in any tense.
  Did you like me when we first met? (= past simple)
  Have you been there before? (= present perfect)
- It's also possible to use a question word with this structure.
  Where did you meet each other?

> **Remember!**
> Auxiliary verbs always come before the subject.

Negative questions
- Use negative questions when you expect your listener to agree, to confirm something is correct, or to express surprise or annoyance.
- Form negative questions with auxiliary verb + *not* + subject + main verb.
  Isn't that the friend you lost touch with?
  Didn't she forget to invite you?
- It's also possible to use a question word with this structure.
  Why don't they talk anymore?

Short answers
- To form short answers to questions, use the auxiliary verb from the question.
  A: *Did Shilpa move back to New York?*
  B: *Yes, she did.*

Short questions
- Use short questions to respond or react to something someone says and keep a conversation going.
- If the statement is positive, the short question is also positive.
  A: *I've got a really good relationship with my brother-in-law.*
  B: *Have you?*
- If there is not an auxiliary verb in the first sentence, use the correct form of *do* to form the question.
  A: *I saw Maxine yesterday.*
  B: *Did you?*

Tag questions
- Tag questions are short phrases that are added to the end of a statement to check information or ask for confirmation.
- Form tag questions with auxiliary verb + pronoun. If the statement is positive, use a negative tag question and if the statement is negative, use a positive tag question.
  You didn't graduate, did you?
  She has a degree in psychology, hasn't she?

Agreement
- Use *so* + auxiliary verb + subject to agree with a positive statement. The auxiliary verb is in the same tense as the statement.
  A: *I have school tomorrow.*
  B: *So have I.*
- If no auxiliary is used in the statement, use the correct form of *do*.
  A: *I graduated from Berkeley.*
  B: *So did I!*
- Use *neither* + auxiliary verb + subject to agree with a negative statement.
  A: *I haven't seen anyone from school in years.*
  B: *Neither have I.*

Adding emphasis
- Use an auxiliary verb to add emphasis to present or past simple tenses.
- Use the auxiliary verb before the main verb.
  I did phone you, but you didn't answer.
  She does think things will get better.

1 Find and correct the mistakes.
1. A: You and Giovanni don't have a lot in common, don't you?
   B: No, we don't.
2. A: My sister is a real inspiration to me.
   B: Has she?
3. A: He is your colleague?
   B: He is, but I don't know him very well.
4. A: I've revised really hard for the end-of-year exams.
   B: Neither have I!
5. A: Why you don't go back to university to get your degree?
   B: I don't really have the time or money.
6. A: I think do studying abroad is a good choice.
   B: So do I.

2 Put the words in order to make positive sentences (+) and questions (?).
1. haven't / have / you / you / been / to / Australia / before (?)
2. think / I / met / do / I've / before / you (+)
3. didn't / you / like / each other / when / school / why / you / at / were (?)
4. the / same / do / you / both / for / company / work (?)
5. really is / doing / Yaniv / job / good / a (+)

1C Focus on: Short questions

- Use short questions to keep a conversation going and to show interest. Use them to ask for more details.
- You can form short questions with just a question word.
  A: *My sister just got a new job.*
  B: *Where?*
- You can also form short questions with a question word + preposition.
  A: *I'm going on holiday next week.*
  B: *Who with?*
  A: *I just bought this beautiful bag.*
  B: *Where from?*
- Other common examples are: *Who for? Who by? Who from? What with? Where to? How long for? What for?*
- Similar to a question tag, you can use auxiliary verb + pronoun to form a short question.
  A: *That was such a hard exam this morning.*
  B: *Was it?*
  A: *I don't think I remember telling you that.*
  B: *Don't you?*
- Some short questions don't follow a pattern. Some common examples are: *How come? Such as? In what way? Why's that? What sort/type of …? Was it?*
  A: *I'm not going to school tomorrow.*
  B: *Why's that?*

1 Complete the conversations with these short questions.

Haven't you?   Was it?   What for?   Where?
Who from?   Why not?
---

1 A: I've finally found some evening classes I'm interested in!
   B: _____
   A: At the college in town.
2 A: I'm moving to Lisbon!
   B: _____
   A: To teach English in a school there.
3 A: I don't think spending time with my colleagues is a good idea.
   B: _____
   A: Because I'm the manager, so I need to be professional.
4 A: I haven't met Laura's parents yet.
   B: _____
   A: No, but I will soon, hopefully.
5 A: Did you receive that message?
   B: _____
   A: Your old school friend you were telling me about.
6 A: Today was such a bad day.
   B: _____
   A: Yeah … work was so stressful.

UNIT 2

2B Grammar: Past tenses

Past simple

- Use the past simple to describe past, finished events. It can be used to list past events or tell the actions in a story.
- Form the past simple with *-ed* verbs or irregular verbs.
  Eliza **checked** *her homework before she* **handed** *it in.*
  I **didn't eat** *enough at the restaurant, so I* **went** *home and* **made** *food.*
  Did *you* **lock** *the back door before we* **left** *the house?*

Past continuous

- Use the past continuous to show that a longer action was interrupted by a shorter action in the past simple. The time expression *when* is often used.
- Form the past continuous with *be* (*not*) + verb + *-ing*.
  I **was cooking** *dinner when my phone* **rang.**
  I **wasn't listening** *so I* **missed** *what the teacher said.*
  Were *you* **getting** *ready for the party when you* **heard** *the news?*

Past perfect

- Use the past perfect to describe the order of two past events. The past perfect describes the first action in the past, and the past simple describes the second action.
- You can use time expressions such as *before, by the time* and *when*.
- Form the past perfect with *had* + past participle.
  I **had left** *the house when I realized I didn't have my wallet.*
  I had no idea that my phone **had been** *stolen.*
  Had *you* **met** *him before you joined the class?*

Past perfect in reported speech

- You can use the past perfect to report what someone says in the past simple or present perfect.
- A reporting verb is also used, such as *said, mentioned, stated, reported, explained, described,* etc.
  'I've already sent the email,' Filip said. → *He* **explained** *that he* **had** *already* **sent** *the email.*
  'I've booked the flights,' my sister said. → *She* **said** *she* **had booked** *the flights.*

Past perfect in the third conditional

- Use the past perfect in a third conditional sentence to describe a situation that didn't happen, and to imagine the result of this unreal situation.
- Form the third conditional with *If* + past perfect, … *would/ could* + *have* + past participle.
  If *I* **hadn't noticed**, *the hacker* **could've stolen** *even more information from my computer.*
  I **wouldn't have been** *found guilty* **if** *I'd had a better lawyer.*

141

Grammar reference

1 Write whether the sentences use past simple (PS), past continuous (PC) or past perfect (PP).
1. The police would have caught the robbers if they'd arrived just five minutes earlier.
2. Vicente had to pay a fine of $50.
3. Had you already left work when I called you?
4. I was running so fast that I went straight past my house.
5. We heard that the woman had been found guilty.

2 Complete the story using the correct form of the verbs in brackets.

Local police finally ¹_____ (catch) the robber last night, after six months of searching. He was found at his grandmother's house. When the police arrived, the criminal ²_____ (play) video games, and his grandmother ³_____ (sleep).

His grandmother told reporters he ⁴_____ (be) at the house for the past few weeks, then said, 'If I ⁵_____ (know) he was wanted by the police, I wouldn't have let him in. He told me he ⁶_____ (lose) his job and just needed somewhere to stay for a while. He's my grandson, so of course I ⁷_____ (believe) him.'

The officers ⁸_____ (search) the house for the stolen jewellery but didn't find anything.

2D Focus on: *be/get used to* + something / doing something

Get used to
- Use *get used to* to describe the process of becoming familiar with something. Often, this is something strange or unusual for the speaker.
- You can form it with *get used to* + verb + *-ing* or *get used to* + something/someone.
  *I'm finally **getting used to driving** on the other side of the road.*
  *I **got used to her Welsh accent** after a while.*

Be used to
- Use *be used to* if you have often experienced something. It is not strange, new or difficult.
- You can form it with *be* (not) *used to* + verb + *-ing* or *be used to* + noun phrase / someone.
  *I**'m used to working** night shifts. I don't mind it.*
  *I**'m not used to my new job** yet. I don't really know what I'm supposed to be doing!*

Used to
- Use *used to* to describe a habit or state in the past.
- Form it with *used to* + infinitive.
  *When I was young, I **used to go** fishing with my dad.*
  *I **didn't use to have** much free time as a teenager.*
  ***Did** you **use to walk** to school?*

1 Read the information. Write sentences using *be used to* or *get used to*.
1. Li has just moved to the UK and has not used the money before. It is strange for him.
   Li needs to get used to the money in the UK.
2. Emily lives in Japan. She needs to become familiar with speaking Japanese.
   _____
3. Subin lives on her own now. Before she lived with her parents. After a while, she became practised in washing her own clothes.
   _____
4. It is not strange for Rashid to wake up early in the morning. He often does.
   _____
5. Igor is not using social media anymore. He is adjusting to life without it.
   _____
6. It is not unusual for Max and Fraser to look after their little sister. They often do.
   _____

UNIT 3

3B Grammar: Talking about predictions

Will
- Use *will* + infinitive to talk about the future, when a decision is made at the time of speaking.
  *I**'ll go** and get some bread – we've run out.*
- You can also use *will* to make predictions about the future based on opinion.
  *I think it**'ll rain** later.*

Going to
- Use *going to* + infinitive to talk about the future, when a decision is made before the moment of speaking.
  *I'm **going to go** out later to the supermarket.*
- You can also use *going to* to make predictions about the future based on evidence.
  *France have just scored a goal. They're **going to win**!*

Probably/Possibly
- You can use *possibly* and *probably* with *will* and *going to* to talk about an uncertain future situation. Use *probably/possibly* before or after *will/going to*.
  *She's **probably going to tell** us her news at some point, but I don't know when.*
  *They**'ll probably call** you later.*

Modal verbs

- Use *may* or *might* + infinitive to talk about the future when we are not certain of something.
  *The party **might be** cancelled if they can't organize the food.*
  *I'm tired, so I **may go** to bed early tonight.*

Future clauses

- When a sentence has two clauses, use the future tense in the main clause and the present simple in the time clause. The future tense cannot be in both clauses. A time clause shows that an event will happen at a specific time.
- Words that introduce time clauses in the future include: *as soon as, before, if, once, when, unless* and *until*.
  *I'll **tidy** the kitchen **after I cook**.*
  *I'll **have** the house decorated **by the time you bring** her back for the surprise.*
- You can invert the clauses with no change in meaning.
  *I **won't go** home **until I finish** this presentation.* = *Until I finish this presentation, I **won't go** home.*

Present perfect

- Use the present perfect to talk about the future when one event can only happen if another event finishes. Use the present perfect for the action that follows the time clause.
- Common time clauses include: *after, as soon as, before, when* and *until*.
  *You'**ll need** to restart your computer **when** the program **has finished** downloading.* (= the program hasn't downloaded yet, but when it has, you'll need to restart)

1 Match the beginnings of the sentences (1–6) with the endings (a–f).

1 The weather's quite warm this morning, so I think it …
2 I think humans …
3 After the invites are sent to the guests …
4 We're probably …
5 I'll need my laptop back …
6 Looking at the data, there's …
a might live on other planets in the future.
b going to plan our wedding for next year.
c when you've finished using it.
d will be nice for our barbecue later.
e I'll feel much more relaxed.
f going to be a fall in student numbers next month.

2 Find and correct the mistakes.

1 In the future, there will to be much more advanced technology than today.
2 I'll let you know what I thought of the food after I'll have eaten it.
3 Probably there will be driverless cars on the roads in the next few years.
4 I think it's going snow tomorrow.
5 I'll make dinner as soon as I'll finish typing this up.
6 Once I know if I passed my driving test, I call you.

3C Focus on: Talking about data: Prepositions

Noun phrases

- You can use noun phrases to describe changes in an amount of something, or a situation.
- Form noun phrases with *a/an* + noun + preposition.
- Some common noun phrases include: *a rise, a fall, a decrease, an increase, a decline* and *a growth*.
- You use *in* after the noun when you are saying what has changed.
  *There has been **a sharp decline in** (the amount of) sales this month.*
  *We've seen **an increase in** (the number of) enquiries this week.*
- You use *of* after the noun when you are saying how much something has changed.
  *There's been **a rise of 10%**.*
  *We've seen a **decline of** around **100 members** per week.*

Verbs

- You can use verbs to describe changes in an amount or situation. Some common verbs include: *rise, fall, decrease, increase, decline* and *grow*.
- You can use *by* after the verb to say how much something will, or has, changed.
  *The population is expected to **grow by 2%** over the next five years.*
  *Registrations have **declined by half**.*
- You can use *to* after the verb to give a specific amount. You can also use *to* to describe the minimum or maximum level of change in a situation.
  *The business has **grown to 1,000 employees**.*
  *We expect the prices to **fall to the lowest** ever seen.*

1 Choose the correct option to complete the sentences.

1 The number of crimes in the area has increased *by / to* 25% over the last year.
2 The profits are expected to grow *of / to* over a million dollars in three years.
3 We've had an increase *of / in* the number of applications since we advertised the job.
4 There's been a rise *in / of* the number of people buying their first house this year.
5 The number of viewers has risen *to / by* double the number we had last year.
6 The increase *of / in* 30% in sales this year was unexpected for the company.

Grammar reference

UNIT 4

4B Grammar: Modifying comparative and superlative adjectives

Comparative adjectives

- Use comparative adjectives to compare different things.
  *Your meal is **spicier than** mine!*
- Use *a bit* or *slightly* before a comparative adjective to express a small difference.
  *I think this restaurant is **a bit nicer than** that one.*
  *I think he's **slightly older than** me.*
- Use *a lot*, *much* and *so much* to express a big difference.
  *You're a **much better** cook **than** me.*
  *This place is **a lot more expensive than** I thought.*
- Repeat the comparative with *and* to emphasize something or show that a situation keeps changing.
  *It's becoming **hotter and hotter** every summer.*
  *This day keeps getting **worse and worse**.*

Superlative adjectives

- Use superlative adjectives to describe the upper or lower limit of something.
  *That's **the biggest pizza** I've ever seen!*
- Use *by far* and *easily* before a superlative to stress an extreme of something.
  *You're **easily the tallest** person in the class.*
  *This is **by far the best** film I've ever seen.*
- Use *one of* + superlative to describe a plural noun that is part of a group.
  *She's **one of the kindest** people I've met.*
  *This is **one of the nicest** meals I've had in a long time.*

Comparative phrases

- To say two things are equal, use (*just*) *as* + adjective + *as*.
- Use *not as* + adjective + *as* to say the first thing is less than the second thing.
  *I can run **(just) as fast as** you.*
  *My English is **not as good as** yours.*

Adverbs

- Adverbs can be used instead of adjectives in comparatives and superlatives.
- To form the comparative with adverbs ending in *-ly*, use *more* + adverb + *than*. The adverb describes the verb.
  *You dance **more beautifully than** I do.*
  *He drives **more carefully than** me!*
- To form the superlative with adverbs ending in *-ly*, use *most* + adverb.
  *He eats the **most slowly** out of all of us.*

- As with adjectives, there are also irregular adverbs. Some common examples are:

Adverb	Comparative adverb	Superlative adverb
badly	worse	worst
far	further	furthest
little	less	least
much	more	most
well	better	best

*Our team played **better than** yours.   Our team played **the best**.*

1 Complete the sentences with the correct form of the word in brackets.
  1 Hyeon is one of the _____ (friendly) people in our class.
  2 My brother's cooking is not as _____ (good) as mine.
  3 Could you speak a bit more _____ (quiet), please?
  4 Your school photo is much _____ (nice) than mine.
  5 This is by far the _____ (bad) song I've heard in a while.
  6 Your laptop plays music much more _____ (loud) than mine.

2 Look at the first sentence in each pair. Complete the second sentence so that it has the same meaning.
  1 This pair of shoes is the same price as that pair of shoes – they are both expensive.
    The shoes are as _____ each other.
  2 We both started our homework at 5 p.m., but he finished at 6 p.m. and I finished at 6.30 p.m.
    He finished his homework more _____ me.
  3 The food in this restaurant is nice, but the food in the other restaurant is nicer.
    The food in this restaurant is _____ as in the other one.
  4 I've eaten a lot of spicy food, but this dish is very spicy.
    This is one _____ dishes I've ever eaten.
  5 I'm 21 on 2nd December, and my best friend is 21 on 4th December.
    My best friend is a _____ than me.

144

4C Focus on: Negative prefixes for adjectives

- A prefix is a syllable which has a specific meaning. You can add a prefix to the start of a root word to change its meaning.
  Honest ➜ **Dis**honest (not honest)
  Legal ➜ **Il**legal (not legal)
  Happy ➜ **Un**happy (not happy)
- Some common prefixes for adjectives are: *dis-, il-, im-, in-, ir-* and *un-* All of them mean 'not', so they change an adjective to a negative, or opposite, meaning.
  Agree ➜ **Dis**agree
  Flexible ➜ **In**flexible
  Perfect ➜ **Im**perfect
  Professional ➜ **Un**professional
- You usually add *il-* before an adjective starting with 'l'.
  Logical ➜ **Il**logical
- You add *im-* before adjectives starting with 'b', 'm' and 'p'.
  Possible ➜ **Im**possible
  Patient ➜ **Im**patient
- You usually add *ir-* before an adjective starting with 'r'.
  Regular ➜ **Ir**regular

1 Complete the sentences with the correct prefix.
  1 Why are you so ____patient? You have to wait in the queue to get an appointment!
  2 Joe, this work is ____complete. You'll need to take it home and finish it.
  3 I'm ____able to come in to work today. I'm not feeling well.
  4 That man I just spoke to was so ____helpful. He didn't give me any information I didn't already have.
  5 My brother is so ____responsible. He forgot to lock the door before we left the house.
  6 This chair is so ____comfortable. I can't sit here for a whole hour.
  7 My phone has ____appeared. Have you seen it?
  8 I think it's ____legal to park here.

UNIT 5

5B Grammar: *Could have, should have* and *would have*

Expressing ability or possibility in the past

- Use *could have* + past participle to describe something that was possible in the past.
- You can also use *could have* to express an ability to do something in the past that didn't happen.
  I **could have scored** that goal if she'd passed me the ball.
  With more time, she **could have done** better in the exam.
- Use *could not + have* + past participle to say something was not possible in the past, even if the speaker had wanted it to be.
  I **couldn't have done** a better job. I worked so hard.
  He **couldn't have studied** any harder than he did.

Expressing regret

- Use *should have* + past participle to express regret about something that didn't happen.
  I **should have taken** the job when I had the chance.
  She **should've gone** travelling. She would've been much happier.
- Use *should not + have* + past participle to express that a past action was not a good idea, but it happened anyway.
  He **shouldn't have spent** so much money on that jacket.

Past results

- Use *would (not) have* + past participle to express an imagined result, if something had been different in the past. Often, this is used with *if* in a third conditional sentence.
  If I'd left earlier, I **would have arrived** on time. (= I didn't leave early, so now I'm late.)
  They didn't have the best player on the pitch. He **would've won** the match for them.

1 Choose the correct option to complete the sentences.
  1 He *couldn't have / would have* been on your flight, because he's not due home until next week.
  2 If I'd been told it was your birthday, I *would have / should have* got you a present!
  3 She *shouldn't have / could have* gone to any university she wanted to.
  4 I really *should have / would have* asked to borrow my brother's car. Then we wouldn't have to walk.
  5 If I had known you were vegetarian, I *wouldn't have / shouldn't have* made chicken burgers.

Grammar reference

2 Rewrite the sentences using the correct form of the modal verb in brackets.

1 I didn't bring an umbrella with me. Now I regret it because I'm wet. (should)
   I should have brought an umbrella with me.

2 Joining the volleyball team was not a good idea because it takes all of my time, but I joined it anyway. (should)
   _____

3 I didn't work hard so I didn't get the promotion at work. (would)
   _____

4 It was possible for me to learn to play the violin when I was young, but I didn't want to. (could)
   _____

5 It wasn't possible for me to win the singing competition, even If I wanted to. (could)
   _____

6 I haven't learned to play chess, but I'm sure I'd be good at it. (would)
   _____

5C Focus on: Talking about past ability: *could*, *was able to* or *managed to*?

Could

- *Could* is the past form of *can*. Use *could* + infinitive to talk about general abilities in the past.
- Use *could not* + infinitive to talk about things a person was not able to do.
  *When I was young, I **could read** for hours.*
  *I **couldn't cook** until I was living alone.*
  ***Could** you **sing** well when you were little?*
- Use *could* to describe single events that happened in the past with verbs to describe senses: *think, feel, look, see, touch, taste, smell*, etc. and thoughts: *believe, remember, understand*, etc.
  *Dinner was horrible. I **couldn't taste** anything.*
  *I **could feel** someone was standing behind me.*

was/were able to / managed to

- Use *was/were able to* and *managed to* if something is achieved at a specific time in the past.
  *I **was able to** get the ball in from the far side of the pitch.*
     (= had the ability to)
  *I **managed to** contact the manager directly.* (= succeeded in doing something difficult)
- Use *wasn't/weren't able to* and *didn't manage to* to talk about a specific time in the past when something was unsuccessful, or when you didn't have the ability to do something. *Couldn't* is also possible in this situation and is less formal.
  *I **wasn't able to** find the number for Petrina.*
  *I **didn't manage to** finish the presentation on time.*

- To make questions with *was/were able to*, change the position of the subject and *be*. Use *did* + subject + *manage to*.
  ***Were you able to** get in touch with him?*
  ***Did she manage to** get a ticket to the show?*

1 Write sentences using the information. Make them positive (+), negative (−) or questions (?).

1 Tina / manage / finish the project on time (?)
   _____

2 Roberto / be able to / drive / until he was 30 (−)
   _____

3 I / could / remember where I'd seen him before (−)
   _____

4 You / be able to / get the decorations (?)
   _____

5 Ichika / manage to / find the dress she wanted (−)
   _____

6 We / be able to / communicate well / even though we speak different languages (+)
   _____

UNIT 6

6B Grammar: Reporting what people say

Direct and indirect speech

- Use reported speech to tell someone what another person has said. It's also known as indirect speech.
- Form reported speech with pronoun + reporting verb + (*that*) + reported clause. Use a reporting verb such as *say, tell, explain, mention, decide, suggest*.
  'I want to make a complaint.' (direct speech)
  She decided (that) she wanted to make a complaint.
     (indirect speech)

> **Remember!**
> The sentence meaning stays the same with or without *that*.
>   *They said **(that)** they think they know each other.*

- You 'move' the tense of the verb in indirect speech 'further back' to the past than the tense of the verb in direct speech.
  *'**I'm not coming** to work today.'* (direct speech, present tense)
  *He told me (that) he **wasn't coming** to work today.*
     (indirect speech, past tense)
- The present simple usually changes to the past simple.
  *'I **love** trying new food.'* (present simple)
  *She said (that) she **loved** trying new food.* (past simple)

- However, if the information in direct speech is a fact or general truth, the indirect speech usually remains in the present tense.
  *'The oven **is** hot,'* said mum. (present simple)
  *Mum said (that) the oven **is** hot.* (present simple)
- If something was said very recently, for example two minutes ago, the indirect speech usually stays in the same tense as the direct speech.
  *'**I'm** hungry,'* said Florencia. (present tense)
  *Florencia said (that) she**'s** hungry.* (present tense)
- The present continuous usually changes to the past continuous.
  *'**I'm living** with my sister.'* (present continuous)
  *She told me (that) she **was living** with her sister.* (past continuous)
- The past simple and the present perfect usually change to the past perfect simple.
  *'We **went** to the same school.'* (past simple)
  *They told me (that) they **had gone** to the same school.* (past perfect simple)
  *'I**'ve made** soup for lunch.'* (present perfect)
  *He mentioned (that) he**'d made** soup for lunch.* (past perfect simple)
- *Will* usually changes to *would*.
  *'I**'ll** make dinner tonight.'*
  *He said he **would** make dinner tonight.*
- *Can* usually changes to *could*.
  *'I **can** be quite clumsy.'*
  *She told me she **could** be quite clumsy.*

Expressions of time and place
- Expressions of time and place may change depending on when the information was heard, and when you report it.
  *'I'm starting my new job **today**,'* said Ellie. (said on Monday)
  *Ellie told me she was starting her new job **yesterday**.* (reported on Tuesday)
  *'I love **this** restaurant,'* said Khun. (Khun is in the restaurant)
  *Khun said he loved **that** restaurant.* (the speaker is not in the restaurant)

Some common time changes:

Direct speech	Indirect speech
now	then / at that time
today	yesterday / that day
yesterday	the day before
last night	the night before
last week	the week before / the previous week
tomorrow	today / the next day / the following day

Questions
- You can also report a question someone has asked.
- If you report a question, it becomes a statement. You do not need to use a question mark.
- The tense changes are the same as in reported statements.
  *'**Have** you **been** here before?'* (present perfect)
  *She asked whether I **had been** there before.* (past perfect)
- To report a *yes* or *no* question, change it to a statement using *if* or *whether*.
  'Are you creative in the kitchen?'
  *She asked me **if** I was creative in the kitchen.*
- For open questions, change it to a statement using the question word (*who, what, where, when* or *how*) said by the speaker.
  *'**When** did you smash your phone screen?'*
  *He asked me **when** I had smashed my phone screen.*
  *'**Where** do you live?'*
  *She asked me **where** I lived.*

1 Match the direct speech tenses (1–6) with the indirect speech tenses (a–f).

1 can
2 present continuous
3 will
4 present perfect
5 present simple – general truth
6 present simple

a present simple
b past continuous
c could
d past simple
e past perfect
f would

2 Rewrite the sentences using reported speech.
1 'I have really bad luck,' said Charlotte.
   Charlotte said she had really bad luck.
2 'Did anyone get seriously injured?' asked Riko.
   _____
3 'I'm staying at my friend's house,' she explained.
   _____
4 'When did you lose your wallet?' he asked.
   _____
5 'I'll make a complaint,' Becky said.
   _____
6 'Water boils at 100 degrees Celsius,' the teacher told the class.
   _____

Grammar reference

6C Focus on: Discussing present habits

Habits

- Use the present simple to talk about things you usually do, or habits.
- You can use adverbs of frequency, for example *always*, *occasionally*, *every day*, *often*, *sometimes*.
  I **walk** to work **every day**.
  My sister **always picks** me **up** from school.
- You can also use *tend to* + infinitive to talk about habits.
  I **tend to go** to the gym in the evenings.
  I **tend to make** mistakes with my pronunciation.
- You can also use *will* + infinitive without *to* to talk about habitual actions, but not states.
  Lily **will** always **help** you if you need something.
  My mum **will send** me a message every morning to see if I'm ok.

States

- The present simple is used to talk about states that exist at the time of speaking.
- A state is a feeling or a condition that someone or something is in at a specific time.
  She **lives** in Beijing.
  I **love** cooking.

1 Find and correct the mistakes.
1 He tend to eat dinner at 6 o'clock.
2 Dad will like gardening.
3 I tend to will make mistakes when I try to express my opinion in another language.
4 Marianne is late usually for everything.
5 Ibrahim and I often to go for a coffee on Fridays.
6 She tends listen to podcasts to practise her listening skills in English.

UNIT 7

7B Grammar: *have/get something done*

- Use *(not) have/get* + object + past participle to talk about something that someone does for you. This structure can be used in any tense.
  We can **get the windows cleaned** professionally.
  I'm **not having my nails done** until next week.
  Did you **get your laptop repaired**?
- The subject of the sentence caused the action to happen but didn't do the action themselves. They may have paid someone, asked someone or persuaded someone to do the action, for example.
  She **got her car fixed** yesterday. (= she didn't fix it; she asked someone else to fix it for her)

I **haven't had my hair cut** for a long time. (= I don't usually cut my hair; I pay someone to do it for me)
Garrett, have you **had your room painted**? (= the speaker is asking if someone else painted their friend's room)

- You often use this structure when you want to focus on the action, rather than who did it. However, you can add who did the action by using *by*.
  I got my essay checked **by** Mr Thomas.
  I had my phone screen fixed **by** the shop across the street.
- You can also use *get* + object + past participle to say when someone does something to us, or when something bad happens to someone.
  My sister **got her bag stolen** last week.
  My teammate **got his leg broken** by another player.
- Use *need* + gerund to talk about things you think should be done. Often, these are things you can pay or ask someone else to do. It can be used in any tense.
  The bed sheets **need changing**.
  The carpet **needed cleaning**.

> **Remember!**
> A gerund is verb + *-ing*.

1 Put the words in order to make positive sentences (+), negative sentences (–) or questions (?).
1 a / once / Mehmet / washed / his / car / gets / month (+)
2 internet / her / did / your / get / fixed / sister (?)
3 photos / fire / in / lost / their / the / got (+)
4 getting / delivered / are / not / we / again / tonight / food (–)
5 had / have / eyes / tested / recently / you / your (?)
6 needs / garden / a / professional / the / clearing / by (+)

2 Match the beginnings of the sentences (1–6) with the endings (a–f).
1 The dog is muddy so he needs …
2 Abasi is so pleased he got his …
3 Logan's hair is really long, but he's …
4 Selina got her …
5 I need to get my car …
6 Victoria had …

a computer hacked, and all her data was stolen.
b home designed by his favourite architect.
c flowers delivered to her mum's house for her birthday.
d having it cut this afternoon.
e washing. Would you mind doing it, please?
f checked – it's making a strange noise!

7C Focus on: cost, price, worth

Cost

- Use *cost* as a noun to say how much money you need to buy, make or do something.
- Use *cost* as a verb to say how much something is to buy, make or do.

  The **cost** to make the website was £100. (= the amount of money to produce the website)

  Tickets **cost** £12. (= the amount of money to buy the tickets)

- Use *how much + do + subject + cost* to ask someone about the amount of money something was bought for.

  A: How much did your holiday **cost**?
  B: The holiday **cost** a lot of money.
  A: How much does this painting **cost**?
  B: It **costs** £350.

Price

- Use *price* as a noun to talk about the amount of money you have to pay for something. Often, *price* is used in a shop or shopping situation, for example at a market.

  A: What's the **price** of this phone?
  B: The **price** is £322.

- Use *what + be + the price (+ of)* to ask a question. It can be used in any tense.

  Excuse me, what's the **price** of these flowers?
  What will the **price** be for six people?

Worth

- *Worth* is an adjective. Use *worth* to talk about the value of something. It can be a specific or non-specific amount.

  This diamond is **worth** thousands.
  Your designer handbag isn't **worth** as much as you think.

Cost, price and worth

- You can use *cost* to refer to things other than money. Often, these are the negative consequences of an action.

  If more trees are cut down, the **environmental cost** is huge.
  That project **cost** me a lot of **time**, and it wasn't even appreciated.

- You can use *price* to talk about something someone had to give up in order to get something else.

  Earning less money is a small **price** to pay if it means he's happier in his job. (= he earns less money but he's happy now)

  Their win against the other team came at a heavy **price**. One of the players was seriously injured. (= the player was injured, but they won)

- You can use *worth* to talk about something someone deserves, or something that is or isn't important.

- If *worth* is followed by a verb, use the gerund form.

  You should be paid what you're **worth**. (= you should be paid what you deserve)
  The food was **worth waiting** for. (= we had to wait a long time for the food, but the food was very good)

1 Complete the sentences with the correct form of *cost*, *price* or *worth*.

1 The subscription _____ $8 a month.
2 It _____ hundreds of pounds to hold this event, but I think it was _____ it.
3 House _____ have risen over the past year. It's not _____ buying a property at the moment.
4 Not having privacy is often the _____ you have to pay for being famous.
5 I paid £2000 for this car, but I think that was too much. Online it says it's only _____ £1000.
6 How much did the building work _____?
7 The money for the job wasn't _____ the time he put in.
8 What's the _____ of this jumper, please?

UNIT 8

8B Grammar: Noun phrases

- A noun phrase is a group of two or more words that contains a noun plus other words, e.g. a preposition, the infinitive with *to* or a relative clause.
- You can use noun phrases to add more information to a noun in a sentence.

  I need to write an **apology for how I acted**.
  I'd really like a **manager to train me**.
  I have a **job that I don't enjoy at all**.

Noun + preposition

- You can use certain prepositions with a noun to connect ideas, emphasize something or provide clarification.
- Use the preposition directly after the noun.
- Some of the most common prepositions to use are: *to, for, of, in, on, at, from, with, about* and *between*.

  I feel **sorry for** him. He didn't get the job.
  I got a job **offer from** the school in Japan.
  My **relationship with** my boss is great.
  Have you heard the **story about** the man I sit next to at work?

Noun + infinitive with *to*

- You can use the infinitive + *to* after abstract nouns.
- Use infinitive + *to* directly after the noun.

  The manager gave the employee the **opportunity to explain** himself.
  My first day was a **chance to demonstrate** my abilities.

> **Remember!**
> An abstract noun is an idea, quality or state rather than something concrete or physical, e.g. love, fear, excitement, luck, patience, clarity, happiness, etc.

149

Grammar reference

- Use the infinitive + *to* after an indefinite pronoun such as *something, someone, anyone, anything, everybody, everything, nobody* or *nothing*.
  *This discussion has **nothing to do** with me.*
  *I need to ask **someone to help** me find these files.*

Noun + relative clause
- You can use a relative pronoun after a noun to add more information to a sentence and connect ideas together.
- Use a relative clause to give more information about a person, thing or situation.
- Use the relative pronoun directly after the noun.
  *That's the **place where/that** I used to work.*
  *I want a **job which/that** pays well and has flexible working hours.*

Remember!
Relative pronouns

who/that	person
when/that	time
where/that	place
which/that	thing

- You don't need to use a relative pronoun when it is the object of the clause.
  They're the people (who/that) I saw at the interview.
  Here's the restaurant (which/that) I was telling you about.

1 Choose the correct option to complete the sentences.
  1 This is a position *that requires / to require* you to support the whole team.
  2 Ahmet didn't have the patience *to wait / which waits* in the queue.
  3 What's the reason *that / for* your unhappiness at work?
  4 It's a job *that / who* you'll love if you just give it a chance.
  5 There's a problem *with / to give* the email address you gave us.
  6 We're looking for someone *who is / to be* willing to work Tuesday to Saturday.

2 Complete the noun phrases in the sentences.
  1 Can you give me an example _____ how you've been flexible in your previous roles?
  2 It's a pleasure _____ meet you. But haven't we met before?
  3 This is my friend Zena, _____ I was talking about yesterday.
  4 When I work at home, I always have music on, or something _____ listen to while I work.

  5 Isn't that the bank _____ you used to work?
  6 What's the reason _____ your call, please?

8C Focus on: Compound words

- Compound words are two or more words which are put together to create one new word.
- Compound words often have a different meaning to the two individual words.
  life + guard = lifeguard
  news + paper = newspaper
- You write some compound words with a hyphen.
  check-in, part-time, full-time
- You write other compound nouns as one word.
  hairdresser, headteacher, babysitter
- You can also write compound nouns as two words.
  police officer, shop assistant, flight attendant
- You can use any word forms together to make a compound word.
  courthouse (noun + noun)
  driving licence (verb + noun)
  haircut (noun + verb)
  public speaker (adjective+ noun)

1 Match the words 1–8 with words a–h to make compound nouns.

  1 sales   a coach
  2 zoo   b star
  3 sports   c person
  4 building   d agency
  5 train   e site
  6 employment   f keeper
  7 home   g driver
  8 pop   h work

UNIT 9

9B Grammar: *Pronouns*

Subject pronouns	Object pronouns	Possessive pronouns	Reflexive pronouns
I	me	mine	myself
you	you	yours	yourself
he/she/it	him/her/it	his/hers/its	himself/herself/itself
we	us	ours	ourselves
you	you	yours	yourselves
they	them	theirs	themselves

Subject pronouns
- Use a subject pronoun to replace a noun which performs the action in a sentence.
  He invented the lightbulb.
  They were an advanced civilization.

Object pronouns
- Use an object pronoun to replace a noun which receives the action of a verb.
  Send the details over to me.
  I forgot to invite her.

Possessive pronouns
- Use a possessive pronoun to replace a noun phrase and to avoid repeating words.
- You can use a possessive pronoun after *of*.
  Whose book is this? Is it yours?
  They're friends of ours.

> **Remember!**
> You don't need to use an apostrophe with a possessive pronoun.
> *This is hers. This is her's.*

Reflexive pronouns
- Use a reflexive pronoun to refer back to a person or thing.
- You can use a reflexive pronoun when the subject and object of the verb are the same.
- You can use a reflexive pronoun to emphasize that someone does something personally, not anybody else.
  My laptop keeps turning itself off.
  Did he drive there himself or take a taxi?
- Use *by* + reflexive pronoun to mean *alone*.
  She went travelling by herself.
  Do you often study by yourself?

Indefinite pronouns

Person	Place	Thing
anybody, anyone, everybody, everyone, nobody, no one, somebody, someone	anywhere, everywhere, nowhere, somewhere	anything, everything, nothing, something

- An indefinite pronoun does not refer to a specific person, thing or amount.
- You can use an indefinite pronoun as the subject or object of a sentence.
- Use a singular verb after an indefinite pronoun.
  Somebody told me, but I can't remember who.
- You usually use *some-* in positive sentences.
  He's someone I used to work with.
  There's something on the table for you.
- Use *any-* in questions and negative sentences.
  Is there anything I can help you with?
  Don't tell anyone, please.

- You can use *some-* in questions when it is an offer or request, or when you think the answer will be *yes*.
  Shall we go away somewhere for the weekend?
  Can I help you with something?
- In negative clauses, use pronouns with *no-*, not *-any*.
  Nothing happened. ~~Anything happened.~~
  Nobody had heard the news yet. ~~Anybody had heard the news yet.~~

One
- When you talk about countable things, you can use *one* or *ones* if it is clear what you are talking about.
- Use *one/ones* to replace a noun and avoid repeating yourself.
- Use *one* for singular countable nouns.
  I asked to borrow a pen, but he didn't have a spare one.
- Use *ones* for plural, countable nouns.
  These coins are older than the ones they found here before.

1 Complete the sentences with these words.

---
anyone   anything   herself   him   I   mine   no one
one   ones   ourselves   someone   you
---

1 Dongmei settled in a rural area, quite far from the city. She lives by _____.
2 Will you visit any historic sites while you're in Asia? There are some beautiful _____ in Cambodia.
3 I haven't told _____ that we're going away to get married by _____!
4 Can I get you _____ to eat?
5 I forgot my pencil. Do you have _____ I can borrow?
6 I'm looking for _____ to help me paint the spare bedroom, but there seems to be _____ available.
7 _____ saw Davide this morning, and invited _____ over for dinner later.
8 Do _____ remember the Thompsons? They're friends of _____ from the sports club.

2 Complete the sentences with a pronoun. There is sometimes more than one possible answer.
1 She gave _____ a well-deserved day off and went shopping.
2 Did you go _____ this weekend?
3 Here's a photo of the twins. Nicole is the _____ on the left.
4 The archaeologists were very proud of _____ discovery.
5 I visited the ruins by _____.
6 The teacher asked _____ why she was always late for class.

151

Grammar reference

9C Focus on: The passive voice with *by*

- Use the passive voice to emphasize the person or object that experiences the action, rather than the person that does it.
- You can use the passive voice when you don't know who or what did the action.
- The object of an active sentence becomes the subject in a passive sentence.
  Active: *My sister bought the house.* (subject + verb + object)
  Passive: *The house was bought.* (subject + *be* + past participle)
- If you know the agent, use *by* to say who or what performs the action in the passive voice.
- The focus of the sentence shifts to the object, not the subject.
  Active: *The red team won the game.* (= who won is the focus of the sentence)
  Passive: *The game was won by the red team.* (= the game is the focus of the sentence)
  Active: *Howard Carter discovered the tomb of King Tutankhamun.* (= Howard Carter is the focus)
  Passive: *King Tutankhamun's tomb was discovered by Howard Carter.* (= the tomb is the focus)
- It is very common to use the passive voice + *by* in academic writing.
  The breakthrough was made by researchers at Cambridge University.
  The health of the economy is determined by growth.

1 Rewrite the sentences using the passive voice with *by*.
1. The children baked a chocolate cake.
   _____
2. Romulus and Remus founded Rome in 753 BCE.
   _____
3. Arthit cooked dinner this evening.
   _____
4. The Chinese emperor Shen Nong discovered tea.
   _____
5. Thirty students took the test.
   _____
6. Augustus Pugin designed London's Big Ben.
   _____

UNIT 10

10B Grammar: Quantifiers

- Quantifiers express a quantity of something and answer the questions *how much?* and *how many?*
- Use these quantifiers with both countable and uncountable nouns: *all*, *any*, *most*, *no* and *some*.
  Most of my evenings are spent relaxing.
  He's got no time to practise this weekend.

Any and some

- You often use *any* in negative sentences and questions.
- You can also use *some* in questions. Use *some* for offers and requests if you think the answer will be *yes*.
  Did you bring any snacks?
  I didn't see any reason to lie.
  Would you like some water? (= offer)
  I'd like some time to myself, please. (= request)
- Use *any* in positive sentences when you want to say 'it doesn't matter which'.
  You can come and see me any time. (= doesn't matter what time)

No, none, all, most and many

- Use *all* + plural countable/uncountable nouns to talk about everything or every person in a group.
  All decisions were made by the teachers.
  All visitors should report to reception.
- Use *most* + plural countable/uncountable nouns to talk about nearly all of a number of people or quantity of something.
  Most days are spent working outside.
  His advice is usually helpful in most situations.
- Use *no* + singular countable nouns, plural countable nouns and uncountable nouns to say something does not exist or is not present.
  The company had no plans to offer any discounts.
  There was no job for her.
- Use *no/all/most* + uncountable/plural noun to talk about everything or nothing in general.
  Almost all the seats were filled.
  The answer is the same in most cases.
- Use *none/all/most* + *of* (*the*) + uncountable/plural noun to talk about everyone or everything in a specific group.
- *All of* is usually followed by pronouns *us*, *them*, *this*, *that*, *these*, *those* and *which*.
  All of us are graduating this year.
  All of those people work in my office.
- Use *most of* (*the*) to refer to the majority of a specific group of something.
  Most of my friends live nearby.
  Most of the inhabitants live in the city centre.

152

- Use *none of* before *this*, *that*, *the*, *my*, *your* or pronouns.
  None of us knew what we were looking at.
  None of that made sense.
- Use *(too) much* with uncountable nouns and *(too) many* with countable plural nouns.
  Many of our users saved more than 80 dollars.
  Much of the money was spent on advertising

All and *every*
- Both *all* and *every* refer to the total number of something.
- *All* refers to the whole group.
- *Every* refers to individual members of a group.
  I'm friends with **every**one I work with. (= every individual person)
  I'm friends with **all** my colleagues. (= as a group)
- You can use *all* on its own without a noun.
- You cannot use *every* on its own without a noun. Use *everyone*, *everybody* or *everything* instead.
  All are welcome to come for a coffee at lunch.
  Everyone is welcome to come for a coffee at lunch. ~~Every are welcome to come for a coffee at lunch.~~

Both, *either* and *neither*
- Use *both*, *either* and *neither* to talk about two people or things.
- Use *both/either/neither* with object pronouns.
- Nouns with *both* have a plural verb.
- Nouns with *either* and *neither* have a singular verb.
  Both restaurants **were** closed.
  Neither restaurant **was** open.
  I don't think **either** restaurant **was** open.

1 Choose the correct option to complete the sentences.
1. *Both / Neither* my sister and I are good at hiding our emotions.
2. There were too *many / much* people in front of Prisha for her to be able to see the stage.
3. Could I have *any / some* cake, please?
4. There was *none / no* space for Hafiz to park his car.
5. *Every / All* person in this team has helped us make the company the success it is today.

2 Find and correct the mistakes. Rewrite the sentences.
1. Neither of us are able to come to the meeting as we'll be with a client.
   _____
2. I didn't receive some invitation from her.
   _____
3. I really don't mind which you choose – I like every of it.
   _____
4. No of the guests have confirmed they're coming.
   _____
5. Both Arjun and Mila has fact-checked the article.
   _____

10C Focus on: Verbs of the senses: *looks, sounds, smells, feels, seems*

- *Look*, *sound*, *smell*, *feel* and *seem* are all verbs. They describe the impressions we receive through our five senses.
  It **seems** as though he's trying to blame it on someone else.
  He **sounds** like he's lying.
- *Seem* and *look* both relate to appearance but have a difference in meaning.
  You **look** tired. (= my impression from seeing your face)
  You **seem** tired. (= my impression from your actions, e.g. behaviour, tone of voice, etc.)
  You **look** beautiful. ~~You seem beautiful.~~
- *Look*, *sound*, *smell*, *feel* and *seem* are all non-action verbs, which means they cannot be used in a continuous form.
  It **looks** as if it's going to rain. ~~It's looking as if it's going to rain.~~
  You **smell** lovely. ~~You are smelling lovely.~~
- Use verbs of the senses + adjective.
  She **sounds** happy.
  He **looks** angry about something.
- Use verbs of the senses + *like* + a noun.
  You **look like** your dad.
  That **smells like** a perfume I used to wear.
- Use verbs of the senses + *as if / as though / like* + verb phrase.
  You **look as if** you've seen a ghost.
  It **feels as though** we've met before.
  That photo **looks like** it's been edited.

1 Look at the first sentence in each pair. Complete the second sentence so that it has the same meaning using the word(s) in brackets. Use 1–4 words.
1. Jeremy appears to be making up excuses for not doing his job properly. (seem, as)
   Jeremy _____ he's making up excuses for not doing his job properly.
2. From Mr Yang's voice, we can tell he's annoyed. (sound, like)
   Mr Yang _____ annoyed.
3. My impression from seeing Leon's face is that he's stressed. (look, as)
   Leon _____ he's stressed.
4. Pia thought the description of the film was interesting. (sound)
   Pia thought the film _____ interesting.
5. The dentist told him he might experience a sharp pain. (feel)
   'You might _____ a sharp pain,' said the dentist.

Irregular verbs

INFINITIVE	PAST SIMPLE	PAST PARTICIPLE
be	was / were	been
beat	beat	beaten
become	became	become
begin	began	begun
bite	bit	bitten
break	broke	broken
bring	brought	brought
build	built	built
burn	burned/burnt	burned/burnt
buy	bought	bought
catch	caught	caught
choose	chose	chosen
come	came	come
cost	cost	cost
cut	cut	cut
deal	dealt	dealt
do	did	done
dream	dreamed/dreamt	dreamed/dreamt
drink	drank	drunk
drive	drove	driven
eat	ate	eaten
fall	fell	fallen
feel	felt	felt
fight	fought	fought
find	found	found

INFINITIVE	PAST SIMPLE	PAST PARTICIPLE
fly	flew	flown
forget	forgot	forgotten
forgive	forgave	forgiven
get	got	got
give	gave	given
go	went	gone/been
grow	grew	grown
have	had	had
hear	heard	heard
hide	hid	hidden
hit	hit	hit
hold	held	held
hurt	hurt	hurt
keep	kept	kept
know	knew	known
lay	laid	laid
lead	led	led
leave	left	left
learn	learned/learnt	learned/learnt
lend	lent	lent
let	let	let
lie	lay	lain
lose	lost	lost
make	made	made
mean	meant	meant

Irregular verbs

INFINITIVE	PAST SIMPLE	PAST PARTICIPLE
meet	met	met
pay	paid	paid
put	put	put
read	read	read
ride	rode	ridden
ring	rang	rung
rise	rose	risen
run	ran	run
say	said	said
see	saw	seen
sell	sold	sold
send	sent	sent
set	set	set
shake	shook	shaken
shine	shone	shone
shoot	shot	shot
show	showed	shown
shut	shut	shut
sing	sang	sung
sit	sat	sat
sleep	slept	slept
smell	smelled/ smelt	smelled/ smelt
speak	spoke	spoken
spell	spelled/ spelt	spelled/ spelt
spend	spent	spent

INFINITIVE	PAST SIMPLE	PAST PARTICIPLE
spoil	spoiled/ spoilt	spoiled/ spoilt
spread	spread	spread
stand	stood	stood
steal	stole	stolen
stick	stuck	stuck
swear	swore	sworn
swim	swam	swum
take	took	taken
teach	taught	taught
tell	told	told
think	thought	thought
throw	threw	thrown
understand	understood	understood
wake	woke	woken
wear	wore	worn
win	won	won
write	wrote	written

Extra speaking tasks

PAGE 19, 1D, EXERCISE 9
Student A: You are from São Paulo, Brazil, but you've been living in Singapore for three years. You are an MA Engineering student. So far you love both the university and Singapore, but once you graduate, you hope to go back to Brazil and work as a civil engineer. You know Singapore pretty well. The party host is your friend's colleague. You've known him for a few months, but aren't too close. Your friend really insisted on coming to the party, so you couldn't say no.

PAGE 27, 2B, EXERCISE 9
Student A

> **Criminal:** Attila Nemeth, a 26-year-old man from Hungary
>
> **His plan:** persuade a large hotel chain to give him the job he'd applied for previously
>
> **What he did:** hacked the security system, introduced a virus into their system, told the hotel chain he would do more damage unless he got the job
>
> **Hotel chain's response:** told US Secret Service, prepared a fake job offer
>
> **What happened:** Attila applied, all his information went to US Secret Service, he was caught

PAGE 100, 8C, EXERCISE 1

> Kunal Kelhar wasn't able to go to Italy to work, but he decided to do the shoot anyway … at home! He used a toy model car and a treadmill (running machine) instead of a real car and road. He also used some table tennis nets and water spray.

PAGE 120, 10A, EXERCISE 7
Pair A

Look at the optical illusion and discuss the questions.
1. What do you see when you look at it for the first time?
2. Look more closely. Are the circles still or moving?

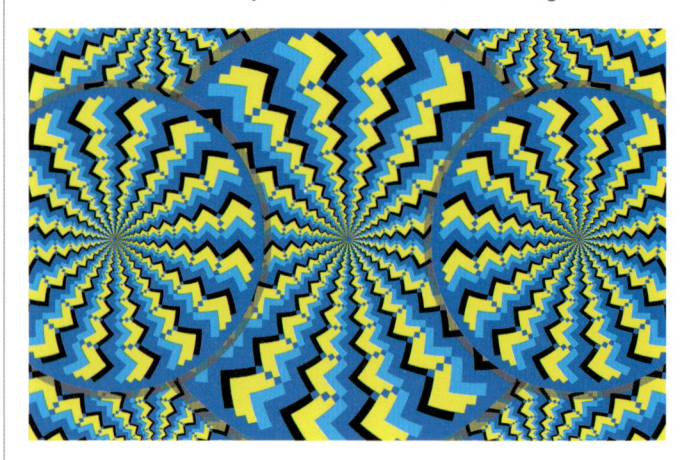

PAGE 43, 3D, EXERCISE 10
Student C

Give feedback on the feedback!					
Award Student A a score out of 5 for each statement.					
A asked whether B wanted feedback.	1	2	3	4	5
A focused on the future, not the past.	1	2	3	4	5
A limited the negative feedback to 2 or 3 points.	1	2	3	4	5
A included some positive points and helped B to feel good.	1	2	3	4	5
A offered B future help and support.	1	2	3	4	5

PAGE 108, 9A, EXERCISE 7
Use these questions to help you 'build' your world.
- Is your world like the real world but with added elements or completely invented?
- Is it based on history, the present or the future?
- What kind of people and animals live there?
- Are there things that happen in your world that are not possible in this world?
- What about the politics, culture, architecture, geography, clothes and technology?

Our world is based on ancient Japan, at the time of the Shogun. But a few people have special powers which they use for …

Extra speaking tasks

PAGE 56, 4E, EXERCISE 2

Student B

> **Ha-neul L.**
> 17 reviews • 2 photos
>
> ★ a month ago
> **A complete let-down!**
>
> Last night we went to La Havana, a new Cuban restaurant in the neighbourhood. Having read some of the reviews, I expected so much more from this place. But unfortunately, it turned out to be totally overpriced.
>
> The first thing that made a negative impression was the service. Even though we'd reserved a table for four people, they only had one for two available. So we had to wait for about half an hour for our table to be free. The staff weren't helpful at all, and we didn't even get an apology.
>
> The second let-down was the food. I expected it to be full of flavour, but it was completely tasteless. I would not recommend it at all.
>
> The design of the restaurant doesn't live up to expectations either. Just as with the food, it's completely inappropriate. I think they tried to make it look really posh, you know expensive-looking, but it just didn't work. And anyway, I didn't go there for the design but for the food!
>
> So all in all, I had a dreadful experience. I'd definitely discourage you from going there. It's not worth your time or money at all!
>
> 👍 Like

PAGE 120, 10A, EXERCISE 7

Pair B

Look at the optical illusion and discuss the questions.

1 Which blue circles seem bigger?
2 Look more closely. Are the blue circles really different sizes?

PAGE 19, 1D, EXERCISE 9

Student B: You are from Tokyo, Japan. You have just moved to Singapore. You moved here with your family to work for an international company. You work in marketing. Your partner is an engineer. So far you've enjoyed Singapore. It's a big city like Tokyo, where you're from, and that's something you like. You haven't had much time to explore it yet and would like to get to know it better. The party host is a friend of a friend. You wanted to come to the party because you want to make new friends.

PAGE 31, 2D, EXERCISE 7

Key

1 a low	b medium	c high
2 a medium	b high	c low
3 a medium	b low	c high
4 a high	b low	c medium

PAGE 27, 2B, EXERCISE 9

Student B

> **Criminal:** a group of hackers from San Francisco, US
>
> **Their plan:** hack electronic road signs, make a joke
>
> **What they did:** hacked into electronic road signs, changed the signs, showed funny phrases such as 'GODZILLA ATTACK! TURN BACK!'
>
> **Drivers' reactions:** some reacted with surprise, thought it was an advert for a new Godzilla movie; others reported it to police
>
> **What happened:** hackers never caught, government tried to make the sign systems more secure

PAGE 120, 10A, EXERCISE 7

Pair C

Look at the optical illusion and discuss the questions.

1 What do you see immediately: a rabbit's or a duck's head?
2 Look more closely. Can you see both a rabbit's and a duck's head depending how you look at the drawing?

157

Audioscripts

UNIT 1

🎧 1.1

A = Aleksander, E = Evelina

A: Do you remember that friend Jacek I told you about?
E: Yeah, I think I do. Was he the friend you used to go to swimming with?
A: Yes, he was. We met when we were about six or seven and quickly became best friends.
E: But you two lost touch a while back, didn't you?
A: We did, yes. We moved to different cities to study. Then started working. And you know, before you realize, fifteen years have passed … Anyway, he contacted me the other day, wants to meet up …
E: Does he? That's great! But isn't he living abroad now?
A: He was, but I think he moved back recently.
E: Brilliant news! When are you going to see him?
A: I'm not sure yet, but …

A = Alisa, H = Harika

A: I was going to ask you, have you heard from Biyu at all?
H: Yeah, I have. Er … I haven't spoken to her for a while, but we messaged last week. She changed jobs about a month ago.
A: Oh, did she? Where is she now?
H: Same company, but now she's in Carlton.
A: That's not far from where I live.
H: No, it isn't. Maybe you'll bump into her.
A: You know, we haven't spoken since she left.
H: Haven't you? I think that's a shame.
A: Yeah, so do I. We were good friends. I do think that if we bumped into each other, I'd want to see her again, you know, catch up over a coffee or something.
H: Oh, you should! She does ask about you, you know.
A: Does she? That's good to know.

🎧 1.3

I = Interviewer, T = Tsiory

I: Would you say you were a good student at school?
T: I think so, I paid attention in class most of the time. Except during mathematics and physics classes, when I was terrified …
I: Terrified?
T: When I didn't have the answer and I was sure the teacher noticed.
I: Right.
T: And during gym class … Oh, and the afternoon class. I lived about 1 kilometre from school, and walked that distance back and forth four times a day, and I got pretty tired. The afternoons are hot in Madagascar, and there were 60 students in the classroom! I had to make a big effort to stay focused and not fall asleep!
I: Why didn't you pay attention in gym class?
T: I never felt comfortable. I was not good at it – I was petite, shy and chubby. One of the worst feelings I had was when forming a team, I would be among the last people to be chosen. I never felt I belonged to a sports team and I wonder how I got through it!
I: Is there anything you would have changed about the way you studied?
T: On the one hand, I have the career I wished for and it was through hard work and dedication. If I changed the way I studied, I would not be the person I am today. But on the other hand, I feel like I spent all of my life studying. I saw my friends socializing and having more fun than me. And that is something I couldn't catch up on, even if I wanted to.

I = Interviewer, M = Mike

I: What didn't you like about school?
M: I hated 'busy work' that required no imagination or thought to complete. Unfortunately, much of it was busy work – that was how the public education system worked where I grew up – so, I just got it done quickly and moved on to do fun things, like hanging out with friends and playing sports. I think a major turning point for me, when I realized that there was far more to learning than just 'getting good grades', was when I studied abroad in Australia. I took a field course in ecology on an island in the middle of the Great Barrier Reef, and seeing my subject matter come to life made me hungry to learn.
I: Did you use to study a lot for exams?
M: I was good about revising for exams, but I was always 'cramming': waiting until the last minute to memorize everything. I would just repeat the information I'd learned by heart and then forget most of it nearly immediately.
I: Is there anything you would change about the way you studied?
M: I wish I would've taken more time to try to establish a deeper understanding of my subjects. We were taught to memorize so many specific things, but I think that, in doing so, I would often miss the big picture.

🎧 1.6

J = Janet, M = Matt, G = Guide

J: Are you here for the astronomy night?
M: Yes, for the star tour. Is it your first time here?
J: Yes, I thought it might be interesting.
M: It is. You learn a lot about the stars and planets.
J: Wonderful! Well, we've been very lucky with the weather.
M: Yes, perfect. But that usually means it'll get really cold after dark. I hope you've got some warm clothes?
J: Don't worry about me. So … what do you do?
M: I'm a student. I'm studying business and economics.

J: Business, eh? And what are you thinking of doing after university?
M: I'm not sure. To be honest, I don't think business is for me. I'd quite like to be a chef. What about you?
J: I'm retired now, but it's funny you mention cooking, because I worked in restaurants most of my career.
M: Really? Which ones?
J: You might know 'The Lemon Tree'?
M: Of course! It's got a really good name! Were you the chef there?
J: No, I was a business manager there. I did the money side of things.
M: Right! That's interesting …
G: OK, everybody, if you can all gather round … I see there are a few new faces here this evening, so welcome all …
J: I see you've got your binoculars. Was I supposed to bring some?
M: No, there's no need. They have some extra equipment you can borrow. But you're welcome to borrow mine, too.
J: That's very kind! Thank you.

1.7

1
A: Where in Australia do you live?
B: I live in Melbourne now, but I was in Perth before. I moved last year.
A: I've heard Perth is beautiful. Why did you move?
B: For work. There's not much for me in Perth, it's a quiet place. But yes, I miss Perth – it's a great place to live: clean, there's a nice mix of people there, good food …
A: Speaking of clean cities, what do you think of Moscow?
B: It's incredible! So clean! I don't think I've seen any rubbish in the street since I got here!

2
A: How well do you know the museum? Have you been here before?
B: Oh, yes, several times. I think it's my favourite museum in Colombia.
A: Why do you like it so much?
B: Well, I'm a big fan of Gabriel García Marquez. And the garden views are great.
A: I think it's the house itself I love. Such great architecture.
B: It's funny you mentioned the house, because I have a photo of this house before it became a museum hanging on my wall.
A: Really? That's fascinating.

3
A: How did you and Bouchra meet?
B: I was working in a port in Tangiers, and Bouchra owned a company there.
A: Tangiers. That must have been nice. How long were you there?
B: For a couple of years. I came back last year. I loved Morocco, but Tangiers is a busy industrial city, it's not very pretty. Going back to what you were saying about escaping the city, we used to go to a place in the hills called Chefchaouen. It's not far from Tangiers. Do you know it?
A: No, I've never been to Morocco. I'd like to go, though …

UNIT 2

2.1

I = Interviewer, A = Alyea
I: If you could change two rules in your city, what would you change?
A: If I was in charge, there's a lot I'd like to change. But if I could only make two rules in my city, I would make sure there was equal, free access to educational resources, lessons, buildings and teachers. I know this is a big request because to make sure everyone got the same learning opportunities, it would involve proper salaries for teachers, and rebuilding many communities so that there are not such big differences in the level of education between cities.
Secondly, I would give everyone time in the afternoon for a siesta, because I think a short sleep after our mid-day meal would certainly help us operate better. After all, we are all still growing kids and we need our rest!

2.3

O = Olivia, A = Alfie
O: So today on the show we're going to talk about the least talented criminals on the planet. So, who's the first criminal on our list?
A: This a really funny one. This guy was caught at his home with a stolen phone and an expensive watch, worth £4,000. And that's only an hour after he'd stolen them.
O: No way! That was quick!
A: Well, he gave the police a lot of clues – he broke into the house and stole the watch. Then he saw a phone on the table and grabbed it, too. And then …
O: … he called the owner?
A: Almost, but no. He took a selfie of himself wearing the watch and sent it to the victim's friends by mistake!
O: No way!
A: I know. Unbelievable! He was sentenced to four years in prison. OK, what's your story?
O: So this one is hilarious as well. This guy didn't even get to steal anything!
A: What do you mean?
O: He was planning to rob a local supermarket. But before he did it, he posted a photo of himself on social media with a caption: 'Robbing a supermarket right now.'

159

Audioscripts

A: What a genius!

O: I know! Anyway, the police caught him before he even got to the supermarket.

A: So he was innocent, wasn't he? I mean, he didn't really break the law.

O: You're absolutely right. He was only guilty of using social media!

A: So did the police just give him a warning?

O: Well, actually, they found several thousand pounds in his house from a previous robbery. So he was given seven years in prison.

A: Wow! OK, OK, I think we have time for one more.

O: All right, I've got an interesting one. So one day this couple came back from holiday and found their house completely clean. But the thing is, they had left it in a complete mess when they left. And they also found something, or rather someone, else in the house.

A: A robber?

O: Sleeping on the couch! So the couple called the police. It turns out the man wasn't even planning to rob the house. He just wanted to sleep somewhere.

A: So he didn't steal anything, then?

O: That's right. And not only did he not steal anything, he also cleaned the entire house and washed the dishes after cooking!

A: So what did the police do? I imagine it's against the law to break into people's houses to sleep, even if you clean up afterwards.

O: Yes, that's true. But he didn't steal anything. So they gave him a fine of £200.

A: I'd rather they sent him to my house. It needs a good clean!

2.6

D = Dirk, Z = Zainab

D: So I told you I met Abner last week?

Z: Is that your new friend from Iraq?

D: Yes, we're in the same class and now we're doing a project together. I think we'll work well together. But I'm going over to his house tomorrow to work on it, and he's invited me for dinner. The thing is, it's with his family, and I'm really nervous.

Z: Why are you nervous?

D: Well, he told me his family are really traditional.

Z: So? You'll be fine. Just be polite.

D: What should I call them, his mum and dad?

Z: Well, what would you normally call other friends' parents?

D: Back home I used to call them by their first name. Is that also how it normally is in Iraqi families?

Z: Some maybe, but it's probably better to start with 'Mr' and 'Mrs', if you're not sure.

D: OK, good. I'll need to get used to being more formal then. And will they mind if I bring a present? Chocolates, say?

Z: I'm sure they won't. That would be very nice. Be aware that you're the special guest, so you'll probably sit next to his dad.

D: Oh no!

Z: It's fine! Abner will be there.

D: You're right. It's just that I'm not used to such special treatment. But I'm sure it will be fun. And I just need to learn a few things so that there are no surprises.

Z: There you go! Now, what else, oh yes, one thing that's a bit rude is helping yourself to a second serving. Usually people don't serve themselves …

2.8

Alyea: I love reading and watching crime stories. I find them to be extremely captivating and so interesting.

First, I think a good crime story should always have conflict and disagreement. Conflict is the centre of any good story.

Second, make sure your characters are interesting. You don't have to like them. Some of the best stories I have read have fantastic characters who aren't the kindest, coolest or most beautiful. But they do have depth. Also ask yourself: is your main character going to be the criminal or the detective?

Third, try to show the action, don't tell it. For example, don't tell your readers that the criminal is nervous; show them, by describing the way he is shaking, or how his eyes kept moving to the door.

Fourth, in order to get started try working backwards. Most crime stories begin with the crime which can be very captivating for your reader, so definitely try to describe that scene as well as possible.

Lastly, make sure there is always a reason to keep reading. Every story needs suspense and drama because those are the things that keep us reading. As readers, we want to know if they will make it, if they will finally fall madly in love, or if he will find his long-lost sibling. As readers, we want to know what happens next.

UNIT 3

3.1

Mary: The library on wheels is such a wonderful project! So many of us take reading and having access to books for granted and it is such a luxury in so many parts of the world! Access to books is vital for education! I love that this project also encourages an entire community to join. Using motorbikes and volunteer time means that everyone is supporting kids to learn to read.

What a fantastic idea! Cities all around the western world have centres with lots of empty spaces that are no use for building on and are surrounded by people who are experiencing food poverty because there are just not enough supermarkets nearby. Urban farming is a wonderful solution, I really love these sorts of projects because they're about communities leading the way and making changes that are right for where they live. They can really cause change on so many different levels.

I love the Ocean Sole project because it is a really nice example of what we call the circular economy, so where you take products at the end of their life and give them a new life as something else, instead of throwing them away. It is what we need to do to use resources better and protect our oceans from plastic pollution.

🎧 3.4

1

H = Host, G = Guest

H: According to UNESCO, between 1950 and 2010, 230 languages became extinct.
G: Yes, and what's more worrying is that, like, one third of languages in the world have 1,000 or fewer speakers left. It is estimated that between, erm, 50 and 90 percent of these languages will be extinct by the next century.
H: Really? That is kind of …
G: Concerning? Yes, it is. On a more positive note, there have been many success stories of languages being saved from extinction, you know, such as Māori and Cornish.
H: That's incredible!
G: Yes! And more recently, projects such as Wikitongues are using technology to save languages from extinction.
H: How are they doing that?
G: By trying to make recordings of every single language in the world. And they are doing really well. I mean, they have nearly 1,000 recordings in over 400 languages in their archive so far, and they estimate that they will soon have recordings of, like, 1,000 languages.
H: Wow! How did they manage that?
G: Well, they invited volunteers to upload videos of themselves speaking their native language and they now have an impressive collection of videos, including unusual languages like, erm, Bora, which only has a few thousand speakers in the Amazon region of, you know, Colombia and Peru.
H: So it gives the speakers of these languages the power to save them?
G: Exactly. Basically, the hope is that by recording these languages, they are preserving them. They hope this will save them from extinction.

2

H = Hondo, S = Sofia, A = Amira

H: I read an interesting article yesterday. Did you know that about 70 percent of all films in the US are in English?
S: That doesn't surprise me. It's an English-speaking country, after all!
A: Well, the US actually has 62 million Spanish speakers, making it the second biggest Spanish-speaking nation in the world.
H: Yes, right after Mexico.
S: So do you think Spanish-language films will, like, start growing a lot, you know?
H: Yes, it's possible. I mean, it probably depends on the population growth of …
A: I'm not so sure, if we compare it to, like, French-language films, for example, they're on the decline.
H: But, you know, it's predicted that the popularity of films in languages other than English is set to grow because of the recent Oscar wins of films like *Roma* or *Parasite*.
A: In fact, I've heard somewhere, that erm, there has already been a slight increase in the number of Korean films released in the US.
S: That kind of makes perfect sense, after *Parasite* won the Oscar.
H: I also heard that films featuring more than one language are becoming more popular.
A: Ah, yes, that's right – I heard that too. In fact, there's one film called *Life in a Day* that features over twenty different languages!
S: Twenty? That's amazing!

🎧 3.7

R = Rosa, J = Julieta

R: Excuse me, Julieta?
J: Yes, Rosa. How can I help you?
R: I wanted to ask you about my essay grade. I'm disappointed I only got 55 percent. Have you got a minute?
J: Of course. I think the main problem was one of organization. For example, your paragraphs have lots of different ideas in them. Instead, each paragraph should be about one main idea. How much time did you spend planning before you started writing it?
R: Er, not long. I prefer to just get writing.
J: OK. You might want to spend longer at the planning stage next time. Think about paragraphs, so for an essay of this length, I'd suggest five or six paragraphs.
R: Right. But how do I know what to include in each paragraph?
J: Well, you made some good points in this essay, so they are in your head! So before writing the essay, you could try noting down all your ideas on a big piece of paper, and then use different colours to join all the related ideas together.
R: I see.
J: And listen, I know it isn't always easy to do something new. So don't hesitate to ask me if you need help.

R: Thanks. What if I make the notes, and organize them with colours, as you suggest, and then could I show you before I start writing?
J: Of course! That's a great idea. I'll be happy to talk about it any time.
R: Thank you, Julieta.

UNIT 4

4.1

Imogen: My favourite meal is just down the road from my flat. I live in a seaside city called Plymouth, which is in the south-west of the UK. In my opinion, it has probably the best fish and chip shops in the country. The fish is by far the most delicious I've ever had. I can't think of anywhere else I've been to where the fish is nearly as fresh as it is there.

I was once on a research sailing boat in Maine, in the US, and we took turns to cook food. One evening, when it was my turn, I decided to make a green Thai curry. When putting some salt in the curry, the whole lid accidentally fell off and a mountain of salt went into the dish. The more I tried to get rid of the taste of salt, the worse the meal tasted. I remember people pulling a face when they ate it. It must have been the saltiest meal they have ever tried! I was so embarrassed!

Paola: I was doing research in San Andrés, Colombia, where I had what they call *vijahoó* or *fruta del pan* for the first time, which literally translates as 'fruit of the bread'. In San Andrés and nearby Caribbean islands, potatoes or rice are a lot less common than *fruta del pan* with your meal. It has a sweet and savoury taste. It's possibly the most delicious fruit I've ever tried. And probably the most addictive too!

I'll never forget a completely vegetarian Christmas dinner my mum cooked for me a few years ago. You might think that it's no more special than a regular Christmas dinner, but not long before that I went on a strict no meat diet because of some health issues and I was eating more carefully than usual. So my mum decided to learn how to cook vegetarian food for me and made that Christmas extra special for me. And it was one of those meals that just gets more and more tasty with each mouthful. I could have eaten another plate.

4.2

A: It's a fantastic restaurant. And a lot bigger, too.
B: A lobby? What do you mean?
A: No, a lot bigger. It's a lot … bigger.

B: Oh yeah, of course. I get you now. Much bigger. So many tables!

4.6

I = Interviewer, Im = Imogen, P = Paola

I: Today I want to ask about your experience of food and other cultures. Imogen, what are some of the main differences that you noticed between your home country and other countries?
Im: Well, I've actually noticed quite a lot of similarities. In any country I've been to, people get together for a meal on a birthday or another celebration.
I: Ah, yes, it's the same where I'm from. And what about table manners? Have you noticed any differences?
Im: I was researching in India and Bangladesh last year and there were quite a few differences. The main thing was that rather than a knife or fork, a lot of people ate with just their right hand. Everyone made it look far more graceful than me when I tried to do it!
But you know, even in your home country people might have different table manners. One thing that annoys me a bit is people using their phone.
I: I'm probably guilty of this myself sometimes! What about hospitality? What does hospitality mean for you?
Im: For me it's allowing others to relax. I love to have friends over and treat them to a big meal. It is a fantastic time to relax yourself and to talk and catch up.
I: One last thing I want to talk about is offending others or being offended. Do you remember making any cultural blunders related to food?
Im: This is actually a memory I remember from when I was younger. Sometimes, I used to put salt and pepper on my food before I had tried it. I remember my dad telling me I should not do that because it looks rude. You are assuming that the cook already hasn't seasoned it enough before trying it!
I: Good point – I've never thought of that! Thanks Imogen! Now let's talk to Paola. Paola, have you noticed any difference between your home country and other countries you've visited?
P: Yes, for me it's the meal times! What most people in other countries call lunch, we call *comida* and you eat it around 2 or 3 in the afternoon. So, when I go to another country and lunch arrives at midday or 1pm, I don't feel like eating.
I: I'd be starving if I didn't have lunch until 3! And what would you say hospitality means to you?
P: Hospitality for me means inviting friends and family to my home, which is common. We get together many times to eat and talk. When a friend needs to talk, my house is open without them having to let me know beforehand.
I: Finally, do you have any stories of making a cultural blunder during a meal?

P: Well, I don't eat red meat, but often out of politeness, I'll have it, so I don't offend the host. But then I might get sick. So the host feels bad their food made me sick, and I feel bad I offended them by being sick …

4.7

P = Patricia, G = Gabi

P: Hi Gabi, Michael tells me you're really good at baking cakes. Is that right?
G: Er, yeah. Why?
P: I've got to make something to take to a party next week, and I was wondering if you'd help me tomorrow.
G: Yeah, sure. Do you want me to send you a recipe? There's one I do that's really easy.
P: Oh, I've got lots of recipes. But I'm a disaster in the kitchen. So I was hoping you could help out.
G: Oh, I see.
P: It wouldn't be too much work, only a couple of hours, and I'd be …
G: A couple of hours?
P: … really grateful.
G: Er, it's just that I'm not really that good at cakes. I do more bread and that sort of thing.
P: That's not what I heard. Everyone says that cake you made for Natsuki was fantastic. I can watch and take notes. And then I can do it exactly like you do it the day of the party. With your magic touch, I'm sure we can do a great job.
G: You know what, I'm not sure I'll be free tomorrow.
P: It doesn't have to be then. Tuesday or Wednesday's fine.
G: Erm, well, let me think. Have you got my number?
P: Yes, right here. So I'll text you when I've chosen the recipe, and then you can come over any time to help.
G: Um, yeah. Sure.
P: Thank you!
G: Hmm.

UNIT 5

5.1

Anusha: In school, I used to play an Indian sport called 'throwball' that mostly girls play. It's mainly a school sport that doesn't really get carried on to college, so I haven't played since the 12th grade! You have to throw a ball over the net. It's a bit like volleyball except that you use a heavier ball, and players catch the ball. The opposing team has to stop the ball from hitting the floor. The rules are quite complicated about how you can catch, handle and throw. I loved it because I was good at it, and it was a team sport. It made me feel free and strong!
Another one I like is a game – 'Carrom', which I played a lot as a kid. It's similar to pool, but on a board, and you flick little round pieces with your fingers. To play, you need a wooden board with four holes in the four corners. You also need some black pieces, an equal number of white pieces and a single red piece. Either two people can play, sitting on opposite sides of the board, or four people can play, in teams of two. Each team aims for either the white pieces or the black pieces, and the aim of the game is to hit all of your pieces into one of the four holes in the corners. You're only allowed to win the red piece if you get one of your pieces at the same time. I loved playing with my family and trying to improve my striking technique. Yeah, I really miss playing it!

5.2

1
A: Perez with the ball. He goes past the defender, shoots! But the ball goes far from the target.
B: That was a good effort, but he really should have passed the ball. He had Martinez there on the right wing making a great run.
A: And you could see the frustration on Martinez's face. He knows he would have been in a much better position to shoot.

2
What a race that was! Let's rewatch the last 50 metres. Kovacs really could have won this race with an earlier attack. Yu swam the first 150 metres brilliantly, leaving everyone behind, but she had no energy left for the last 50. Being beaten by a 16-year-old Hungarian we hadn't even heard about before this World Cup would have been a huge surprise for the current world record holder. Still, it's a huge success for Kovacs!

3
A: Oh what a ball! Ivanov looks stunned. He can't believe he lost this point.
B: And it's now a break point for Schulz.
A: This should have been an easy point for Ivanov. He could have played the ball left. He could have played it right. He had the whole court open.
B: But instead he thought he'd surprise Schulz by playing it close to the net. Why would you do something like this?
A: I don't think even he knows the answer to that question!

5.4

Anusha: I was once in a dance competition in high school. This was a competition between schools, with other schools in similar grades. There were four or five of us on my team from my school, and we were all ready with our performance. But we had never

Audioscripts

practised in the full skirts that we wore the day of the competition. The others entered the stage ahead of me, and I was the last to enter. As I entered, I tripped on my skirt. I could have fallen right on my face, but thankfully I got my balance and started dancing. But then I tripped again! We obviously didn't have any chance of winning because clumsy me was falling all over the place! We really should have practised in our final costumes! I'm pretty sure I wouldn't have tripped then! I learned that day that if I was ever going to be on stage again, I should carefully plan my outfit and test it out before the big day!

5.5

We're witnessing history here. 23,700 people have come to Arthur Ashe Stadium today to watch the Fortnite World Cup. This will surely go down as one of the biggest events in esports history, especially with over 2 million people watching it live online.

And it's not only the huge audience that is making this event historic; the total prize money is said to be 30 million dollars, one of the highest ever in a video game competition. According to the organizers, over 40 million gamers took part in the qualifiers to get to this World Cup. Only one, sixteen-year-old Kyle 'Bugha' Giersdorf, took home the top prize of 3 million dollars, more than Tiger Woods did for winning the golf Masters.

5.6

I = Igor, J = Ji Soo, A = Adam

- **I:** What if I told you that we may soon be seeing esports at the Olympics? For some of us, this will probably come as quite a shock, but for millions of gamers, it's about time that esports were recognized by the wider sports community. To discuss this, I have Ji-Soo …
- **J:** Hi Igor.
- **I:** … and Adam.
- **A:** Hello!
- **I:** Let's start with you, Ji-Soo. You're a bit of a gamer. What do you think about this?
- **J:** I think it's great! So good to see a sport that's so popular with young people finally recognized …
- **A:** It's not a sport! Where's the physical activity? They're sitting on the sofa in front of the TV!
- **J:** OK, and since when have sports needed to be physical? Have you ever watched snooker?
- **A:** True. I'm not sure snooker is a sport, to be honest! But at least they're standing up to play. And there's a lot of skill involved.
- **J:** Good games require great skill. You can only become a professional if you practise for eight hours a day. Gamers need to be really talented. It's a serious business, like any sport.
- **A:** Eight hours of sitting in your bedroom in front of a screen doesn't sound like a life I want to encourage!
- **I:** Ji-Soo, you say it's a serious business. How does it compare to other sports?
- **J:** Igor, it is huge! Millions of dollars in prize money, teams with sponsorship from large companies who will win at any cost, lots of excited spectators travelling from tournament to tournament …
- **A:** I know it's popular. But just because there are big crowds and sponsorship money doesn't mean it qualifies for the Olympics! For me, the Olympics is all about inspiring people to go out there and do exercise. The traditional sports were all physical: running, jumping, throwing …
- **J:** Not true. Shooting has been an Olympic sport since the modern games began. And you beat your opponent by skill, not physical fitness, just like gaming.
- **I:** OK, but Adam has a point about being healthy. A lot of the big esports are fighting games, like *Fortnite* and *League of Legends*, so as well as keeping people indoors, they're violent, so they're not healthy mentally, either.
- **J:** The argument that video games make people violent just isn't true! And anyway, so many Olympic sports glorify violence, like boxing, judo and karate.
- **I:** That's a good point. Adam?
- **A:** I think if you combine the facts that esports aren't physical, they make kids lazy and they glorify violence, then the Olympics shouldn't be going near them! They're only interested in gaming because of the money it will bring in.
- **I:** Ji-Soo?
- **J:** Esports are competitive, hugely popular, take a lot of skill to win, oh and in team play modes, they encourage working together. I think we should give esports a chance!

5.9

R = Rudy, P1 = Player 1, P2 = Player 2, C = Coach

- **R:** Hi everyone!
- **P1:** Hey! Here he is! The man of the moment.
- **R:** What? Oh, thanks!
- **P2:** What's going on?
- **P1:** It's Rudy's birthday.
- **P2:** Well happy birthday, pal! We should celebrate after practice. What do you say?
- **R:** Yeah, sure …
- **P1:** Afternoon, coach!
- **C:** Hello gentlemen. And happy birthday, Rudy!
- **R:** How did you know?
- **C:** It's in your player information from the Tigers, and that's still on my desk.
- **R:** Ah, OK. Thank you.
- **P1:** So? Come on Rudy, where's the cake?
- **R:** Um, what?
- **P2:** Yeah! Cake! Cake!
- **R:** When you say 'cake', I guess you mean birthday cake?

P1: Did you not bring it?
R: Oh, ha ha, very funny, guys.
P2: Er, yeah! It is really your birthday, isn't it?
R: Of course.
P2: Well?
R: Just to clarify, are you telling me that it's my job to bring cake today?
P1: That's exactly what he's saying.
R: You seem to think that I should know about this tradition, but I don't!
P2: Surely the Tigers bring cake when it's their birthday?
R: No, why would we ask the birthday boy to bring his own cake?
C: Woah! Let's go back a bit here. I think you're both assuming our traditions are the same as they are everywhere else?
P1: Not all traditions, but birthday cake? Come on!
C: Well, I think that since Rudy is new to the team we'll let him off. I'll go out and buy some cake.
R: Thanks, Coach.
P2: As long as we still get cake, that's OK.

UNIT 6

6.1

1

I read this story recently. It's about these two high school friends, Amy and Kyle. Amy asked Kyle whether he'd ever been to London. And he said he'd been there twice, once when he was about ten years old and again when he was older. She told him that the reason she was asking was because she'd found some pictures from when she was a kid and there was a boy in one of the pictures that she thought looked like him. She said she would bring it in …

2

So this was in a podcast I heard recently. There was this couple – her name was Esther, that's important, but I don't remember his name. Let's call him Mike. They were in the early stages of their relationship, and he was paying for something in a shop one day, and he was given change in dollar bills. And one of these bills had the name 'Esther' written on it, the name of his girlfriend. So he said to himself that he would give it to her, in a frame. It was all very romantic. When he gave it to her, she looked amazed and told him to ask her about it later. But he forgot, and that was that. Anyway, they got married, and everything was great, and then one day, they were moving apartments when Mike found the dollar bill in a box. So he asked her what the story was, and she told him …

3

So there's this one about phone numbers. I'm not sure how true it is. It might just be an urban myth. So there's this guy, Lucas, at the shopping centre doing questionnaires – what's your favourite washing up liquid, that sort of thing. He had to ask everyone for their phone number. This one lady he was surveying – it quickly became obvious she was making up a number. The lady started telling him a number, 9-3-3-4-6-0-… And then before she finished, Lucas asked her if the last number was 8. The lady nodded, slightly surprised. And then he told her that it couldn't be her phone number. The lady asked him why not …

1

She said she would bring it in … and there he was, next to her, both of them feeding pigeons together in Hyde Park. The weird thing is that they lived in different parts of the United States at the time, and they didn't become friends until about four years later. What are the chances of that happening, I wonder?

2

So he asked her what the story was, and she told him … that she had written her name on a dollar bill, and had told herself that whoever gave her that dollar bill would be the man she married. So she said she had known that they were going to be married that day, early in their relationship.

3

The lady asked him why not … and Lucas said, 'Because that's my phone number. The number you just made up, it's actually my phone number.'

6.3

A: Hey! You're back! How was your trip?
B: We had great fun. And you're not going to believe this, but we met someone you know!
A: Who?
B: Marcos.
A: No way!
B: I swear it's true.
A: What on earth was he doing there? I thought he was living back in Brazil?
B: He was, but he's back, and now he's working at the campsite! He's the manager or something.
A: You're joking!
B: I know! Weird, right. Totally out of the blue.
A: That is such a coincidence!
B: It's a small world, isn't it? But there's more. You'll never guess what.
A: What?
B: He's about to move into an apartment … on the same street as you!
A: He is? That's amazing!
B: What are the chances of that happening?

Audioscripts

6.6

Joe: As my team and I were travelling across Gabon, it was always hot. One of the amusing things we did was jumping off of our raft into the water to cool down. The raft is big and bouncy, so it was fun to jump really high and bounce into the water. Slowly we became more confident, and we started doing spins and even flips into the water. Megan, our expedition photographer, was really good at doing front flips off the raft, and soon we'd started a little competition. We took turns filming one another jumping off the raft. And when it came time for me to try a backflip, I slowly climbed into the front of the boat and up onto the inflated tube. But when I bounced, I slipped. As I lost control and started to fall into the water, I tried to backflip anyway. So I was falling into the water head-over-heels. I don't think you could call it a backflip, maybe a back-flop. I produced a big splash as I hit the water head-first. And as I popped up to the surface I saw that Megan was laughing and had been filming the whole thing.

Paola: As a marine biologist I tend to dive a lot, and although we always try to be very careful, we can get hurt. About five years ago during a field trip we were carrying the tanks to the boat, and a couple of days before I had bought new sandals. But something I did not notice is that they can be quite slippery. So when I was going down the ramp, I slipped. My first instinct was to protect the tank I was carrying, so it did not hit the floor as it could explode. However, what happened was that it hit my hand. I was quite lucky I didn't break it completely, but the bone was still fractured. All my colleagues and students were very sorry when they saw me. But the funny thing is they all said: 'Lucky it was your left hand and not the right one!' And in fact I am left-handed.

Joe: I love fish. Over my ten years of freshwater research in Central Africa I've collected tens of thousands of fish, but every time it's just like the first time. I get so excited every time I see a fish, it can get me into trouble. This one time I ended up with a big swollen hand for the rest of the day. On my first expedition in Gabon we'd caught about 350 fish. Of course, I jumped into action to remove the fish from the net and transfer them into an ice chest. But I didn't realize that almost every fish in the net was a spiny, venomous catfish! As I reached into the net, I felt a stabbing pain like a bee sting. As I pulled my hand back out of the net, I was poked several more times. And it hurt! I looked at my hand and realized I had about six tiny catfish stuck in my hand, injecting venom from their spines! I've now learned to check for dangerous fish before sticking my hand into any fishing net!

6.8

Paola: I am not a person who likes to cook, however I will do it as a daily activity. Often, when cooking, I will get distracted and start thinking about other things. My husband likes knives to be sharp, so he keeps them in great shape. This for anyone who cooks must be good, however for me it is a danger since by not concentrating I tend to cut myself. Sometimes I am cutting vegetables, I get distracted, and instead of staring at what I am cutting, I start a conversation or I pay attention to something else. So it is very common that while I'm cooking I will have a napkin wrapped around my finger. My husband always says 'Again! You should stop fighting with the knives or I will give you a child's knife to cook with!'

6.9

1

So brother has an accident other day, was really funny, I couldn't finish laughing. Anyway, so our parents buyed a new skateboard for him. And he really want to, you know, show he's an amazing skateboarder, so he riding the board and not looking ahead, just waving at me, and then, it was hilarious, he just hits tree. Fortunately, he not going very fast, so not very hurt, just some scratches and a bruise.

2

I really love cooking, but I tend to be a bit … oh, what was that word? … Clumsy. That's it. I am clumsy. So I was mixing some ingredients in a bowl, and I … trip? Tripped. I tripped over one of my daughter's toys, and the bowl flyed … No, sorry, not flyed, the bowl FLEW out of my hands and the ingredients spill … no, spilled … all over my husband, who was furious!

UNIT 7

7.1

1

So I really wanted to see this football game. It was going to be the biggest game of the season. But getting the tickets would be a nightmare. People had camped in front of the stadium the day before in order to get a good place in the queue to buy tickets. I wasn't going to wait that long. I mean, I love football and everything, but camping for over a day in front of the ticket office isn't my idea of fun. So I decided to get the tickets bought for me. You can basically pay someone to wait in line for you! But, you're not going to believe my bad luck, my professional queuer got robbed! So I lost the money AND ended up with no tickets!

2

Some time ago my parents decided to buy a new house. It was exactly what they wanted, but the only problem was the garden. It was a little bit overgrown, to say the least. The grass definitely needed cutting and the bushes and trees some serious trimming. But it's an expensive business. I decided to help them and after days of searching on the internet, I finally had their garden cleared. How did I do it? I hired goats! Yes, you heard it right. Goats. The weeds were gone in a day for half the normal price. And all eco-friendly, too.

7.3

Popi: I was in Paris and decided to visit the Saint-Ouen antiques market just outside the city. Since I love antiques, I try to visit the flea market of every city I visit. In these kinds of markets, bargaining is a must because there are no clear reference points for the prices of unique pieces. So the seller will often charge you whatever they feel like for the item. You can also get a better price if you pay in cash and not by credit or debit card. A long time ago I felt embarrassed when bargaining but now I am used to it and I think it is a normal market practice.

The article I bought was the arm guard of a 17th-century Persian suit of armour. It was not for sale; it belonged to the owner of the store and was hanging on the wall for decoration. It had no sale price, but as I was interested he asked for just over 140 euros – that was approximately 160 dollars in those times. But we bargained back and forth a bit and finally, I bought it for just under 100 dollars.

I think it was an absolute bargain, because some time later, I saw a similar piece in the London Portobello antiques market. I can't remember its exact price, but it was about 1,000 pounds, which is well over 1,000 dollars, probably around 1,300 dollars.

On the other hand, I have also made some bad purchasing decisions. For example, I bought a dress online for my wife. The description of the dress for sale and the pictures shown in the promotion looked really good. The dress was on sale and the price was around 40 dollars or so, which seemed to be good value for money for the product shown in the promotion. However, it turned out to be a terrible deal, a complete rip-off. The dress had nothing to do with the promoted product. The quality and type of the fabric was completely different to what was shown online. While the design was kind of similar, it was a bad copy and definitely not the same one for sale. It looked like a very low quality article. It was such a bad article that my wife could never use it. She was disappointed since she saw the dress offer online before I bought it, and she really liked it then. She was looking forward to wearing it. At least I did not waste too much money on it.

One thing for sure is that I will never buy anything from that online store again and I warned my friends not to do so either.

7.7

A = Aidah, K = Kang, J = Jack, M = Milly

A: All right, so what do you all say for camping in the countryside?
K: I'm not sure. I still have a back problem, so I really need a good bed to sleep in.
J: That's completely understandable. You'd feel more comfortable in a hotel, Kang.
A: But I've never been camping! I really want to go.
K: I see where you're coming from, but I really want some place comfortable to sleep …
M: Can I suggest something?
A: Go on.
M: How about we go glamping?
J: Glamping? What's that?
K: Yeah, I've never heard of it.
M: Well, it's more glamorous camping: 'glamping'. You know, like camping, but fancy. Comfortable. Nice beds in the tents. Showers.
K: Sounds more like what I need.
A: But are we still in nature?
M: For sure. We'll still have a great time together outside, in nature.
J: So can we all agree on glamping then?
A: I'm in.
K: Me too.
M: Great! Let's do it!

UNIT 8

8.1

S = Samira, P = Paco

S: All these jobs look so boring. I want to do something different.
P: Why don't we look for some more unusual jobs and see what we can find?
S: OK, good idea.
P: OK, here we go, so how about 'nail polish namer', Samira?
S: What? That's just silly, Paco!
P: But look, it says it's a job for art lovers. And someone who has a good sense of language. That's basically you!
S: Well, thank you. But no, I don't think that's a rewarding way to spend your life.
P: OK. What about colour expert?

Audioscripts

S: Hmm, that sounds similar. They're looking for someone with a passion for colours.
P: And knowledge of current design trends including colour psychology …
S: Colour psychology? I don't even know what that means! Next!
P: OK. How about a golf ball diver? They're looking for someone who enjoys diving and being outdoors to pick up golf balls from the bottom of ponds on golf courses.
S: But I can't dive, Paco!
P: Well, I guess you could learn, couldn't you?
S: I need a job now! This is useless … Hold on, what's this: Gravity Bed Sleeper for NASA … you'll take part in an experiment to research sleeping in space.
P: If it's a job that requires you to sleep all day, then you're the perfect candidate!
S: You're so funny. Wow! Guess how much you get paid.
P: Can't be much …
S: $18,500!
P: That can't be right!
S: How do I apply?

8.4

I = Interviewer, N = Nirupa, B = Brian

I: Where do you normally work?
N: For the past five years, I have been working from my home studio. Ordinarily, I would travel once every couple of months to my field locations to sketch and study my subjects, and then come back to the city to work on my paintings. Recently, I haven't been able to travel so much.
B: I work in different places, but recently I have been mostly working from home and going on trips into the field, and not going into my office.
I: What do you enjoy the most about working from home? What do you not like about it?
N: I love the flexibility of being able to finish up my housework during my breaks from work. If I had a 9 to 5 job, I would have to come home after a long day's work to a mountain of housework! But I dislike the fact that you don't end up meeting many people, and it can get lonely at times.
B: I enjoy not having to take the bus to work, but sometimes my children will run and shout in the room while I am teaching on Zoom, surprising the students! I think in the future we will all work from home more. This is generally a positive change, I believe, because fewer people will need to commute and fewer commercial buildings will need to be heated and cooled. This will all reduce carbon emissions, fighting climate change.
I: Do you have a flexible schedule or do you mostly work from 9 to 5?
N: I have a flexible schedule. I find that the flexibility helps me achieve a better work-life balance. Plus for those of us in creative fields, it can be quite difficult to force moments of inspiration into a 9–5 timeslot. I often let my work spill over onto Saturday and Sunday, since I prefer to take breaks to read or go for a run.
B: I try and work regular times. I find that a fixed schedule is better for me, because it means I am in the habit of working productively and I am less distracted. I generally wake up at 5.30 a.m. and start working around 6 a.m., and then finish mid-afternoon.
I: What effect will technology have on the way we work and what skills will people need to succeed?
B: In general, technology is improving working conditions for many, but it also makes some jobs less secure. Perhaps the most important skill to succeed is the ability to learn new technologies in the future. There will always be new tools, and to be successful people should be able to learn how to use those tools in their work.
N: I think the skill people most need is adaptability – to new technologies, changing production and consumption patterns and more. We all have to constantly learn to stay relevant!

8.6

1

Working from home allows you to be flexible in your work-life balance, but people can suffer from not seeing other people. Creative work may benefit from taking place at home. It may be better to spread your work out, even working seven days a week.

2

Working from home prevents you having to travel to work and lets you choose when you work and when you do other things. It's also good for the environment. Disadvantages include being interrupted by family, greater distractions and loneliness.

3

Working from home means you can start work earlier than you would if you had to travel to work. You don't have to take public transport to your place of work, which saves time and is good for the planet. However, family might interrupt your work.

8.7

C = Carlos, L = Lek
C: Good morning!
L: Hi Carlos!
C: How was your weekend?
L: Er, fine.

C: It was your birthday, wasn't it?
L: Er, yes. How did you know?
C: I saw it on social media.
L: Ah, yes, of course.
C: Did you do anything special?
L: Er, not really. Went out for a meal.
C: Great! Out of interest, where did you go?
L: Um, a little restaurant near my house. Gosh, is that the time? I really need to get started.
C: Oh, right. Yeah sure.
L: It's just that we've got that report to finish today, and I really need to get on with work …
C: Yeah, I get it. Anyway, happy birthday!
L: Thanks Carlos.
C: I'll take a look at the sales figures from last year, shall I? And then together we can see how this year compares …
L: Good idea. But, er … I think we'll probably get more done if we work separately for now.
C: Oh, OK. Well, if you need any help …

UNIT 9

9.1
1
K = Kveta, F = Fran
K: That's a beautiful photo, Fran. Where was it taken?
F: Oh, thanks. That was on a school trip in the mountains, part of my geography course.
K: Did you take it yourself?
F: No, someone else took it on their phone. I dropped mine that holiday. Can't remember who … um … I know they sent it to me because they knew I'd like it … Kati, maybe?
K: So how old were you there?
F: I must have been seventeen then. So, 2015. Summer 2015.
K: That was when I bought my motorbike. Actually, which mountains did you go to? In Poland?
F: Yes, the Carpathians.
K: What? I was there too that summer! We drove up from Kiev in … August, I think.
F: Wow! We were probably there at the same time! You didn't go to that nature reserve, did you? What was it called …

2
S = Sam, X = Xing
S: I wonder what's going on in the world today …
X: Sam! You're not still reading the news, are you? It's all so depressing! Can you remember the last happy news story you heard?
S: I know what you mean. A happy one? Let's see … There were those boys in Thailand who got caught in that cave …
X: That was ages ago! 2018, I think, or around then.

S: I know, but it was so emotional! I think I watched the news non-stop for a week!
X: Me too. Do you remember where you were when you watched it?
S: Yes, I was staying with my grandfather. He wasn't very well.
X: Those kids were incredible, weren't they? So brave!
S: Absolutely! They were real heroes. What about you? Where were you?
X: I remember I was still living at home because my brother was really affected by it.
S: Poor thing. He was only … what? About ten then?
X: Ten or eleven, yes. And your grandfather? Was he OK?
S: Yes, he recovered. I mean, he's very old now, but he's looking after himself pretty well.
X: That's good!

9.4
I = Interviewer, F = Francisco
I: So you study the Maya civilization. Who were they?
F: They were the inhabitants of what is now Southern Mexico, Guatemala and parts of Honduras. Their civilization dates back to around 2000 BCE. But I'm most interested in what is called the Preclassic Maya, which was from 1000 BCE to 250 CE. It's a period when Maya civilization really started developing fast. By the fall of the civilization, many of the now famous historic sites like Tikal had been built.
I: So what fascinates you most about the Maya?
F: One really interesting thing is that they left very little writing. So there is still a lot of uncertainty about how they lived and so on. And we learn most from studying the ruins of the cities they left, but also everyday objects, like jewellery.
I: So tell us, were their lives very different from ours?
F: In some ways, yes, the lives of ordinary people were very different from ours. For example, their way of life was much more sustainable than today's. Their diet was dominated by corn, beans and other vegetables grown in their household plots, so no industrial food and no plastic trash!
I: That's fascinating. It sounds like we've got a lot to learn from them!
F: Absolutely! I think one of the lessons we are now learning from the Maya is that they lived a well-balanced life, with a very keen knowledge of their environment and how to get the best of it while maintaining harmony with its parts, especially in terms of clean water and rich soil.
I: And in what ways were their lives similar to ours?
F: For example, much like today, family was very important and formed the base of Maya society. People that were related to one another tended to live together, forming large family groups. They also had similar occupations. In rural areas, they would be farmers; in the cities, writers or

merchants, all based on their family relations. And they were ruled by powerful kings – and who became king was all down to being born into a certain family.

Another similarity is that they moved a lot for work, just as many of us have to do now. For example, they might move to the city and settle down to find better job opportunities. There were also those that travelled across the Mayan territory buying and selling rare products, like minerals, salt, precious stones, textiles and, importantly, chocolate.

Finally, one of the favourite past times of the ancient Maya were board games. Chess-like patterns known as patolli have been found etched in the floors of houses and temples suggesting that as a board game it may have served as family entertainment. Just like how many of us enjoy board games with family and friends in the present day.

UNIT 10

10.1

F = Fatima, H = Host

H: Thanks for coming on the show today, Fatima.
F: It's great to be here.
H: So you study advertising. And you also design adverts, is that right?
F: Correct.
H: Would you agree that all adverts are just trying to make you buy the product?
F: Yes and no. It's true that the main goal of most of the adverts that you'll see is to sell a product. But some adverts might also aim to, for example, educate the customer, give them advice or simply make the brand more well-known among the customers.
H: And I imagine advertisers have a lot of tricks, right?
F: Tons of them! For example, statistics are very common, something like 'Many of our users saved more than 80 dollars per month.' It's also common to talk about other happy users of the product to build trust, like 'Hundreds of athletes trust our products.'
H: And now it's also common to pay famous people to give positive reviews of your product on social media, right?
F: Absolutely. It's called celebrity endorsement, and it's a very effective technique. I'm sure everyone who uses social media has seen posts by celebrities or influencers endorsing a product, saying how fantastic it is and encouraging us to buy it.
H: So the question is, can we believe it?
F: I think it's important that as a consumer you are aware that none of these celebrities or influencers do those posts for free. They are paid by the brand. That's not to say that no celebrity actually likes any of the products they advertise, but the fact they're being paid thousands of dollars to do it should make you slightly sceptical.
H: Sure, I mean, I'd happily endorse a brand on social media for a few thousand dollars! And as a practising advertiser, which technique is most effective? For example, are statistics better or reviews from celebrities?
F: It's difficult to say. Both techniques you mentioned can be effective. It all depends on your product, target audience and how you use the technique. I'd also say that neither of them on its own will give you great results. It's best to combine different techniques.

10.4

1

Jeff: After a research expedition once, I was travelling home with samples of sediment collected from the bottom of the ocean. When the airport security officers saw the samples, they thought it might have been soil from a farm, which you're not allowed to bring into the country. I had the correct paperwork, and even showed the officer photos of our ship, but they still didn't believe me even though I was telling the truth. I was very nervous that the officers were about to take my precious samples, but finally they decided to call my university. When they learned I was being honest, the officers became very curious and asked many questions about what we hoped to learn from the bottom of the ocean. I told them all about the microorganisms, worms and fish on the seafloor. In the end I made it to my flight, but with just a few minutes to spare!

2

Jeff: Where I grew up, the winters were very cold, and the ponds and lakes would freeze over so you could walk or skate across. One winter, my friends and I were passing one of these ponds, and I wondered if the ice was thick enough yet to walk on. One friend said yes – he said he had seen several people out on the ice earlier that day having a snowball fight. He encouraged me to go out on the ice to be sure. But after I took a couple of steps onto the ice, it began to crack, and I ran back to the sidewalk before I fell into the cold water. Later, my friend told me he had made up his story about the snowball fight, and just wanted me to test the ice before he walked out onto the pond too. I was angry with him for being dishonest because he had put me in danger and hadn't thought about the risks of his lie.

3

Jeff: A few geologist friends and I were on a road trip once, and we stopped the car to look at some rocks that had all kinds of old fossils in them. It was exciting to imagine the animals crawling through mud millions of years ago! We climbed over a fence to take some pictures, but the woman who owned the land rode over on her horse to ask what we were doing. I was worried that she might have thought we were thieves trying to steal from her, so I made up a story that our map had blown onto her land. She helped us look and even offered to get us a flashlight, as it was getting dark. I felt terrible, knowing the map didn't exist and that the landowner was being so generous. Looking back, it would have been better just to be honest with her. She just wanted to help!

10.5

1
- **A:** Do you like these? They're new.
- **B:** Er, yes. They're very … unusual. Are they to go with your dress for tomorrow?
- **A:** Yes, they are. I haven't tried them on yet, so I hope they fit OK.

2
- **A:** He's late again! Can you believe it?
- **B:** I know! He'd better get here soon or it'll get cold … Oh, here he comes. I wonder what he's going to say this time?
- **C:** Hiya! Sorry I'm a bit late. No hot water again. I had to wait half an hour for them to fix it.

10.6

I = Interviewer, C = Cara, P = Peng

- **I:** Your partner has bought you an expensive jacket as a gift, but you hate it. What would you say?
- **C:** Oh, that's happened to me actually. It was a jumper, but the same thing. And on that occasion I think I told him it was a bit small even though it wasn't, but that meant we could go back to the shop and I chose a different one. So yeah, I'd do the same again.
- **I:** In a restaurant, you are served a fairly poor meal. The waiter asks you 'How is everything, sir?' Do you tell them the truth?
- **P:** No way! I hate it when people I'm with complain in a restaurant. My dad does that and it embarrasses me so much. It isn't the waiter's fault the food's bad – he's just doing his job.
- **I:** You walk past a colleague's computer and notice an open email on the screen. You notice that the email mentions you by name. Do you take a closer look, even though the email is not addressed to you?
- **C:** Ha ha! I'd like to say no, but if I'm honest, I almost certainly would. I mean, it could be important, couldn't it? But then what if they catch you doing it? If I knew they were going to be gone for a few minutes I'd do it, but I wouldn't want to get caught.
- **I:** A friend has lent you their car but just as you're about to take it back you hear an unhealthy sound coming from the engine. What do you do?
- **P:** Oh, yeah, that's going to be expensive, isn't it? I could pretend it wasn't making the noise while I had it, right? But then it's going to be obvious that something happened while I had it. I think I'd tell them. And it's my friend, so yeah, of course I'd tell them!
- **I:** A friend tells you that they are moving away. They ask you to keep it secret for now. Two weeks later, a mutual friend finds out and tells you about it. They will be upset if they find out you already knew. What do you say?
- **C:** That sort of thing happens to me all the time, and the problem is I'm really bad at lying. But I think I'd be OK here, because you only need to say: 'Really? Wow! I had no idea.' Yeah, it's not like it's a big lie, is it?
- **I:** Your uncle invites you to dinner. You say you'll come. The next morning a friend calls offering you a free ticket to a concert you'd like to attend. Will you change plans?
- **P:** Depends on which uncle! I'm really close to one uncle, and he's cool. If I told him the truth, he'd understand. We could just have dinner another day. But I'd probably tell my other uncle that I was sick or give him some other excuse. Then I could go to the concert without offending him.

Acknowledgements

The Voices publishing team would like to thank all of the explorers for their time and participation on this course – and for their amazing stories and photos.

The team would also like to thank the following teachers, who provided detailed and invaluable feedback on this course.

Asia

SS. Abdurrosyid, University of Muhammadiyah Tangerang, Banten; Hằng Ánh, Hanoi University of Science Technology, Hanoi; Yoko Atsumi, Seirei Christopher University, Hamamatsu; Dr. Nida Boonma, Assumption University, Bangkok; Portia Chang, SEE Education, New Taipei City; Brian Cullen, Nagoya Institute of Technology, Nagoya; David Daniel, Houhai English, Beijing; Professor Doan, Hanoi University, Hanoi; Kim Huong Duong, HCMC University of Technology, Ho Chi Minh; Natalie Ann Gregory, University of Kota Kinabalu, Sabah; Shawn Greynolds, AUA Language Centre, Bangkok; Thi Minh Ly Hoang, University of Economics – Technology for Industries, Hanoi; Mike Honywood, Shinshu University, Nagano; Jessie Huang, National Central University, Taoyuan City; Edward Jones, Nagoya International School, Nagoya; Ajarn Kiangkai, Sirnakarintrawirote University, Bangkok; Zhou Lei, New Oriental Education & Technology Group, Beijing; Louis Liu, METEN, Guangzhou; Jeng-Jia (Caroline) Luo Tunghai University, Taichung City; Thi Ly Luong, Huflit University, Ho Chi Minh City; Michael McCollister, Feng Chia University, Taichung; Robert McLaughlin, Tokoha University, Shizuoka; Hal Miller, Houhai English, Beijing; Jason Moser, Kanto Gakuin University, Yokohama; Hudson Murrell, Baiko Gakuin University, Shimonoseki; Takayuki Nagamine, Nagoya University of Foreign Studies, Nagoya; Sanuch Natalang, Thammasart University, Bangkok; Nguyen Bá Học, Hanoi University of Public Health, Hanoi; Nguyen Cong Tri, Ho Chi Minh City University of Technology, Ho Chi Minh; Nguyen Ngoc Vu, Hoa Sen University, Ho Chi Minh City; Professor Nguyen, Hanoi University, Hanoi; Dr Nguyen, Hao Sen University, Ho Chi Minh City; Nguyễn Quang Vịnh, Hanoi University, Hanoi; Wilaichitra Nilsawaddi, Phranakhon Rajabhat University, Bangkok; Suchada Nimmanit, Rangsit University, Bangkok; Ms. Cao Thien Ai Nuong, Hoa Sen University, Ho Chi Minh City; Donald Patterson, Seirei Christopher University, Shizuoka; Douglas Perkins, Musashino University Junior and Senior High School, Tokyo; Phan The Hung, Van Lang University, Ho Chi Minh City; Fathimah Razman, Northern University, Sintok, Kedah; Bruce Riseley, Holmesglen (Language Centre of University Of Muhammadiyah Tangerang for General English), Jakarta; Anthony Robins, Aichi University of Education, Aichi; Greg Rouault, Hiroshima Shudo University, Hiroshima; Dr Sawaluk, Sirnakarintrawirote University, Bangkok; Dr Supattra, Rangsit University, Lak Hok; Dr Thananchai, Dhurakijbundit University, Bangkok; Thao Le Phuong, Open University, Ho Chi Minh; Thap Doanh Thuong, Thu Dau Mot University, Thu Dau Mot; Kinsella Valies, University of Shizuoka, Shizuoka; Gerrit Van der Westhuizen, Houhai English, Beijing; Dr Viraijitta, Rajjabhat Pranakorn University, Bangkok; Dr Viraijittra, Phranakhon Rajabhat University, Bangkok; Vo Dinh Phuoc, University of Economics, Ho Chi Minh City; Dr Nussara Wajsom, Assumption University, Bangkok; Scott A.Walters, Woosong University, Daejon; Yungkai Weng, PingoSpace & Elite Learning, Beijing; Ray Wu, Wall Street English, Hong Kong.

Europe, Middle East and Africa (EMEA)

Saju Abraham, Sohar University, Sohar; Huda Murad Al Balushi, International Maritime College, Sohar; Salah Al Hanshi, Modern College of Business and Science, Muscat; Victor Alarcón, EOI Badalona, Barcelona; Yana Alaveranova, International House, Kiev; Alexandra Alexandrova, Almaty; Blanca Alvarez, EOI San Sebastian de los Reyes, Madrid; Emma Antolin, EOI San Sebastian de los Reyes, Madrid; Manuela Ayna, Liceo Primo Levi, Bollate, Milan; Elizabeth Beck, British Council, Milan; Charlotte Bentham, Adveti, Sharjah; Carol Butters, Edinburgh College, Edinburgh; Patrizia Cassin, International House, Milan; Elisabet Comelles, EIM - Universitat de Barcelona, Barcelona; Sara De Angeles, Istituto Superiore Giorgi, Milan; Carla Dell'Acqua, Liceo Primo Levi, Bollate, Milan; John Dench, BEET Language Centre, Bournemouth; Angela di Staso, Liceo Banfi, Vimercate, Milan; Sarah Donno, Edinburgh College, Edinburgh, UK; Eugenia Dume, EOI San Sebastian de los Reyes, Madrid; Rory Fergus Duncan; BKC-IH Moscow, Moscow; Ms Evelyn Kandalaft El Moualem, AMIDEAST, Beirut; Raul Pope Farguell, BKC-IH Moscow, Moscow; Chris Farrell, CES, Dublin; Dr Aleksandra, Filipowicz, Warsaw University of Technology, Warsaw; Diana Golovan, Linguist LLC, Kiev, Ukraine; Jaap Gouman, Pieter Zandt, Kampen; Maryam Kamal, British Council, Doha; Galina Kaptug, Moonlight, Minsk; Ms Rebecca Nabil Keedi, College des Peres Antonines, Hadath; Dr. Michael King, Community College of Qatar, Doha; Gabriela Kleckova, University of West Bohemia, Pilsen; Mrs Marija Klečkovska, Pope John Paul II gymnasium, Vilnius; Kate Knight, International Language School, Milan; Natalia Kolina, Moscow; David Koster, P.A.R.K., Brno; Suzanne Littlewood, Zayed University, Dubai; Natalia Lopez, EOI Terrassa, Barcelona; Maria Lopez-Abeijon, EOI Las Rozas, Madrid; Pauline Loriggio, International House London, London; Gabriella Luise, International Language School Milan, Milan; Klara Malowiecka, Lang Ltc, Warsaw; Fernando Martin, EOI Valdemoro, Madrid; Robert Martinez, La Cunza, Gipuzkoa; Mario Martinez, EOI Las Rozas, Madrid; Marina Melnichuk, Financial University, Moscow; Martina Menova, PĚVÁČEK vzdělávací centrum, Prague; Marlene Merkt, Kantonsschule Zurich Nord, Zurich; Iva Meštrović, Učilište Jantar, Zagreb; Silvia Milian, EOI El Prat,

Barcelona; Jack Montelatici, British School Milan, Milan; Muntsa Moral, Centre de Formació de Persones Adultes Pere Calders, Barcelona; Julian Oakley, Wimbledon School of English, London; Virginia Pardo, EOI Badalona, Barcelona;

William Phillips, Aga Khan Educational Service; Joe Planas, Centre de Formació de Persones Adultes Pere Calders, Barcelona; Carmen Prieto, EOI Carabanchel, Madrid; Sonya Punch, International House, Milan; Magdalena Rasmus, Cavendish School, Bournemouth; Laura Rodríguez, EOI El Prat, Barcelona; Victoria Samaniego, EOI Pozuelo, Madrid; Beatriz Sanchez, EOI San Sebastian de los Reyes, Madrid; Gigi Saurer, Migros-Genossenschafts-Bund, Zurich; Jonathan Smilow, BKC-IH, Moscow; Prem Sourek, Anderson House, Bergamo; Svitlana Surgai, British Council, Kyiv; Peter Szabo, Libra Books, Budapest; Richard Twigg, International House, Milan; Evgeny Usachev, Moscow International Academy, Moscow; Eric van Luijt, Tilburg University Language Centre, Tilburg; Tanya Varchuk, Fluent English School, Ukraine; Yulia Vershinina, YES Center, Moscow; Małgorzata Witczak, Warsaw University of Technology, Warsaw; Susanna Wright, Stafford House London, London; Chin-Yunn Yang, Padagogische Maturitaetsschule Kreuzlingen, Kreuzlingen; Maria Zarudnaya, Plekhanov Russian University of Economics, Moscow; Michelle Zelenay, KV Winterthur, Winterthur.

Latin America

Jorge Aguilar, Universidad Autónoma de Sinaloa, Culiacán; Carlos Bernardo Anaya, UNIVA Zamora, Zamora; Sergio Balam, Academia Municipal de Inglés, Mérida; Josélia Batista, CCL Centro de Línguas, Fortaleza; Aida Borja, ITESM GDL, Guadalajara; Diego Bruekers Deschamp, Ingles Express, Belo Horizonte; Alejandra Cabrera, Universidad Politécnica de Yucatán, Mérida; Luis Cabrera Rocha, ENNAULT – UNAM, Mexico City; Bruna Caltabiano, Caltabiano Idiomas, Sao Paulo; Hortensia Camacho, FES Iztacala – UNAM, Mexico City; Gustavo Cruz Torres, Instituto Cultural México – Norteamericano, Guadalajara; Maria Jose D'Alessandro Nogueira, FCM Foundation School, Belo Horizonte; Gabriela da Cunha Barbosa Saldanha, FCM Foundation School, Belo Horizonte; Maria Da Graça Gallina Flack, Challenge School, Porto Alegre; Pedro Venicio da Silva Guerra, U-Talk Idiomas, São Bernardo do Campo; Julice Daijo, JD Language Consultant, Rua Oscar Freire; Olívia de Cássia Scorsafava, U-Talk Idiomas, São Bernardo do Campo; Marcia Del Corona, UNISINOS, Porto Alegre; Carlos Alberto Díaz Najera, Colegio Salesiano Anáhuac Revolución, Guadalajara; Antônio César Ferraz Gomes, 4 Flags, São Bernardo do Campo; Brenda Pérez Ferrer, Universidad Politécnica de Querétaro, Querétaro; Sheila Flores, Cetys Universidad, Mexicali; Ángela Gamboa, Universidad Metropolitana, Mérida; Alejandro Garcia, Colegio Ciencias y Letras, Tepic; Carlos Gomora, CILC, Toluca; Kamila Gonçalves, Challenge School, Porto Alegre; Herivelton Gonçalves, Prime English, Vitória; Idalia Gonzales, Británico, Lima; Marisol Gutiérrez Olaiz, LAMAR Universidad, Guadalajara; Arturo Hernandez, ITESM GDL, Guadalajara; Gabriel Cortés Hernandez, BP- Intitute, Morelia; Daniel Vázquez Hernández, Preparatoria 2, Mérida; Erica Jiménez, Centro Escolar, Tepeyac; Leticia Juárez, FES Acatlán – UNAM, Mexico City; Teresa Martínez, Universidad Iberoamericana, Tijuana; Elsa María del Carmen Mejía Franco, CELE Mex, Toluca; José Alejandro Mejía Tello, CELE Mex, Toluca; Óscar León Mendoza Jimenéz, Angloamericano Idiomas, Mexico City; Karla Mera Ubando, Instituto Cultural, Mexico City; Elena Mioto, UNIVA, Guadalajara; Ana Carolina Moreira Paulino, SENAC, Porto Alegre; Paula Mota, 4 Flags, São Bernardo do Campo; Adila Beatriz Naud de Moura, UNISINOS, Porto Alegre; Monica Navarro Morales, Instituto Cultural, Mexico City; Wilma F Neves, Caltabiano Idiomas, Sao Paulo; Marcelo Noronha, Caltabiano Idiomas, Sao Paulo; Enrique Ossio, ITESM Morelia, Morelia; Filipe Pereira Bezerra, U-Talk Idiomas, Sao Bernardo do Campo; Florencia Pesce, Centro Universitario de Idiomas, Buenos Aires, Argentina; Kamila Pimenta, CCBEU, São Bernardo do Campo; Leopoldo Pinzón Escobar, Universidad Santo Tomás, Bogotá; Mary Ruth Popov Hibas, Ingles Express, Belo Horizonte; Alejandra Prado Barrera, UVM, Mexico City; Letícia Puccinelli Redondo, U-Talk Idiomas, São Bernardo do Campo; Leni Puppin, Centro de Línguas de UFES, Vitória; Maria Fernanda Quijano, Universidad Tec Milenio, Culiacan; Jorge Quintal, Colegio Rogers, Mérida; Sabrina Ramos Gomes, FCM Foundation School, Belo Horizonte; Mariana Roberto Billia, 4 Flags, São Bernardo do Campo; Monalisa Sala de Sá 4 Flags, São Bernardo do Campo; Yamel Sánchez Vízcarra, CELE Mex, Toluca; Vagner Serafim, CCBEU, São Bernardo do Campo; Claudia Serna, UNISER, Mexicali; Alejandro Serna, CCL, Morelia; Simone Teruko Nakamura, U-Talk Idiomas, São Bernardo do Campo; Desirée Carla Troyack, FCM Foundation School, Belo Horizonte; Sandra Vargas Boecher Prates, Centro de Línguas da UFES, Vitória; Carlos Villareal, Facultad de Ingenierías Universidad Autónoma de Querétaro, Querétaro; Rosa Zarco Mondragón, Instituto Cultural, Mexico City.

US and Canada

Rachel Bricker, Arizona State University, Tempe; Jonathan Bronson, Approach International Student Center, Boston; Elaine Brookfield, EC Boston, Boston; Linda Hasenfus, Approach International Language Center, Boston; Andrew Haynes, ELS Boston, Boston; Cheryl House, ILSC, Toronto; Rachel Kadish, FLS International, Boston; Mackenzie Kerby, ELS Language Centers, Boston; Rob McCourt FLS Boston; Haviva Parnes, EC English Language Centres, Boston; Shayla Reid, Approach International Student Center, Boston.

Credits

Illustration: All illustrations are owned by © Cengage.

Cover: © Julia Wimmerlin; **3** © Michael Friedel; **4** (tc1) Reuters/Alamy Stock Photo, (tc2) Ehsan Ahmed Mehedi/Shutterstock.com, (c) © Lynn Johnson/Ripple Effect Images, (bc1) Markus Kirchgessner/laif/Redux, (bc2) Lucas Barioulet/AFP/Getty Images; **6** (tc1) © Graeme Guy/Comedy Wildlife Photography Awards, (tc2) Mladen Antonov/AFP/Getty Images, (c) Stephen Alvarez/National Geographic Image Collection, (bc1) Photo 12/Universal Images Group/Getty Images, (bc2) © Michael Friedel; **8** (tl) Courtesy of Alyea Pierce, (tr) Courtesy of Francisco Estrada-Belli, (cl) Courtesy of Anusha Shankar, (cr) © Imogen Napper, (bl) © Brian Buma, (br) Courtesy of Jeffrey Marlow; **8-9** (spread) Robert Harding Picture Library/National Geographic Image Collection; **9** (tl) © Sébastien Lavoué, (tr) © Global Penguin Society, (cl) © Mary Gagen, (cr) © Alok Shetty, (bl) © Mike Gil, (bc) © Tsiory Andrianavalona, (br) © Paola Rodriguez-Troncoso; **10-11** (spread) Reuters/Alamy Stock Photo; **11** (br1) © Mike Gil, (br2) © Tsiory Andrianavalona; **13** (t) Kucher Serhii/Shutterstock.com, (tr) (br) ozgurdonmaz/iStock/Getty Images; **14** (tl) Owen Franken/Corbis Documentary/Getty Images, (tr) kali9/E+/Getty Images, (cl) Jetta Productions Inc/DigitalVision/Getty Images, (cr) Klaus Vedfelt/DigitalVision/Getty Images; **16** (tc) Creative Stall/Shutterstock.com, (tr) Belozersky/Shutterstock.com, (c) (cr) T. Lesia/Shutterstock.com, (br1) (br2) (br3) ProStockStudio/Shutterstock.com, (br4) IhorZigor/Shutterstock.com; **18** Monkey Business Images/Shutterstock.com; **20** Tang Ming Tung/DigitalVision/Getty Images; **22-23** (spread) Ehsan Ahmed Mehedi/Shutterstock.com; **23** Courtesy of Alyea Pierce; **25** Anjuman Sharma/iStock Editorial/Getty Images; **26** (b1) Mega Pixel/Shutterstock.com, (b2) leungchopan/Shutterstock.com; **28** RichLegg/E+/Getty Images; **30** (tl) (tr) © Josy Bloggs/NB Illustration Ltd/Cengage; **32** (b) yukipon/Shutterstock.com, (br) © Szilvia Szakall/Beehive Illustration/Cengage; **34-35** (spread) © Lynn Johnson/Ripple Effect Images; **35** © Mary Gagen; **37** (tr) Sian Cain/Guardian/eyevine/Redux, (cl) Ben Curtis/AP/Shutterstock.com, (br) © Stephen Zeigler, Bright Black Studio; **38** © David Moore/Deborah Wolfe Ltd/Cengage; **40** (bgd) peiyang/Shutterstock.com, (tl1) ASAG Studio/Shutterstock.com, (tl2) frikota/Shutterstock.com, (cl1) charnsitr/Shutterstock.com, (cl2) Piyaboot Jaikamlue/Shutterstock.com, (cl3) Martial Red/Shutterstock.com, (bl1) Anna Vector/Shutterstock.com, (bl2) Sudowoodo/Shutterstock.com; **42** Cultura Creative RF/Alamy Stock Photo; **45** Courtesy of Mary Gagen; **46-47** (spread) Markus Kirchgessner/laif/Redux; **47** (br1) © Imogen Napper, (br2) © Paola Rodriguez-Troncoso; **49** Guadalupe Polito/Shutterstock.com; **50** (tr) stockstudioX/E+/Getty Images, (cr1) Ivan/Moment/Getty Images, (cr2) Reuters/Alamy Stock Photo, (br) Emmoth/Dreamstime.com; **53** © John Stanmeyer; **54** Klaus Vedfelt/DigitalVision/Getty Images; **56** Klaus Vedfelt/DigitalVision/Getty Images; **58-59** (spread) Lucas Barioulet/AFP/Getty Images; **59** Courtesy of Anusha Shankar; **61** Design Pics Inc/National Geographic Image Collection; **62** © Moto Yoshimura/Getty Images; **65** Johannes Eisele/AFP/Getty Images; **66** Rick Neves/Moment/Getty Images; **68** Dario/Alamy Stock Photo; **70-71** (spread) © Graeme Guy/Comedy Wildlife Photography Awards; **71** (br1) © Paola Rodriguez-Troncoso, (br2) © Sébastien Lavoué; **73** (tl) VictoriaArt/Shutterstock.com, (cl1) VeselovaElena/iStock/Getty Images, (cl2) Pictorial Parade/Staff/Archive Photos/Getty Images, (bl) hlphoto/Shutterstock.com; **74** (tl) MD_Photography/Shutterstock.com, (cl) Alexey Fedorenko/Shutterstock.com, (bl) Jeffrey Isaac Greenberg 13+/Alamy Stock Photo; **76** Courtesy of Joe Cutler; **78** (t) bekulnis/Shutterstock.com, (br1) (br2) © Caterina Baldi/Lemonade Illustration Agency/Cengage; **79** Multigon/Shutterstock.com; **80** Javier Joaquin/Beehive Illustration/Cengage; **82-83** (spread) Mladen Antonov/AFP/Getty Images; **83** © Global Penguin Society; **85** (tr1) (tr2) (cr1) (cr2) (br1) (br2) © Lindsey Spinks/Mendola Ltd/Cengage, (bl) AP Images/Kyodo; **86** (tl) Maskot/Getty Images, (cl1) Yves Lanceau/Nature Picture Library, (cl2) SetsukoN/E+/Getty Images, (bl) Luke MacGregor/Bloomberg/Getty Images; **87** © Javier Joaquin/Beehive Illustration/Cengage; **88** (bl) (br) © Pablo Borboroglu; **90** dowell/Moment/Getty Images; **92** (bl) Leszek Czerwonka/Alamy Stock Photo, (br) L A Heusinkveld/Alamy Stock Photo; **93** (bl) Jeffrey Isaac Greenberg 12+/Alamy Stock Photo, (br) Wil Batista/Alamy Stock Photo; **94-95** (spread) Stephen Alvarez/National Geographic Image Collection; **95** (br1) © Brian Buma, (br2) © Alok Shetty; **97** Mike Luckovich/The Cartoonist Group; **98** Peter Jordan/Alamy Stock Photo; **100** © Kunaal Kelkar; **102** (cl) (bl) 10'000 Hours/DigitalVision/Getty Images; **104** (tl) Macrovector/Shutterstock.com, (cl) Unitone Vector/Shutterstock.com, (cr1) Sapann Design/Shutterstock.com, (cr2) Vadym Nechyporenko/Shutterstock.com; **105** Courtesy of Brian Buma; **106-107** (spread) Photo 12/Universal Images Group/Getty Images; **107** Courtesy of Francisco Estrada-Belli; **109** (tr) (br1) (br2) Image courtesy of R.K. Lander, (t) ustas7777777/Shutterstock.com, (b) Oleg Golovnev/Shutterstock.com, (bl) Cristina Romero Palma/Shutterstock.com; **110** (tl) Busran Baka/Shutterstock.com, (cl1) Vectors Bang/Shutterstock.com, (cl2) Eva Speshneva/Shutterstock.com, (cl3) juliare/Shutterstock.com, (cr1) vectorpouch/Shutterstock.com, (cr2) Danilo Sanino/Shutterstock.com, (br) maak/Shutterstock.com; **112** © Bruce Smith/Holmul Project; **114** (tl) Stefano Bianchetti/Bridgeman Images, (tr) Bettmann/Getty Images; **116** (tl1) Alain BUU/Gamma-Rapho/Getty Images, (tl2) Art Directors & TRIP/Alamy Stock Photo, (tc1) Sueddeutsche Zeitung Photo/Alamy Stock Photo, (tc2) Photo 12/Universal Images Group/Getty Images, (tr1) charistoone-images/Alamy Stock Photo, (tr2) Imagno/Hulton Fine Art Collection/Getty Images; **118-119** (spread) © Michael Friedel; **119** Courtesy of Jeffrey Marlow; **120** (cr1) (cr2) Peter Hermes Furian/Alamy Stock Photo, (cr3) SeamlessPatterns/Shutterstock.com; **121** (tr) Digital Image Library/Alamy Stock Photo, (cl) © Duncan Caldwell, (bl) Alan Oliver/Alamy Stock Photo, (br) © Cecilia Bleasdale; **122** (bl1) (bl2) (bl3) (br1) (br2) © Lindsey Spinks/Mendola Ltd./Cengage; **123** Ray Evans/Alamy Stock Photo; **124** © Javier Joaquin/Beehive Illustration/Cengage; **126** fizkes/iStock/Getty Images; **128** (tc) Annanahabed/Dreamstime.com, (tr) pking4th/Shutterstock.com, (br) iadams/Shutterstock.com; **129** kali9/E+/Getty Images; **130** (tl) Reuters/Alamy Stock Photo, (tr) Ehsan Ahmed Mehedi/Shutterstock.com; **131** (tl) © Lynn Johnson/Ripple Effect Images, (tr) Markus